To my mother, Dida Rockley—a librarian—who instilled in me her love of books, her desire for knowledge, and her ability to organize information. And to my father, J.W. Rockley (Rock)—a management consultant—who became my mentor in business.

Dedicated to my mother, Elizabeth Cooper, who passed her love of exploring the world through books and reading to me, and to my father, Earl Cooper, who instilled in me the love of examining the world around me, taking bits apart, and attempting to put them back together—just a bit better.

Table of Contents

About the authors and book team

It's not possible to write a book without the help of a lot of different people. The following provides information about the authors and the people who helped make this book happen.

The authors

Ann Rockley is president of The Rockley Group, Inc. She has an international reputation for developing XML-based content strategies. She has been instrumental in establishing the field in eContent, content reuse, intelligent content strategies for multiplatform delivery, eBooks, and content management best practices. Rockley is a frequent contributor to trade and industry publications and a keynote speaker at numerous conferences in North America, Europe, and Asia-Pacific.

Known as the "mother" of content strategy, she introduced the concept of content strategy in 2002 with the first edition of this book. Ann was ranked among the top five most influential content strategists in 2010.

Ann led Content Management Professionals (CM Pros), an international organization that fosters the sharing of content management information, practices, and strategies to a prestigious eContent 100 award in 2005. Ann was cochair of the OASIS DITA for Enterprise Business Documents subcommittee in 2009–2011.

Ann is a fellow of the Society for Technical Communication (STC) and has a master of information science from the University of Toronto. She is also the primary author of *DITA 101: Fundamentals of DITA for Authors and Managers*, and coauthor of *eBooks 101: The Digital Content Strategy for Reaching Customers Anywhere, Anytime, on Any Device*.

Charles Cooper is vice president of The Rockley Group, Inc.

Cooper has over 20 years' of experience in quality assurance and over 15 years' of experience in eContent, user experience, taxonomy, workflow design, composition, and digital publishing. He teaches, facilitates modeling sessions, and develops taxonomy and workflow strategies.

Charles has assisted companies by analyzing their content, current workflow, and taxonomy systems; helped to create new ones; and worked to ensure that they are maintained on a consistent basis. He not only understands process, he understands production tasks and can design a process that works for everyone in an organization. Charles always keeps the voice of the customer in mind when developing solutions.

He has a strong background in process and business planning and believes that taxonomies, structure, organization, workflow, and quality assurance processes must be designed to support the company as they work to provide products and services that their customers need. Charles is a coauthor of *DITA 101: Fundamentals of DITA for Authors and Managers* and *eBooks 101: The Digital Content Strategy for Reaching Customers Anywhere, Anytime, on Any Device.*

Case study contributors

Rahel Anne Bailie is an integrator of content strategy, requirements analysis, information architecture, and content management to increase ROI of product lifecycle content. She is also an aficionado of content structure and standards, founder of IntentionalDesign.ca, and a fellow of the Society for Technical Communication.

Derek Olson is vice president of Foraker Labs. Derek leads the design and development of award-winning iOS apps, web apps, and websites in Foraker's Boulder offices. He also provides usability, content strategy, and information architecture guidance to clients like Breastcancer.org.

Joe Gollner is the director of Gnostyx Research, an initiative he launched for the purpose of helping organizations adopt open content standards and leverage intelligent content technologies. Joe has a BA in mathematics and literature from Queens University and a master of philosophy from the University of Oxford. Joe is a popular keynote speaker at major content management events and for several years chaired the XML World series of conferences.

Richard Thompson is an English-language copywriter/editor, web writer, and content strategist. He lives and works in France, near Paris. When he's not obsessing about content, he's taking pictures and restoring old houses.

B. Noz Urbina is a content strategist, senior consultant, and trainer at Mekon Ltd. With years of experience as a content strategy and content management consultant, he has provided services to Fortune 500 organizations and small-to-medium enterprises. He specializes in helping companies align content processes and infrastructure with their business needs and customer goals.

The reviewers

Scott Abel, aka The Content Wrangler, is an internationally recognized content strategist, publishing process expert, and social networking choreographer whose strengths lie in helping global organizations improve the way they author, maintain, and deliver information. Scott writes regularly for trade and industry publications, blogs, and newsletters. He's a popular presenter at publishing industry events and hosts a weekly webinar series. In his free time, Scott creates dance music mashups under the moniker The Audio Wrangler.

Ingrid S. Goldstein has worked in the publishing sector for more than 20 years and is an expert in the semantic preparation, processing, and cross-linking of content. A computational linguist and art historian located in London and Heidelberg, she advises publishing houses on the development and implementation of forward-looking digital content strategies. She has led industry and research projects for Fraunhofer and realized numerous projects with publishers in Germany and the UK.

Mark Lewis is a contributing author of DITA 101, second edition, by the Rockley Group. He has authored several white papers on DITA Metrics that prove the savings and high content reuse percentages possible with DITA's structured, topic-based architecture. His DITA metrics model was a 2009 competitor for JoAnn Hackos's Rare Bird Award. Mark manages the DITA Metrics LinkedIn group. He has presented on technical writing, DITA, and object-oriented design topics at Doc-Train, STC, DITA North America, and other national conferences. Mark is a member of the Organization for the Advancement of Structured Information Standards (OASIS) DITA technical committee. He and John Hunt are cochairs of the OASIS DITA for the Web subcommittee. He has received Society for Technical Communication (STC) awards for Distinguished Chapter Service and the Florida Technical Communications Competition. Mark is the DITA product manager for usability and a product evangelist for Quark.

Clare O'Brien is a digital marketing and communications professional with a career in several branches of the media. Her mission with digital communications and content strategy consultancy CDA (other than to help get the right content in place to be reached by the right audience when they need or expect it) is to continue to develop standards for digital content management strategies, governance, and evaluation. She speaks internationally and writes widely on the subjects of digital marketing, content strategy, and digital enablement. She was a cofounder of the UK Content Strategy Association and works closely with other industry bodies such as the IAB.

Editorial

Marie-Lynn Hammond is a writer, editor, and proofreader who has edited materials ranging from United Nations reports and academic papers to biographies, novels, and poetry. She has a BA in English and is a longtime member of the Editors' Association of Canada. In her other life, she's a nationally acclaimed singer-songwriter who has also written four plays, all produced.

Laurel Simmons, BA, BEd, has been active in the technical communication industry since the early 1980s, and has worked with hi-tech companies, telecommunication companies, government organizations, defense industries, and financial and marketing companies. She speaks, consults, trains, and yes, still writes, for organizations around the world. She grumbles every time she gets on a plane but she loves it when she gets there.

Illustrations and cover design

Natasha Lessnik-Tibbott began her illustration career at SPY magazine, digitally drawing the numerous tiny charts, maps, and graphs for the first time in the history of magazine publishing. Since then her work has appeared in many publications and books, graced the information kiosks of the International World's Fair in Barcelona and expanded to op-ed pieces for the *New York Times*. She was born in Toronto, worked for over a decade in New York, and currently resides in Nashville, where she is a partner in Our Designs, Inc.

Acknowledgements

A lot of people helped make this book a reality, and we'd like to thank them for all their assistance.

We would like to thank our case study contributors, who provided exemplary examples of projects based on their wide experience in the industry. Rahel Anne Bailie, a content strategist evangelist, shared her experience with the City of Vancouver website redesign. Derek Olson, an innovator with a keen interest in content strategy and intelligent content, shared the story of the development of an app for BreastCancer.org. Joe Gollner, a longtime advocate of XML and intelligent content strategies, shared his story of a government organization that adopted intelligent content technologies. Richard Thompson caught our eye when he posted to the content strategy listserv about a low-tech but highly ingenious content strategy, and we asked him to repeat it for the book. Noz Urbina, a content strategist, content management specialist, and strong proponent of XML, shared the story of Elekta's successful move to DITA and managed translation.

We couldn't have done the book without the help of our reviewers. They each looked at the content from a different industry perspective, ensuring that the book met multiple industry requirements. Scott Abel, aka The Content Wrangler, who knows everything about everything in the content industry, provided his always insightful and laser-sharp comments. Ingrid S. Goldstein drew on her extensive publishing experience to give us industry-specific feedback. Mark Lewis, a DITA evangelist, did an incredibly thorough review, catching problems and making valuable suggestions. Clare O'Brien, a digital marketing and communications professional, provided feedback and identified additional areas of emphasis.

Marie-Lynn Hammond, whom we first got to know as a singer-songwriter before we learned of her editorial skills, provided meticulous copyediting changes. Laurel Simmons, a longtime friend and colleague, did pass after pass after pass to catch editorial issues.

Natasha Lessnik-Tibbott, a graphic designer (and a friend reaching all the way back to high school) created the cover design and illustrations for each of the scenarios.

We'd also like to thank our Peachpit team. Margaret Anderson, our developmental editor, provided much needed hand-holding and guidance, and worked closely with production to make this book happen in a very short period of time. And just when we thought there couldn't be any further edits, Gretchen Dykstra, our proofreader, polished the language further.

Foreword

Ann Rockley has been talking about content strategy and intelligent content for over a decade. Why haven't the rest of us been talking about it, too?

Perhaps Ann's vision of content as a business asset was simply ahead of its time. Maybe the idea of "intelligent content"—content that's free from the constraints of a document or page, and therefore free to adapt to any context or platform—didn't seem as applicable to our challenges as, say, a website redesign or migrating to a new content management system. Of course, none of our tactics seem to have solved the core challenge enterprises have faced: ineffective, poorly organized, and laborious content processes.

So here we are, stuck with the same challenges we had last year, and the year before that, and the year before—you get the picture. On top of it all, we're dealing with the constant introduction of new platforms where we need to (or should) make content available to our customers. There are countless new opportunities to deliver the right content, to the right people, in the right place, and at the right time. How can we take advantage of them without starting from scratch?

The good news is, we don't have to. It's very likely that your organization has at least *some* form of content infrastructure; the question is, how will it need to change? As Ann and her coauthor, Charles Cooper, write, "The processes and best practices to create and manage content are undergoing a dramatic shift as content creators adapt to the increasing demands of a volatile content world." I'd call this an understatement. Content processes and best practices are evolving at the speed of light, and it's not enough just to keep up. If you want your content to truly realize its value as a business asset, you need to be able to look ahead. And the only way you can continue to face forward toward an unknown future is to know your content is truly ready for it—no matter what may come. *That's* intelligent content.

Ann Rockley is nothing short of a visionary, someone who truly understands the value of content as a business asset. Intelligent, adaptive, nimble, or agile content—call it what you will, but without it, you'll stay mired in the content mess that's keeping you from getting ahead. It's time to make intelligent content a reality for your organization. *Managing Enterprise Content: A Unified Content Strategy* will show you how.

Kristina Halvorson

Introduction

A unified content strategy is about much more than just content. It's about how you create content once and how you publish many times from that content. It's about pulling together the best practices, guidelines, and content structure your organization needs to enable you to rapidly design, build, test, and deliver a customer-centric content experience across many channels.

It's about looking back at what worked and looking forward to what can work even better. It's about using all the resources you have in your organization: your people and teams, your departments, your technology, your vendors, your assets, your customers, and the content you have already created and will be creating.

A unified content strategy places the emphasis on "unity"—people and technology coming together to produce content that serves the needs of everyone who reads and uses that content.

Is this an easy task? No. But it's a necessary one as organizations battle it out in competitive markets for the attention of their most precious resource—their customers!

In this book, we will explore all the aspects of creating a unified content strategy. We'll show you the pitfalls to avoid, and we'll explain what you can do and how you can do it to create a unified content strategy that serves your organization's needs now and well into the future.

Who should read this book?

This book was written with a number of audiences in mind. It is designed to assist content managers who are responsible for creating and managing content in many different channels for many types of customers. Content managers will learn what they need to know about what is involved in developing what we call a *unified content strategy*.

This book is also designed for content strategists who are responsible for designing an effective content strategy not for just one channel, but for multiple channels. Content strategists will receive practical advice on analyzing the requirements for and developing a unified content strategy.

This book is also designed for authors, specifically anyone responsible for creating structured, modular content for multichannel products. Authors will receive practical advice on structured writing, writing for multiple channels, and collaborative authoring.

How this book is organized

This book is divided into five sections. Each section focuses on a particular aspect of creating a unified content strategy and how that serves to help you manage your content. You do not have to read this book in chronological order, but it is designed to lead you through the logical stages of implementing a unified content strategy.

Part 1: "The basis of a unified content strategy" (Chapters 1–2)

This section provides an understanding of what makes up a unified content strategy, and why it's such an important foundation for getting content out to the right customer at the right time and in the right format. We also explain the concept of a sustainable and intelligent content strategy—one that will deliver maximum benefit to the users of content while minimizing the cost to the organization.

Part 2: "Where does a unified content strategy fit?" (Chapters 3–6)

In this section, we discuss the implications of what content means for organizations today. We explore the issues of content as a strategic asset, how content can be delivered to customers through multichannel delivery mechanisms, and what content strategists must think about as they prepare for that multichannel delivery. We also talk about the concept of content reuse and how organizations can reuse content to their advantage.

Part 3: "Performing a substantive audit: Determining business requirements" (Chapters 7–11)

Customers are the reason for your business's existence, your products and services, and your content. In this section, we explain how you can understand your customers' needs and your organization's needs for unified content. We show you a discovery process we call the *substantive audit,* which allows you to figure out what processes you are using to produce your content and how you can unify those processes. We'll discuss ways to identify the dangers and the opportunities available to your organization as you begin the process of creating a unified content strategy. We'll show you how to perform a content audit that gets to the heart of the issue—your content and how it suits your audiences. And then we'll help you pull together the big picture as you visualize your unified content strategy and the content lifecycle that is part and parcel of it.

Part 4: "Developing a unified content strategy" (Chapters 12–17)

At the heart of a unified content strategy is the methodology involved in creating models for your content, determining how you want to reuse content, defining how people produce content, and managing all the change that has to take place in your organization to make your content strategy effective. We'll show you what content modeling actually is, and we'll show you what the different types of content reuse are. We'll discuss how you pull together all the tasks and processes that are required for implementing a successful content strategy through workflow. We'll tell you about the information (the metadata) that you'll need to track your content. Then we'll focus on creating the content—why you need to separate format from content and how you can create structured writing guidelines that will help you in setting up collaborative authoring.

Part 5: "Supporting your unified content strategy" (Chapters 18–20)

A unified content strategy depends on the people, and the roles they fill, to support it. We'll discuss the type of roles you'll need—and you'll probably find some new roles that you'll need to introduce to your organization. Along with people, technology also needs to support your unified content strategy, so we'll discuss XML, the underlying technology that makes modern content management systems possible. At the end, we'll wrap up with a discussion about how you can integrate content management into your environment, what types of authoring tools are available, workflow systems you can set up, and delivery mechanisms you can choose.

At what level is this book written?

This book is written with the assumption that readers have some exposure to the concepts of content strategy, but that most readers do not understand the concepts of a unified content strategy and what has to be done to implement one. It is designed to ensure that all the concepts are clear no matter what your existing knowledge level is.

What you should take away

This book will assist you in creating, implementing, and managing your unified content strategy. It will help you define your requirements and build your vision, design your content strategy, understand the tools, and overcome the hurdles of creating and managing content in a multichannel world. We hope that it will help you see the broad spectrum of a unified content strategy and how you can escape the tyranny of format.

Part 1

The basis of a unified content strategy

Content can be considered the lifeblood of an organization; without meaningful content that supports products, services, and business processes, an organization would soon wither away. In Chapter 1, "Content: The lifeblood of an organization," we explore how to get content out to the right customer at the right time and in the right format. We introduce the concept of a unified content strategy and discuss the implications of what the "content silo trap" can mean for an organization's success.

One of the challenges facing anyone considering a content strategy, whether on the scale of a single web offering or a global enterprise, is sustainability. In Chapter 2, "Intelligent content," we discuss how intelligent content supports a unified content strategy. An intelligent unified content strategy doesn't just happen—it's the result of a coherent plan under which content will be designed, developed, and deployed to achieve maximum benefit to the customer and the organization while minimizing the cost to the organization.

Chapter 1

Content: The lifeblood of an organization

Organizations create tremendous volumes of content to support their products, services, and business processes. Getting content out to the right customer at the right time and in the right format is critical to an organization's success. Not only do organizations generate a tremendous amount of content, they have many different audiences, each with its own goals. Some want you to deliver content to them, others are searching for answers to questions that you'll provide, and still others want to be engaged in the content process. Making that content available to them means providing your content in a variety of channels including print, Web, mobile, eBook, app, and more.

This chapter introduces the concept of a unified content strategy, including the causes and effects of the content silo trap and the components of a unified content strategy.

Content: Where does it all come from?

A typical organization has multiple content creation groups who design, create, manage, and distribute information. Virtually every department within an organization touches content in some way. For example, marketing and sales produces information designed to convince both prospects and existing customers to purchase their products and services. They create most of the customer-facing content for the Web, including a wide variety of sales and promotional collateral (newsletters, brochures, white papers) as well as other types of content, including press releases, annual reports, and content destined for use on social networks.

Technical publications is another area where a great deal of customer content is created, managed, delivered, and stored. Technical publications departments create content that assists customers with using products and services, including guides, help, and other reference materials. They also contribute to online customer support centers.

Customer service departments respond to requests for immediate assistance from prospects and customers alike. To help service representatives respond to inquiries, customer service departments typically produce and maintain frequently asked questions (FAQs) and problem-tracking databases, and will often contribute to a knowledge center that may be used by both internal and external customers.

Learning groups assist customers in embracing new products and developing new skills through practical, task-oriented instruction. They produce products such as training (classroom, self-paced, virtual classroom), and a variety of eLearning materials (Web, mobile).

Some organizations exist specifically to produce content. For instance, publishers produce trade books, textbooks and associated learning materials, magazines, and journals. Increasingly they're challenged to produce digital versions of those products such as eBooks, enhanced eBooks, interactive web content, and apps.

While these examples are not all inclusive and not necessarily representative of how all organizations are structured, they serve to illustrate the many possible variations and iterations of content churned into various information products, destined for an increasing array of devices, and consumed by many different audiences.

A unified content strategy brings together the planning and design for all customer-facing content to ensure a seamless customer experience from first contact through purchase, usage, and support. Happy customers who are supported at every point in their content lifecycle are repeat customers. One of the biggest challenges in implementing a unified content strategy is identifying and breaking down the "silos," which is where we'll begin.

Understanding the content silo trap

Too often, content is created by authors working in isolation from others within the organization. Walls are erected between content areas and even within content areas. This leads to content being created, and recreated, and recreated, often with changes or differences introduced at each iteration. No one has a complete picture of the customer's content requirements and no one has the responsibility to manage the customer experience. Organizations fail to understand that content is their product. Content is the lifeblood of the organization. Without content their product or service does not exist. Content is either "tossed over the wall" to the next group in the content creation process or forgotten about in the rush to the next deliverable. We call this the content silo trap (see Figure 1.1).

Figure 1.1
The content silo trap.

The effects of silos

The content silo trap is like plaque in your arteries, inhibiting the blood flow to your vital organs. If silos hinder the flow of information, the organization is unable to function effectively or respond rapidly to threats and opportunities.

Content silos result in increased costs, decreased productivity, reduced quality, ineffective content, and unhappy customers. The effects of content silos are numerous, costly, and insidious, as illustrated below.

Higher cost of content creation, management, and delivery

When content is created multiple times, by multiple people, in multiple departments, and delivered in multiple ways, the costs to create and deliver content increase exponentially. Each and every rendition produces additional expense. When translation is added to the mix, costs escalate each time content is translated.

Duplication of effort

Authors work on many different types of projects. They create content that will be consumed by customers on a variety of devices, such as computers, tablets, and smartphones; for different customers, including decision-makers, influencers, and end users; or for different contexts—marketing, sales, support, training, and more. Authors use their domain knowledge to carefully craft content to meet both the needs of the customer and the requirements of the presentation format.

Because they work in deadline-driven environments, authors often don't share their good ideas, lessons learned, best practices, and finished work with others working on similar projects. They don't expect others to share these things with them. This lack of collaboration results in errors and inconsistencies in the information provided to customers, which in turn causes confusion and aggravation, and harms the customer experience. Poor customer experiences are costly. They increase support costs, damage brand loyalty, and result in lost sales.

For example, a medical devices company created a mobile web app. The marketing department developed all the design and functionality within their own team. However, they were unaware that the product content team had launched a mobile version of the patient content more than six months previously. The product content team had done extensive usability testing and prototyping of the content to meet patients' needs. While the mobile app functioned well, there was no coherence between the two mobile applications. They didn't look as if they were produced by the same company and they functioned differently. The failure to communicate resulted in duplication of effort and confused customers.

Explosion of mobile devices

The content creation world is becoming increasingly complex, with multiple operating systems, differing standards, and an increasing number of devices. Organizations are unable to deliver their content to multiple channels without manually converting the content each time. They don't have enough resources to manage the daily work, let alone the creation of multiple parallel versions. Content is no longer in sync, resulting in errors and customer frustration.

For example, an organization with a very successful website was receiving a growing number of complaints from smartphone users trying to access it. The site is impossible to navigate on mobile. In response to customer complaints, they develop a mobile app for the iPhone, but when they go to reuse the website content they find that even when the issues of navigation are solved, the content is too long and not modular enough to display effectively on mobile. They begin the process of reworking their content for mobile, but end up having two silos of content, one for the desktop version of the website and one for the mobile version. This situation doubles the amount of effort required to produce a single piece of information. Bad news, especially when they're also being asked to support content on tablets and other devices. They don't have the bandwidth to handle another massive project and are finding it difficult to manage the content they have, let alone repurpose it for use on another device.

Poor communication

When walls are erected within an organization, vital information is hidden from all the areas that need it. Poor communication is evident when one group fails to inform another that something has changed, that something exists, that something is wrong, or that something has been discontinued. Poor communication can also occur within a group or department.

For example, a company that sold mobile devices had a very fast product-to-market process. They had been losing ground to the competition, so they put together a marketing campaign to sell a new device at a significant discount. They worked rapidly to get the campaign materials out onto their social network properties, on the radio, in the newspaper, to retail outlets, and on the Web; however, they failed to communicate the promotion to customer service. The morning of the campaign kickoff the phone lines were flooded and customer service representatives had absolutely no information about the promotion. As a result they were unprepared to help customers who wanted to take advantage of the offer.

Reduced awareness of other initiatives

Seldom are content challenges limited to one area or department within an organization. All too often, the problem that negatively impacts one department is the
same problem being experienced in another. Because they operate in silos, each
group launches its own independent initiatives to solve its issues. Disparate initiatives waste time and money.

The content silo trap prevents organizations from collaborating in significant ways.
If each group solves its problems independently, and all the initiatives come to
fruition, they'll likely result in incompatible technology solutions, disparate process changes, and increased costs. In addition, one group may be forced to use a
product or to implement a process that's inappropriate for their purposes.

For example, in one organization, the web team needed a content management
system. They carefully specified their requirements, solicited proposals from software vendors, and made a selection. Customer support, which encompasses
product content, training, and frontline customer support, also needed a content
management system. After careful research, they presented their business case to
management for the product they decided to purchase. Because the web team had
already purchased a content management system, the company decided against
purchasing a second one and told the customer support area to use the same system. While the selected web content management system met the needs of the
web team, it wasn't the right solution for customer support. As a result, customer
support was forced to make the wrong type of system fit their needs.

In other situations we see multiple areas purchasing multiple content management
systems with combined costs of millions.

Lack of consistency and standardization

When content is created in multiple areas by multiple authors, it invariably differs,
resulting in mixed or even incorrect information being produced. This not only
causes confusion, it can be expensive, as illustrated in the following example.

A corporation was launching a new product that required both product content
and instructional materials. The technical communications team met with both
the engineering and product marketing groups to learn how the product worked
so they could create a series of deliverables, including the user guide, a reference
guide, and online help. The instructional designers from the learning group also
met with the engineers and product marketing groups. They gathered the information they needed to develop training materials for the new product.

Because the two groups worked in isolation and failed to collaborate with one
another, they created two different experiences for the customer. This lack of

collaboration resulted in significant confusion for customers and extra costs to the organization.

Customers suffer

While organizations suffer from the negative impact of content silos, customers are the real victims. When information exists in multiple areas, it often differs in content, style, tone, and message. Customers don't know which one is correct, most up to date, or comprehensive. When customers encounter these inconsistencies, they become understandably confused. Sometimes confusion leads to aggravation. Inconsistency damages the customer experience.

What causes content silos?

Most organizations don't set out to create silos; rather, silos are a result of organizational structure and other pressures. Frequently, authors lack awareness of what others are doing elsewhere in the organization. They have a lot on their plate—always too much to do, and rarely enough time to do it in. As requirements grow there never seem to be enough resources available to do what needs to be done. There isn't adequate time for them to find out what other groups are doing, especially when those other groups are just as busy focusing on their own activities. And so the content silo trap continues.

All this struggling to get things done can result in isolation and a sometimes deliberate desire to "block out" other activities. Authors are often unaware that their actions may have a negative impact on others and actually damage the profitability of the organization.

Lack of awareness, shortage of time, and inconsistent amounts of information are prime contributors to silos within organizations. However, the content creation process itself is one that often occurs in isolation, leading to potential inconsistencies and extra work.

Authors take great pride in the materials they create. They have strong ideas about what's appropriate for their content areas, how that content should be organized, structured, and displayed, and how it's different from other content being created in the organization. Authors mistakenly believe that the process of creating content should vary based on the audience who'll consume the content or the device on which it will be displayed.

In addition, when creating content, authors often lack the tools or time to search out existing content, perceiving that it's faster to start from scratch than to spend the time figuring out if content already exists. In a typical organization, content is stored in file systems that allow searching only by file name or file date. This makes it very difficult to search through multitudes of files on multiple servers. To find content, authors have to know exactly what they're looking for and where it's likely to be stored. If an organization does have a content or document management system, the content is seldom organized or classified with reuse in mind, so authors may have to search through volumes of incongruent information to identify the piece they want to reuse.

Traditionally, information-reuse opportunities have been difficult for organizations to identify. Generally, each content creation group develops its own processes, and while interrelated processes typically occur for content *review* cycles, they don't occur for content *creation* cycles. Unless groups identify the commonality of their content, content creation processes remain isolated, making it difficult for content to be identified and reused across an organization.

What is a unified content strategy?

A unified content strategy is a repeatable method of identifying all content requirements up front, creating consistently structured content for reuse, managing that content in a definitive source, and assembling content on demand to meet customer needs. A unified content strategy can help organizations avoid the content silo trap, reducing the costs of creating, managing, and distributing content, and ensuring that content effectively supports both organizational and customer needs. A unified content strategy makes it possible to deliver content to any customer, anywhere, and on any device without having to rework the content at every stage.

You start by analyzing your customers, content, organizational needs, processes, and technology. You examine such things as:

*   Who needs and uses what content (what content needs to be created, for whom, and by whom)

*   How effectively the content currently supports the customer

*   How content is currently created, managed, and delivered

Once you have a thorough understanding of all the information needs within your organization and the processes you currently use to create it, you can determine how to start unifying it, first from the authoring perspective.

In a unified environment, departments and authors need to work together as a team to create content "objects" that can be assembled in a number of different "information products," for a number of different platforms that run on a number of different devices. Instead of writing entire documents, authors create "components" or modules of content that are compiled into an information product, such as a website, a training manual, or a marketing brochure. Some components of content comprise the "core," that is, the information that's reused across information products, while other content components are unique.

Unified content strategy benefits

A unified content strategy is a formal and coherent content strategy. When organizations adopt a unified content strategy, they can rely on content being the same wherever it appears, providing both internal and external customers with a consistent experience. No longer do organizations have to worry about contradicting themselves with differing information; where duplication occurs, it's the same content. A unified content strategy is also a coherent customer-focused content strategy that enables an organization to meet customer needs at every point in the content lifecycle. And it allows for the support of the ever-increasing number of devices.

A unified content strategy offers several benefits, including the following:

Faster time-to-market

Faster time-to-market is achieved through shorter content creation and maintenance cycles. When following a unified content strategy, authors spend less time repeatedly writing content because they reuse existing content wherever possible, supplementing it with new or modified content where appropriate. Content is no longer recreated for every channel; content is automatically adapted for the device. Reviewers also spend less time reviewing content because they only have to review new or changed content; existing content has already been reviewed and approved.

Better use of finite resources

In a unified content strategy, resources are optimized because the repetitive processes of content creation and maintenance are reduced. And because people are required to do less repetitive and manual work, everyone involved in the content creation process can spend time adding value to content and responding to new requirements.

Reduced costs

In a unified content strategy, the costs of creating and managing content are reduced. Less work is required to get a product to market, not only decreasing internal costs, but potentially increasing revenue. Content is modified or corrected once instead of multiple times, reducing maintenance costs. Translation costs are slashed because reusable content is translated only once instead of multiple times; derivatives of that content are eliminated or reduced.

Improved quality of content

A unified content strategy helps to improve the quality of content. Content is clearly modeled for consistent structure, increasing its readability and usability. Issues of inaccurate content, inconsistent content, or missing content are reduced or eliminated.

Unlimited device delivery

Unified content isn't limited to one device for delivery. Content can be automatically adapted to multiple devices with little or no human intervention, reducing costs and increasing speed to delivery. When a new device comes along, it's a simple matter of creating another set of rules that adapts the source content to the new device. Gone are the days of handcrafting deliverables and reworking content!

Scope of a unified content strategy

Your unified content strategy can encompass the content created by a single department, across multiple departments, and between organizational groups or divisions, or it can span the entire enterprise. It may include delivering content destined for single output format or device, or for many devices such as Web, print, smartphone, tablet or eReader. You may choose to start in one area of the organization and then expand your efforts to other departments. No matter which path you choose, you need to determine what makes the most sense for your organization, now and into the future. The remainder of this book will help you to identify your organizational needs, the processes for creating a unified content strategy, and the technology for supporting it.

Summary

Content is created in every area of your organization. Unfortunately, if yours is like most, your content is created in silos, by authors working within a single group or department in isolation from one another. This lack of collaboration leads to increased costs, decreased productivity, reduced quality, and increased errors and inconsistencies of content. Working in isolation without collaboration is known as the content silo trap.

A unified content strategy can help your organization avoid the content silo trap, reduce the costs of creating, managing, and distributing content, and ensure that your content effectively supports both organizational goals and customer needs. A unified content strategy is a repeatable method of identifying all content requirements up front, creating consistently structured content for reuse, managing that content in a definitive source, and assembling content on demand to meet customer needs.

A unified content strategy results in:

- Faster time-to-market
- Better use of resources
- Reduced costs
- Increased quality and consistency
- Multidevice delivery

Only a formal unified content strategy can ensure that your organization is addressing all the problems of content in a repeatable, systematic manner. Your customers will benefit from a unified content strategy, and your company will too!

Chapter 2

Intelligent content

One of the challenges facing anyone considering a content strategy, whether on the scale of a single web offering or a global enterprise, is sustainability. It's only with intelligent content that it becomes possible to talk about a sustainable enterprise content strategy. Automation can be used to minimize the time, effort, and money needed to apply a good content strategy. However, automation doesn't just happen; content must be consciously designed to support it. An intelligent, unified content strategy establishes a coherent plan under which content will be designed, developed, and deployed to achieve maximum benefit to the customer and the organization while minimizing the cost to the organization.

What is intelligent content?

Historically, content has been managed as documents. Metadata is applied at the documents level to facilitate document search and retrieval for both the customers and the content creators. Unfortunately, metadata applied to a complete document can only adequately describe the content at a very superficial level; it can't identify the many types of content *within* the document. The searcher must still examine the complete document and extract the desired information.

If we make the content intelligent by tagging and structuring it, designing and preparing it for discovery and reuse, we can be freed from managing it within the "black box" of a complete document. We can move forward to actually managing the content itself once we take the step of making it intelligent.

Intelligent content is content that is structurally rich and semantically categorized, and is therefore automatically discoverable, reusable, reconfigurable, and adaptable.

Too much of today's content is stuck in formats that don't allow you to easily publish to various channels. For example, content destined for a print magazine can't easily be displayed on the Web with the same look and feel unless you store it as a PDF. And you can't easily take interactive content destined for the Web and publish it as an attractive, print-based magazine. The problem is that most content is locked within that formatting and changing it takes a lot of additional work and expense. You can't hope to be responsive to mobile let alone the latest flavor of device to hit the market when your content is wrapped in the straitjacket of format-specific information.

Instead of thinking about how we visually design the content, we need to start thinking about what content is required, by whom, when, in what circumstance, and in conjunction with other content or interactivity. To do this the content has to be structurally rich and semantically enabled.

And it's not just about format. If we're to truly make our content accessible to customers, it has to be discoverable. When you have unstructured, untagged, *unintelligent* content, the information you or your customers are looking for is likely to be hard to find. You have to rely on brute-force search methods to find information. Intelligent content allows you to take advantage of the information contained within the content to make the content more discoverable.

Understanding intelligent content

Let's take a look at each of the pieces of the definition for intelligent content to understand it better.

Structurally rich

To make our content intelligent so that the system can automatically process it, we need to add structure. Structure is the hierarchical order in which content occurs in an information product. An information product can be a web page, a book, an eBook, a brochure, a training course, and so on. Information products have recognizable structures that are repeated each time the information product is created. Information products consist of components (topics) that also have structure within them.

Structurally rich content is easier for organizations to manage across different products, channels, and departments and it's easier for authors to write.

Structure is everywhere in content. The more consistent and detailed the structure, the easier it is for customers to read and use the content, and the easier it is for authors to write it.

Structure also makes it possible to manipulate the content. For example, we can automatically determine how to publish content to multiple channels (print, Web, mobile) by mapping the structure of the content to a particular style in the output. Or we can filter out some content (for example, tables may not work as well in the mobile environment, so we design a different method of displaying the information that doesn't rely on tables). We can perform searches or narrow our search to the particular type of information we're interested in (for example, all occurrences of a word in the context of a specific element such as a positioning statement).

Structure also frees authors to think about the content itself, rather than the way it should be organized and written, because that's already been laid out, for example, through templates and guidelines.

Understanding structure

To understand structure, let's look at the structure of three different recipes:

- Celery salad

- Chocolate-dipped strawberries

- Beer can chicken

In these examples, the semantic structure of the recipes is illustrated.

What does "semantic" mean? It's a word you hear a lot these days, often without much explanation.

The *Oxford English Dictionary* defines the word semantic as:

1. the study of the *meanings* of words and phrases

2. the *meaning* of words, phrases, or systems

We've italicized the key element in both of these definitions—the word *meaning(s)*.

For example, in a Microsoft Word file we have style tags (headers, bullets, and so on), but they're all about what the content *looks like*. Headers are larger than the body copy, bullets are indented, numbered lists have numbers in front of them, and most of the other text is tagged as Normal. You can see what the content looks like, but it tells you nothing *about* the content.

The styles in Microsoft Word imply a hierarchy through the use of font size and indentation, but there is no real hierarchy. For example, a paragraph follows a sec-tion title. You can delete the section title and the paragraph remains and Word displays no error messages. In a structured document, the paragraph would have been inserted in the section as a structure that is "under" (subordinate to) the title. If you attempted to delete the section, the system would warn you that you are also going to delete the following dependent elements: section, title, and paragraph.

Compare that with semantically structured content. The text that may be tagged as Normal (in an unstructured Word file) could be tagged as Ingredient in the structured content. This tagging immediately informs the author what information must be placed in that location, and allows us (in the future) to search those places and know that the information we find there consists of ingredients, not just ran-dom text. It can also enable us to display the ingredients differently depending on the device. Similarly, in Microsoft Word, a numbered list implies a series of steps, but Word doesn't "enforce" this structure. In a structured document, a Step must contain an instruction (chop carrots) or action. So as soon as we say something is a Step, the author knows that an instruction or action is required—just as when we say Ingredient, the author knows exactly what to write.

Recipe 1

See Figure 2.1 for the celery salad recipe and semantic structure.

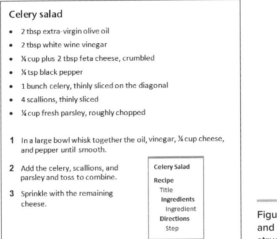

Figure 2.1 Celery salad recipe and associated semantic structure.

Recipe 2

The semantic structure of the chocolate-dipped strawberries recipe is pretty similar to the first one, with one addition. Notice the extra information after the set of instructions. This is a suggestion to the cook, so we've added a semantic structure called Suggestion. Notice as well that the step numbers in this recipe have a period after the number, and they don't in the celery salad recipe. However, the addition of the period is *format* (how it looks), not structure. Format is handled by the stylesheet, so we can ignore this difference. Stylesheets map your structure to a defined layout, for example, all numbered lists are automatically numbered and have a period following the step number.

The combined semantic structure for both Recipe 1 and Recipe 2 is shown in Figure 2.2.

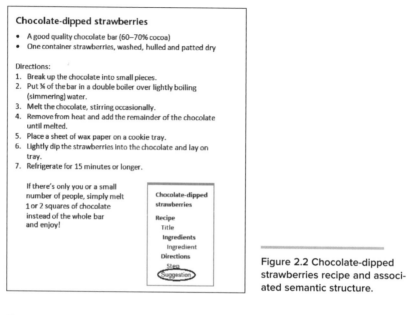

Chocolate-dipped strawberries

- A good quality chocolate bar (60–70% cocoa)
- One container strawberries, washed, hulled and patted dry

Directions:
1. Break up the chocolate into small pieces.
2. Put ¾ of the bar in a double boiler over lightly boiling (simmering) water.
3. Melt the chocolate, stirring occasionally.
4. Remove from heat and add the remainder of the chocolate until melted.
5. Place a sheet of wax paper on a cookie tray.
6. Lightly dip the strawberries into the chocolate and lay on tray.
7. Refrigerate for 15 minutes or longer.

If there's only you or a small number of people, simply melt 1 or 2 squares of chocolate instead of the whole bar and enjoy!

Chocolate-dipped strawberries

Recipe
  Title
    Ingredients
      Ingredient
    Directions
      Step
    Suggestion

Figure 2.2 Chocolate-dipped strawberries recipe and associated semantic structure.

Recipe 3

Look at Recipe 3 in Figure 2.3. There's actually a recipe within the recipe: the beer can chicken recipe contains the rub recipe. So if you create a structured component for recipes, you could then include a recipe within a recipe or use a number of recipes to create a larger recipe.

In addition, both recipes contain a Description at the beginning.

We know, many of you are probably saying your content isn't anything like a recipe. We use recipes to communicate the concepts. Refer to Chapter 12, "Content modeling: Adaptive content design" for a model for a value proposition and Chapter 16, "It's all about the content" for a model for product descriptions.

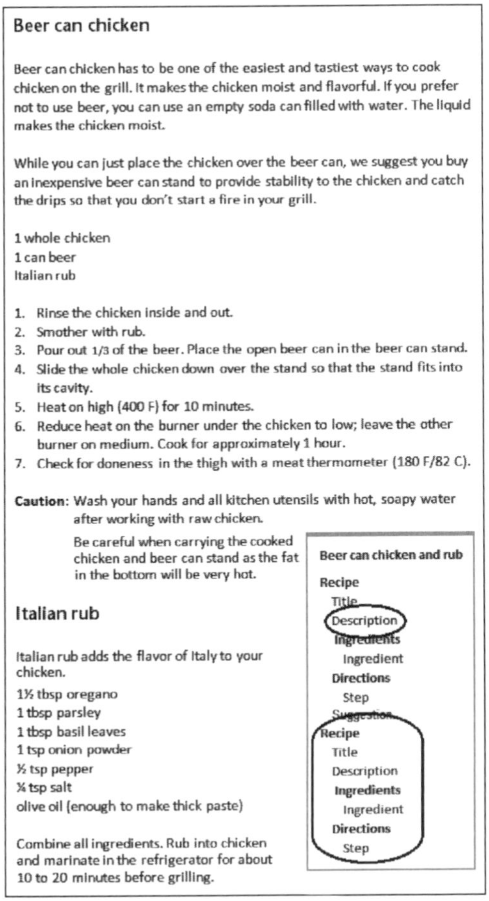

Beer can chicken

Beer can chicken has to be one of the easiest and tastiest ways to cook chicken on the grill. It makes the chicken moist and flavorful. If you prefer not to use beer, you can use an empty soda can filled with water. The liquid makes the chicken moist.

While you can just place the chicken over the beer can, we suggest you buy an inexpensive beer can stand to provide stability to the chicken and catch the drips so that you don't start a fire in your grill.

1 whole chicken
1 can beer
Italian rub

1. Rinse the chicken inside and out.
2. Smother with rub.
3. Pour out 1/3 of the beer. Place the open beer can in the beer can stand.
4. Slide the whole chicken down over the stand so that the stand fits into its cavity.
5. Heat on high (400 F) for 10 minutes.
6. Reduce heat on the burner under the chicken to low; leave the other burner on medium. Cook for approximately 1 hour.
7. Check for doneness in the thigh with a meat thermometer (180 F/82 C).

Caution: Wash your hands and all kitchen utensils with hot, soapy water after working with raw chicken.

Be careful when carrying the cooked chicken and beer can stand as the fat in the bottom will be very hot.

Italian rub

Italian rub adds the flavor of Italy to your chicken.

1½ tbsp oregano
1 tbsp parsley
1 tbsp basil leaves
1 tsp onion powder
½ tsp pepper
¼ tsp salt
olive oil (enough to make thick paste)

Combine all ingredients. Rub into chicken and marinate in the refrigerator for about 10 to 20 minutes before grilling.

Beer can chicken and rub
Recipe
Title
Description
Ingredients
Ingredient
Directions
Step
Suggestion
Recipe
Title
Description
Ingredients
Ingredient
Directions
Step

Figure 2.3 Beer can chicken, Italian rub, and associated semantic structure.

The importance of structuring content

By creating and using well-structured content, you create more opportunities for reuse across information products, product families, audiences, and channels. In a structured-authoring environment, where authors follow the same rules or guidelines for each element of content, the potential for reuse is greatly enhanced.

When content isn't structured, many problems arise. Not only is unstructured content difficult for customers to follow, it's also difficult for authors to create. And it's almost impossible to automate your delivery processes without structure. Content in one format can't be automatically converted to another.

To quote Anne Mulcahy, former CEO of Xerox Corporation, on this subject:

Unstructured content is stupid and old-fashioned. It's costly, complex, and does not generate a competitive advantage.

Benefits of structured content

There are a number of benefits associated with structured content:

- **Reduced costs:** Structured content is less costly to create, manage, and deliver. Authors spend less time creating content, and reviewers spend less time reviewing content. Costs of publishing can be virtually eliminated and the costs of adapting your content for multiple devices can be significantly reduced.

- **Speed:** It's faster to create content when there's a pattern to follow. It takes a lot of the guesswork out of trying to determine if "Every recipe has an introductory paragraph" is a structural rule. A structure guides the author in creating the appropriate content.

- **Consistency:** When we read or use content, we get used to seeing the same types of information in the same place. When things change (when the formatting or structure differs), and there's no obvious reason for the change, our comprehension slows down. Unexpected or unexplainable change reduces the usability of the information. Developing comprehensive, effective structures can eliminate the inconsistencies that drive customers mad.

- **Reuse:** The creation of structured content ensures that reusable components are truly reusable, that their reuse is transparent, and that all content appears unified, whether it's reused or not.

- **Predictability:** Predictability drives consistency. When information is presented and structured consistently, customers get used to the patterns and structures they see. They can find the information faster and understand it more easily because it's predictable. Predictability is also very important for automating publication. It's easier to create stylesheets and automated processing instructions for controlled structures than for ad hoc structures.

Semantically categorized

When we talk about semantically categorized content, we're talking about content that's been identified as "meaning something" and is related to other, similar content. We do this by applying metadata to the content, or tagging the content.

So you might tag your content as being related to a particular industry, for example, industry=medical or industry=pharmaceutical. You might identify it as being written for a particular audience: audience=physician, audience=pharmacist, or audience=patient. Or you might tag it with information defining its subject area: subject=diabetes or subject=hypoglycemia.

Using those metadata, you could later find the pieces of content you need to automatically build customized information sets for the industry, audience, and subject.

Without metadata, it's very difficult to automatically, let alone manually, find the content we need.

Easily discoverable

Every piece of content, including text, video, and audio, can be described and therefore understood if it's tagged with metadata. Metadata makes it possible to discover content.

We use metadata tagging to drive the search engines and we use the intelligence that we've built into the content to allow us to sort through the myriad pieces of information to discover exactly the content we need.

Efficiently reusable

Content reuse is the practice of using existing components of content to develop new materials. Reusable content reduces the time required to create, manage, and publish content, and it also significantly reduces translation costs. We can create modular structured content that can be either easily retrieved for manual reuse or automatically retrieved for automated reuse.

Text-based materials are the easiest to reuse. It's easier to reuse graphics, charts, and media in their entirety than it is to use portions of them, but it is possible to create reusable media.

Most organizations already reuse content by copying and pasting it wherever they need it. This works well until the content has to be updated. It's usually very time-consuming to find and change all those places where the content has been used. Not only does this waste time, but you run the real danger of missing some instances of content, which can result in inconsistencies and inaccuracies. In a recent Substantive Audit (refer to Part 3, "Performing a substantive audit: Determining business requirements") our client indicated that in a recent update they had to manually change content in 48 places! Imagine the consequences of missing one.

Why reuse content?

Reusing content can dramatically improve the way content is created in an organization. Improvements include reduced time and costs for development, review, and maintenance, reduced costs of translation, and increased consistency and quality.

Reduced development, review, and maintenance

Based on our experience, most organizations have a minimum of 25 percent reuse, but it could be as high as 80 percent, depending on how the content is reused. These numbers apply whether you translate content or not.

Development costs are reduced because the amount of content an author has to create is reduced. Authors don't have to research and write it again; they simply reuse it.

In addition to taking less time to create the content, less time is required to review the content. When approved content is reused, it's not necessary to review it again, reviewers need only ensure that the reused content fits or makes sense in the current context. This frees them up to do their "real jobs."

When content is reused, it can be updated automatically everywhere that particular content appears. And if you want to update only certain content but not other content, a smart content management system (CMS) makes it possible to selectively update content (refer to Chapter 20, "The role of content management").

Translation

You can significantly reduce the cost of translation through reuse. Some areas of savings include:

- The cost of translation is reduced by the percentage of reuse (typically a minimum of 25 percent).

- The cost of reviewing the translated content is also reduced by the percentage of reuse.

- Desktop publishing/post-translation formatting is typically reduced by 30 to 50 percent.

- If four or more languages are translated, typically all costs can be recouped in less than 18 months (including the cost of purchasing a CMS).

Translation memory systems (TMSs) use pattern matching to match content that's already been translated so the content doesn't have to be translated again. Every time content is sent for translation, that content is run through the translation memory tool to identify content strings (text) that have already been translated, and as a result, the existing translation is reused. However, each time someone creates and recreates a piece of content, the greater the number of variations that are introduced and the less likely it is that the TMS will find a match. Even if the change is as small as a space or a comma, the TMS will mark it as different. When you ensure that content is reused, translation costs are reduced even further.

Translations vendors charge you a cost to match content, even if the content matches exactly. The cost of matching identical content is a lot less than you pay for actual translation, but it's still a cost. With a good CMS and modular content you send only components that need to be translated, reducing your costs even further.

Translated content can also be rapidly reconfigured and brand new information products can be delivered from existing information products, without ever having to send that content to translation and pay additional costs.

The less easily measured benefits of consistent structure, consistent terminology, and standardized writing guidelines also help to reduce the cost of translation.

When content is formatted with format tags, translation costs you even more. For example, if you have content in HTML for the Web and the exact same content tagged with format for print, the TMS sees the content as different because the formatting is different. In addition, content often has to be reformatted for publication. If you have structured content, particularly if it's in XML, it's easy to automatically reformat content, regardless of language. Translated content is automatically formatted with stylesheets, so only minimal rework is required.

Increased consistency and quality

When there's no reuse, the chances of inconsistencies in content increase, either because the content's been rewritten by many people, or because it's been copied and pasted and some of the occurrences of the content haven't been updated properly. Often, when content is copied and pasted, the versions of the content begin to diverge over time.

When we examine samples of materials, we find examples of content that's similar but not exactly the same. On average, we find five to six variations of content. The worst we've seen is 56! Yet the majority of the time when we and our client really look at the information, we realize that the content could be identical or there could be a limited number of variations.

When content is written once and reused many times, the content is consistent wherever it's used. This consistency leads to higher-quality content.

Reconfigurable

Reusable content is modular content. In today's rapidly changing world, products and customer requirements are constantly changing. Modular, reusable content makes it easy for organizations to rapidly reconfigure their content to meet changing needs. You can easily change the order of modules, include new modules, exclude existing modules, and use modules to build entirely new information products to meet new needs.

For example, a company sold training courses that addressed the issue of diversity in the workplace. They'd been very successful sending their trainers around the world to provide classroom training and had recently developed both virtual training and eLearning. However, more and more customers wanted to license the courses for their own use. Some wanted to have the courses customized for them so all they had to do was deliver them; others wanted access to the source materials so they could customize the courses themselves.

No two companies are alike. Customizations may be as simple as adding a logo, but most companies wanted a learning module or two from one course, a different exercise in a particular module, different terminology, and even localized content. The company ventured into customization but then pulled back. It was too much work and they didn't have the resources to make all the requested changes and still keep their regular content fresh and up to date. They turned to intelligent content, modularizing and structuring their content. Once the content was intelligent, they could respond to a request for customization in a matter of weeks rather than months.

Completely adaptable

Structured content is content in which the look and feel of the content (format) is not embedded in the content. That makes it very powerful. When we know the structure of the content, we can output that content to multiple channels, adapting it to best meet the needs of the channel, or we can automatically mix and match content to provide what customers want when they want it and the way they want it. We can even transform (reconfigure) content from one structure to another, but only if we know what the structure is in the first place.

We frequently create our content for a particular need or audience, but content can be adapted (used in a different way) to meet a new need often without our knowledge. Think of mashups. We don't know how our content is being aggregated, but we know that it can be because we've structured and tagged it intelligently.

Case study: Intelligent content at a national regulatory agency

This National Regulatory Agency was charged with enforcing the national laws designed to maintain a vibrant, open, and fair competitive environment within the country's economy. In performing this function, the Agency drew on extensive expertise and experience in the law, economics, and a very wide range of industrial domains. Well before it was fashionable to consider these things, the management team within the Agency recognized that its knowledge base was endangered by the projected retirement of highly specialized staff. So a strategy was formulated that spanned an array of responses including recruiting campaigns and training initiatives. Some of the responses were directed towards looking at what intelligent content technologies could do.

The Agency launched the first of its intelligent content projects in 1999. As an initial investment, the Agency felt that introducing an integrated case management system would help to establish a more collaborative, and therefore more robust, work environment. The case management systems that were available were highly proprietary so the benefits of collaboration could only be realized if everyone used the same tool. Given the wide range of partners that the Agency worked with, this was clearly going to be a challenge. The Agency adopted the farsighted strategy of designing an independent specification for how the content of cases would be managed and exchanged. In this way, whatever case management system they selected could be integrated with those of key partners like major law firms and judicial tribunals. Leveraging XML, the Agency was able to identify, select, and customize the case management system that best fit their needs and they did so without any fear of vendor lock-in or incompatibilities with partner systems.

With the case management initiative well underway, the Agency then launched a second intelligent content initiative. This time the focus was facilitating the development and use of scenario-based training materials. The challenge lay in the fact that the existing staff members who had the expertise needed to develop training scenarios were specialists in their respective fields. They were not professional communicators with any experience using, or desire to use, the types of authoring tools typically associated with reusable online training materials. Another challenge was that the Agency would not know exactly what types of content would be needed as the project progressed or how the content that was created would need to evolve over time. Sidestepping the trap that many projects fall into, the Agency opted for an open and flexible XML-based environment. Leveraging this flexible data store and a simple-to-use, browser-based editing interface, the project team was able to implement an eLearning environment in a very short time. With the initial capability in place, the team was then able to progressively refine the environment to reflect the input of both specialist contributors and participants in the training programs.

This case study illustrates a number of lessons. One is that open content standards, and specifically XML, can be used to accelerate projects where there is significant complexity in the information being managed and in the range of processes being supported. However, the most important ingredient of success was a sound management approach to addressing a challenge. Such an approach will ensure that specific technologies, including intelligent content technologies, are deployed in a way that best fits into the business environment and that best realizes the long-term goals of the organization.

Joe Gollner, Director of Gnostyx Research Inc.

We can also automatically adapt our content to the device it's delivered to, not just visually, but structurally. Using structure we can identify what content should be displayed when or how. For example, content that is presenting linearly on a web page or in print could be presented as a multitabbed representation of content on a smartphone.

Intelligent content and content strategy

So what does intelligent content have to do with a unified content strategy? Everything! With the speed of change occurring in all industries and with the rate at which new devices for content consumption and interaction are proliferating, organizations must seriously consider how they're going to make their content accessible for their customers. If you go the route of "handcrafting" your content for one channel only, you risk providing only a partial content strategy for your customers. Customers who can't get what they want when they want it and in the form they want it in rapidly go elsewhere despite the quality of your products and services. Just look at the dramatic change in the publishing industry to see how a business can be imperiled by having content locked into old formats and technologies. An intelligent, unified content strategy is adaptable to the known and unknown changes you'll face today and in the future.

Summary

Intelligent content is content that is *structurally rich and semantically categorized, and is therefore automatically discoverable, reusable, reconfigurable, and adaptable.*

- **Structurally rich**: To make our content intelligent so that the system can automatically process it, we need to add structure. In addition, the more consistent the structure, the easier it is for customers to read and use the content, and the easier it is for authors to write it.

- **Semantically categorized**: The word semantic means "meaning." Semantically categorized content is content that has been tagged with metadata to identify the kind of content within it.

- **Automatically discoverable**: If the content has semantic tags and is structurally rich, it's a whole lot easier for customers and systems to find exactly what they're looking for. The addition of semantic tagging makes it possible to zero in on the required content.

- **Reusable**: Reusable content, content which is created once and used many times, reduces the time required to create, manage, and publish it. And it reduces translation costs. We can create modular structured and semantically rich content that can either be easily retrieved for manual reuse or automatically retrieved for automated reuse.

- **Reconfigurable**: Reusable content is modular content. Modular reusable content makes it easy for organizations to rapidly reconfigure their content to meet changing needs. You can easily change the order of modules, include new modules, exclude existing modules, and use modules to build entirely new information products to meet new needs.

- **Adaptable**: When we know the structure and semantics of the content, we can output that content to multiple channels, adapting it to best meet the needs of the channel, or we can automatically mix and match content to provide what the customer wants when they want it and the way they want it.

Part 2

Where does a unified content strategy fit?

It's easy to talk about what a unified content strategy is, but where does a unified content strategy fit into your organization and why should you use one?

In Chapter 3, "Enterprise content: Web and beyond," we discuss the implications of what content means for organizations today. For any organization, content is created by more than one content creator. These creators design, create, manage, and distribute content to customers within and outside the organization. And as delivery methods such as web pages, print, and mobile apps evolve, customers are expecting to be able to do more with content and on multiple devices. In response to those demands, and in recognition that content is a strategic asset, organizations are finding new and different ways to use and leverage that content.

If today's publishers are to survive and thrive as new technologies for delivering content appear, then they have to adapt quickly and adopt digital publishing best practices. It's no longer "good enough" to simply convert a printed book to a PDF and hope for the best. Customers are demanding device-independent delivery processes that will allow them to consume information when and where they want. Chapter 4, "Publishing," discusses the issues that publishers must think about as they prepare their content for multichannel delivery.

The good news is that multichannel delivery is not new; people in the technical communication industry have been developing content using this delivery strategy for years. Technical communicators call reuse "single sourcing," which is a method of reusing content where content is written once, stored in a single source location, and reused many times. In Chapter 5, "Product content," we explain how product content can be created and managed with a unified content strategy.

Teams that build learning materials also benefit from the adoption of a unified content strategy. With tight budgets and timelines, instructional designers need to be able to provide multiple types of training materials for multiple learners. In Chapter 6, "Learning materials," we discuss the advantages of using a unified content strategy to develop reusable content for multiple channels.

Chapter 3

Enterprise content: Web and beyond

A typical organization has multiple content creators who design, create, manage, and distribute customer-facing content. Content is created and delivered on the Web, in print, and on multiple devices. The processes and best practices to create and manage content at an organizational level are undergoing a dramatic shift as content creators adapt to the increasing demands of a volatile content world.

The Web

With more than two decades of website creation behind us, you'd think that the processes for effective website content design and development would be well defined. But content best practices and methodologies have only come into their own with the advent of content strategy.

In the early days of the Web, when large volumes of content had to be uploaded and integrated into the web environment, the focus was on how to achieve this process as efficiently and accurately as possible. Content wasn't considered part of the solution; it was considered more a problem to be solved.

Many organizations felt that if they purchased the right software tool, they could create a great website. Not so. Content management projects have a 30 percent failure rate, with failures occurring when software tools are purchased without a clear understanding of requirements and design. That's because a tool doesn't make a website; a website is only as good as the content you put in.

Ironically, content—the heart of a website—isn't usually coherently designed or managed. It's typically driven by groups saying, "We need content that talks about this, or covers that," rather than by the groups that drive the customer experience. Content is measured by how well it's written, not by how well it conveys the right message or elicits the right response. Content is handcrafted to get the message right as opposed to getting the correct content to the right customer in the right context. Disparate groups across the organization create their own content in isolation, resulting in a disjointed customer experience.

The concept of content strategy has been around since the late 1990s, but it really took off in 2009 when Kristina Halvorson wrote *Content Strategy for the Web*. This book has galvanized web content authors, designers, and editors to put content once again front and center in website design. Kristina defines content strategy as:

Content strategy plans for the creation, delivery, and governance of content.

While not yet fully formalized, the concepts of content strategy have made huge inroads, moving website content creation from an art to a methodology. However, content strategists have fallen into the same trap that print designers fell into before them. They continue to design content for a given platform, a certain screen resolution, or a given size on the screen—the container of "the page." But content is no longer restricted to the page; people expect to be able to consume or use content on the device of their choosing.

Focusing on the issues of screen size, many organizations are adopting responsive web design principles that scale the visual design down for small screen displays and up for very large screen displays. However, responsive web design only resizes a website; it does nothing to provide the right content in the right context for customers. Only adaptive content design can give customers what they want, in the form they want it, and in the right context. Resizing visuals is not the solution to platform proliferation.

The only way to create content that meets changing customer needs is to adopt a unified content strategy. Such a strategy allows you to develop adaptive content that's modular, structured, reusable, and not tied to any device or platform.

Adaptive content automatically adjusts to different environments and device capabilities to deliver the best possible customer experience, filtering and layering content for greater or lesser depth of detail. Adaptive content can:

- Be displayed in any desired order

- Be made to respond to specific customer interactions

- Change based on location

- Integrate content from other sources

Mobile

Mobile is the driving force in the move away from handcrafted content. According to a report published in July 2010,[1] 38 percent of US cell phone users, an estimated 89 million people, accessed the Internet from their phones. The same report identified that more than 47 million US mobile users accessed the Internet daily.

Venture capital firm KPCB has identified a number of mobile Internet trends,[2] including these:

- Combined shipments of smartphones and tablets exceeded that of PCs in 2011

- 60 percent of time spent on smartphones comprises new activities

- Global mobile data traffic is expected to grow to 26 times its current volume over the next five years

There are 5.3 billion mobile subscribers worldwide (77 percent of the world's population) with growth led by China and India.[3]

---

1   Pew Internet & American Life Project. "Mobile Access 2010," accessed December 1, 2011, http://www.pewinternet.org/Reports/2010/Mobile-Access-2010.aspx

2   KPCB. "Top 10 Mobile Internet Trends," accessed December 1, 2011, http://www.kpcb.com/insights/top-10-mobile-internet-trends

3   mobiThinking, "Global mobile statistics 2011," accessed December 3, 2011, http://mobithinking.com/mobile-marketing-tools/latest-mobile-stats

The combination of the volume of mobile devices being sold and the reduction in the number of PCs will result in mobile, rather than the PC, becoming the dominant platform.

Beyond the Web

While the concept of content strategy was popularized with the Web, it doesn't end there. Just as mobile has caused content strategists to rethink their content for mobile devices, the proliferation of other types of customer-facing content is forcing content strategists to rethink their entire corporate content strategy.

Take eBooks, for example, which are creating just as large a shift in content delivery (refer to Chapter 4, "Publishing") as mobile is, and which are not just an alternative delivery vehicle for print books. PDF versions of white papers are being replaced by eBook versions, and annual reports are also being produced as eBooks with interactive graphs, videos, and audio. Anything that potentially requires offline access or encapsulated reading can, and is, being distributed as eBooks or enhanced eBooks.

Likewise, product content such as online help and manuals is starting to see a shift toward mobile access, and there's increasing pressure for learning teams to develop mobile learning materials and eBooks as well.

Content is moving into very different delivery vehicles, such as third-party electronic point of sale (EPOS) apps, which necessitate the integration of extremely modular content that's updated frequently.

Currently, too many organizations create content in something like Microsoft Word, move it into a particular format such as HTML, and then get stuck when it needs to be delivered in another channel such as print. There's a constant churn of preparing content for one format, extracting that content and preparing it for another, and potentially bringing any changed content back to the first format. These processes are incredibly manual, error-prone, painful, and ultimately they're unsustainable.

Case study: Breastcancer.org

Breastcancer.org is a nonprofit organization dedicated to providing up-to-date medical information to women with breast cancer. Their website is the most heavily trafficked breast cancer website in the world (source: Alexa, www.alexa.com).

For many women, the four most frightening words they will ever hear are "You have breast cancer."

Newly diagnosed patients are thrust into a world filled with unfamiliar terminology and concepts normally reserved for advanced biology courses. In addition to dealing with the extreme emotional shock of a breast cancer diagnosis, many people must also navigate employment, financial, insurance, and family issues.

These circumstances create a difficult state of mind for someone trying to understand a complex cancer diagnosis and make informed treatment decisions.

It was obvious that providing an up-to-date website, intuitive information architecture, and powerful search tools was critical. But we realized we had to do more in order to serve our users.

Our goal was to reach breast cancer patients with the information most relevant to their specific diagnosis—even when they didn't know what they should be looking for.

Our user research indicated that the vast majority of patients could not accurately report their own diagnosis. This was true even of highly educated, affluent women with access to some of the best breast cancer doctors in the world.

How could we personalize content to a person's diagnosis when we couldn't be sure the reported diagnosis was correct?

We began this project with a content inventory, which helped us develop a metadata schema that would eventually power content personalization. We needed enough granularity to support medical accuracy,

but we couldn't overwhelm content contributors. Content components were stored as XML, and a rich API (application programming interface) was developed to allow export to other software systems.

As the project progressed, we realized that mobile devices could help us reach women at a critical point in their diagnosis: in the doctor's office. Our content was modular and in XML, making it easy to reuse and share among software systems. This resulted in a smooth transition from website to iPhone app.

In September 2010, we launched the *Breast Cancer Diagnosis Guide*, a free iPhone app that serves three specific goals:

- Provides a 24/7 resource for understanding complex diagnostic tests and terminology

- Gives breast cancer patients a place to record their own diagnosis information for easy reference

- Retrieves up-to-the-minute research findings and news tailored to each breast cancer survivor's unique diagnosis

The app has had over 10,000 downloads, and over two million in-app page views. It was also a 2011 Webby Awards Official Honoree.

People typically don't leave the house without their mobile phones, which means that the Breastcancer.org app is readily available for patients to record correct diagnosis information while in the room with their doctor. This solved one of our major challenges—the accuracy of self-reported diagnoses. Without a robust and evolving content strategy, our leap into the mobile arena would have been cost prohibitive.

Derek Olson, Vice President of Foraker Labs

The role of a unified content strategy

The way content is created today (with multiple versions for different mobile platforms, different versions for different web browsers, tweaks for PDF web distribution, as well as slightly different versions for each eReader environment) is untenable. It's as if we're in the preindustrial age—handcrafting expensive artisanal products. With the proliferation of mobile devices, that task isn't getting any easier.

We have to move to a manufacturing model. We need to be able to build information products the same way Swatch™ makes watches—using well-designed, reusable components in new and interesting ways, producing products that people are happy to purchase.

You might say, "We do that—we send our content out to our web server for automatic distribution, we even send some of the same content out to our manufacturer, our publisher, and our conversion facility to manufacture books and applications."

That's not what we're talking about.

We want to move the manufacturing paradigm all the way back to the beginning of the content design and creation process. Only when we start there will the true benefits of a unified content strategy become apparent.

When a physical product is being designed, the individual components are considered as part of an interconnected whole, not just as small stand-alone pieces. The design is built around the fact that the components are reusable—you don't need to create new components to build new products. When you're manufacturing things, you can't be wasteful, rework is costly, and bottlenecks can kill productivity. We have to create content the same way: considering each component not only as an individual piece of information that has value, but also as a part of a larger information product, or ideally, part of more than one information product.

Doesn't this slow things down?

Not really. There's more upfront design, but less rework and less wasted time and effort. Manufacturers have been working on these ideas for years and we can learn from their efforts. The last 20 years in manufacturing have seen a number of techniques and methodologies come and go. But at the heart of the best of them lie two concepts that drive manufacturing toward making higher-quality products for less cost: lean manufacturing and agile manufacturing.

Lean manufacturing focuses on value; unless an action adds value to a product, it shouldn't be done. Agile focuses on speed. Together they concentrate on eliminating valueless work, errors, rework, and bottlenecks and promote automation to allow people to work smarter, not harder.

This doesn't mean that the quality of the final product will be reduced—it means that content creators will be able to concentrate on creating high-quality content that can then be reused in multiple information products and channels. Think about it: A car manufacturer doesn't recreate all the parts of the car each time they design a new one; they use many prebuilt components. With those components they can build a basic model of a car or a super sport version, and changing the color is a snap. You can mix and match your content the same way, and if you want to make it look different, that's easy—just add a different stylesheet.

That's what a unified content strategy is all about: designing modular, reusable content that can be efficiently "manufactured" into a variety of information products for multiple devices.

Summary

Content strategists have fallen into the same trap that print designers fell into before them. The way content is created today (with multiple versions for different mobile platforms, different versions for different web browsers, tweaks for PDF web distribution, as well as slightly different versions for each eReader environment) is untenable. It's as if we're in the preindustrial age—handcrafting expensive artisanal products. With the proliferation of mobile devices, that task isn't getting any easier.

We have to create content the same way manufacturers do: considering each component not only as an individual piece of information that has value, but also as a part of a larger information product, or ideally, part of more than one information product.

The only way to create content that meets changing customer needs is to adopt a unified content strategy. Such a strategy allows you to develop adaptive content that can be efficiently "manufactured" into a variety of information products for multiple devices.

Adaptive content automatically adjusts to different environments and device capabilities to deliver the best possible customer experience, filtering and layering content for greater or lesser depth of detail. Adaptive content can:

- Be displayed in any desired order
- Be made to respond to specific customer interactions
- Change based on location
- Integrate content from other sources

Chapter 4

Publishing

Digital publishing is fast becoming a critical requirement for publishers. It's no longer just a desirable capability; it's a matter of survival. Most publishers associate digital publishing solely with the production of eBooks and fall short of the mark. The crucial point for publishers today is to prepare their content for multichannel delivery where printed books and eBooks represent only two possible delivery channels.

The digital world offers many more possibilities to use content. Different types of content can now be connected with a wide variety of user experiences (UX): Fiction can be read as digital pages of eBook readers, travel guides can connect their route description to GPS devices, and dictionaries, which provide word definitions within text when and where they're needed, are incorporated into electronic reading devices.

The publishing industry has already changed dramatically, but this is only the start. It will continue to change and the speed of change is expected to increase exponentially. Traditional handcrafted processes are no longer sustainable and automated processes have become an essential requirement.

Content needs to be understood as an asset in its own right, freed from output-based workflows. Device-independent content creation and delivery processes must be adopted instead.

Digital publishing, a tsunami of change

In the last few years the advent of digital publications (eBooks, enhanced eBooks, eBook apps, and digital editions) has started to dramatically change the way publishers do business. Driven by customer demand, slumping print sales, and increasing digital sales, publishers have been racing to convert their backlist to eBooks and simultaneously to publish to print. Some publishers have begun to publish eBook-first, and others have begun to publish eBook-only versions of content. Most eBooks, though, still resemble printed books. This situation keeps publishers happy with the "old world" but is just the first step at the beginning of a radically changing business model.

Aptara's third survey of eBook publishers[1] in 2011 provides insight into the changing field:

- The major driver for producing eBooks is increasing revenue (42 percent), followed by increased customer demand (36 percent).

- The majority of book publishers (85 percent) are printing both eBook and print versions of their titles.

- One out of five eBook publishers generates more than 10 percent of their revenue from eBooks.

- Most eBook production still follows outdated print production models at the expense of significant operational efficiencies.

- The greatest eBook challenge (30 percent) is content format and device compatibility issues.

The publishing process

According to Aptara's survey (see above), the majority of publishers still follow a traditional print process. To achieve full, device-independent publishing, however, the traditional workflow must change.

---

1   http://www.aptaracorp.com/resources/category/white-papers/ eBooks Survey #3: *Uncovering eBooks' Real Impact, 2009-2011.*

Traditional publishing

In a traditional publishing workflow, each book or document is created by one author using some form of text editor or word processor. The document is created, edited, and published as one entity, or possibly a series of chapters, and it doesn't interact with anything else (see Figure 4.1).

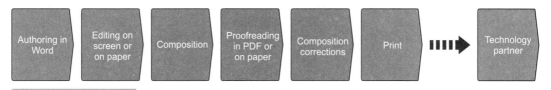

Figure 4.1   Traditional publishing workflow.

Advantages

- Traditional publishing represents a typical, familiar workflow.
- Familiarity makes it easy to use for existing authors and editors.
- eBooks are created by a technology partner skilled in the conversion of print-oriented content to functional eBooks.

Disadvantages

- The file is managed as a complete document.
- Print-oriented content is converted, rather than specifically designed for eBooks.
- Future changes must be done in the production copy, or the content must be exported back out to Microsoft Word and then re-laid out for a new publication.

Note that in this scenario the creation of successful eBooks depends on the publisher's understanding of the nature of the eBook they want to produce and the clear communication of those requirements to the technology partner.

This workflow is very effective for the conversion of the publisher's backlist.

In-house eBook publishing

The in-house publishing workflow for eBooks is very similar to the traditional publishing workflow except for the end product, which is digital, not paper (see Figure 4.2). Publishers use the same publishing software to publish to an EPUB file that they use for print. EPUB, short for electronic publication, is an open standard for electronic books from the International Digital Publishing Forum (IDPF) and is used by the majority of eReaders. In addition, the publishing software may provide the ability to publish to other channels such as Web or mobile.

Figure 4.2   In-house eBook publishing workflow.

Advantages

- In-house eBook publishing represents a typical, familiar workflow.

- Familiarity makes it easy to use for existing authors and editors.

- The publisher creates their own eBooks from the publishing software.

Disadvantages

- The file is managed as a complete document.

- Print-oriented content is converted; it is not specifically designed for eBooks or other channels.

- Future changes must be done in the production copy, or the content must be exported back out to Microsoft Word then re-laid out for publication.

In-house eBook publishing often feels like the easiest route for publishers because they don't have to change any of their process or their technology. However, the content is often constrained by the print paradigm. It's a difficult task to publish in different ways depending on the channel and the device. More often than not, it ends up as a simple conversion (different look-and-feel), rather than optimized output for each channel and device.

In a recent discussion with a new client of ours, they spoke about the challenges of creating eBooks. The output to the EPUB format was pretty simple, but testing on different devices revealed a number of display problems and usability issues.

They were spending weeks "hand tweaking" the output for each device, and with each new device, the job got larger and more arduous.

XML early

Recognizing the challenges they face in publishing to multiple channels and the proliferation of devices, some publishers are choosing to use XML (Extensible Markup Language) in their publishing workflow. XML is a set of rules for encoding documents.

"XML early" means converting your content to XML early on in your workflow to enable you to produce content for multiple channels and to easily reuse content. (See Figure 4.3.)

XML enables you to design and prepare content in a way that's completely portable and open, which in turn enables a wide range of applications that allows you to automate common content tasks such as formatting. If you make the content intelligent by tagging and structuring it, and then if you design and prepare it for discovery and reuse, you're freed from managing content within the "black boxes" of completed books. For more information on XML refer to Chapter 19, "The role of XML."

Figure 4.3   XML early publishing workflow.

Advantages

- Edits can be handled online using collaborative review tools. This speeds up the editing and allows multiple editors to work on the content simultaneously. Change tracking is supported in these tools.

- XML can be configured to support reuse across media (print, eBooks, apps, and so on).

- XML can be optimized to support current and future products (for example, article compendiums, eLearning, and custom books from selected chapters).

- Corrections and changes to content are done in the XML content and "repoured" into each of the outputs. There's no need to transfer content back and forth.

Disadvantages

- Copy editors and others involved in the publishing workflow need to become increasingly comfortable with working largely online and with new software.

- The concept of WYSIWYG no longer exists because content can be published in multiple formats.

- Content is created and managed as components, which may be a paradigm shift for some people.

- Production staff need to learn to work with structured templates and cannot continue to manually tweak content.

- While most people in the organization don't need to understand XML, at least one individual will need a strong understanding of XML.

  Although XML early has the most advantages, XML can be incorporated into your workflow at any point. You might choose to incorporate it somewhere in the middle of your workflow, with content created in Microsoft Word, but converted to XML after the final manuscript was approved. This could be a long-term strategy, or it might be a short-term strategy only—a stepping-stone on the way to creating a full XML-based workflow.

The role of a unified content strategy

To take advantage of new digital markets, you must rethink the way you create, manage, publish, and deliver content. You must reengineer your processes to create a more flexible and sustainable future. You must also reimagine a production process that frees your content to be easily transformed into whatever new formats and devices that your customers desire. In this new world, a publisher becomes a content and service provider, capable of meeting the ever-changing time-to-market requirements. It is not as straightforward as simply incorporating XML into your workflow, because the workflow is only as effective as your content strategy. You also need to determine how you want to create modular, structured content that can be repurposed for multiple information products and services. What's needed is a unified content strategy.

Case study: American Society for Training and Development

The American Society for Training and Development (ASTD) is an association for workplace trainers. We create content to help trainers do their jobs better. We publish 20 books per year, a monthly magazine, and several newsletters. ASTD content is mostly evergreen and not time-sensitive, so reuse is central to our content strategy.

Goals

At ASTD we wanted to increase personalization and findability of our content, to reduce production resources (including time to produce the content and headcount), and to generally make it easier to do business with ASTD.

What we did and why

ASTD started by improving production workflow. We mapped out the current production workflow in a new content management system (CMS) and added automated email notifications, status reporting, and a content repository of XML versions of our books and magazines. We then converted our back catalog and front list into XML, and we integrated our Microsoft Word and InDesign content into XML as well. We added XML format transformations that converted our XML into multiple "flavors" of HTML, PDF, and EPUB. We developed a master taxonomy of training terms and applied that taxonomy to our content down to the article level (for our magazines) and to the chapter level (for our books). We also released this taxonomy for the benefit of the training profession. Finally, with all our rich XML content in the repository, we built a user interface to create custom packages of content.

Outcomes

In addition to meeting our goals, we also experienced other, unexpected outcomes:

- Reduced onboarding time. New ASTD employees became "instant experts"

in training content because they could instantly find everything we've published on a certain topic.

- An integrated language. Our taxonomy is applied across the organization, so how we segment our customers is aligned with how we are segmenting our content.

- Meeting customer expectations. Customers increasingly expect publishers to offer multiple formats to customers. XML-based publishing allows small companies like ASTD to meet those customer expectations in a cost-effective way.

- Agility. With our content already in XML, ASTD is now creating several new (and very cool) content apps. We can concentrate on the app without having to go back and do anything (at all) with the content.

Lessons learned

Start free and small. We started our content management initiative with a company-wide blog. It was a great, stress-free way to get everyone speaking the same language of content management: categories, tags, analytics, search engine optimization (SEO), linking, and findability.

Incentivize the community. ASTD's certified trainers earn recertification credits for tagging our content to our taxonomy. How can you incentivize your volunteers to help you with your content management needs?

Complexity can kill. ASTD integrated XML into the tools that were already being used: Microsoft Word, Excel, and InDesign. Forcing staff to change tools is the surest way of undermining your unified content strategy!

Anthony Allen, Director of Production, American Society for Training and Development

Summary

Digital publishing is fast becoming a critical requirement for publishers. It's no longer just a desirable capability; it's a matter of survival. Most publishers associate digital publishing solely with the production of eBooks and fall short of the mark. The crucial point for publishers today is to prepare their content for multi-channel delivery where printed books and eBooks represent two possible delivery channels.

In a traditional publishing workflow, each book or document is created by one author using some form of text editor or word processor. This document is created, edited, and published as one entity, or possibly as a series of chapters, and doesn't interact with anything else.

The in-house publishing workflow is very similar to the traditional publishing workflow with the exception of the production of eBooks. Publishers use the same publishing software they use for print to publish to an EPUB file.

Recognizing the challenges they face in publishing to multiple channels and the proliferation of devices, some publishers are choosing to use XML in their publishing workflow. "XML early" means converting your content into XML early on in your workflow to enable you to produce content for multiple channels and to easily reuse content.

To take advantage of new digital markets, you must reengineer your processes to create a more flexible and sustainable future. This requires a unified content strategy.

More information on the effective design and creation of eBooks can be found in *eBooks 101: The Digital Content Strategy for Reaching Customers Anywhere, Anytime, on Any Device*, by Ann Rockley and Charles Cooper.

Chapter 5

Product content

Pushed by the need to develop multiple versions of the same information, in multiple languages, in multiple channels, and on tight deadlines, the technical communication industry developed content reuse strategies in the early 1990s.

The technical communication industry calls reuse "single sourcing," which is a method of reusing content where content is written once, stored in a single source location, and reused many times.

Technical communicators have a long track record of multichannel delivery that enterprise and digital publishers can learn from.

The evolution of reuse in technical publications

As the technical communication industry matured, it discovered how to reuse content in different ways.

Multiple channels, multiple copies

Content was made available in multiple channels (for example, print and HTML help). Content was written for one channel and then typically a copy was made for additional channels. The content had to be reformatted for each channel. Little attempt was made to differentiate the content or the presentation of the content to accommodate differences in platform and usage. If the content was modified to fit the channel or to address the fact that online information is used differently than paper-based information, the materials became quite different and were not single sourced (updates had to be made to two sources).

This is similar to the situation faced by many organizations today as they try to convert their content from print to eBooks or from traditional Web to mobile Web.

Single-source publishing

Technical communicators stopped writing long, monolithic documents and started writing content as stand-alone topics that could be published to both print and HTML formats. Vendors created help authoring tools (HAT) to support this process and to eliminate the need to have one copy of the content formatted for print and another format for the Web. These tools resulted in single-source publishing.

Customized content

At the beginning, single sourcing meant identical content and multiple channels, but as authors became concerned about the effectiveness of identical content used in multiple channels, they moved to customized content. This type of content is customized to meet the needs of the customer, the type of content to be developed, and the channel. Content is deliberately built for customized output from the single source to meet specific audience needs or output requirements. Authors select from topics to create customized content (for example, different customers or products).

Although content is customized, it does not mean that the content is rewritten for each usage. Rather, sub-elements (for example, greater or lesser detail, and illustrations of screens in the paper document, but not in the help materials) are used where appropriate.

This form of single sourcing produced much more effective and usable materials, but was also time-consuming.

Dynamic content

With dynamic content, information is assembled only when it is requested. It exists as a series of components that are assembled in response to user requests or requirements. Customers identify required content, or a user profile automatically identifies the requirements and delivers the appropriate content.

This type of reuse does not rely on the author to build the document, but it does rely on effective content models that can predict how to provide the appropriate information at the right time. And it relies on technology. Content can be automatically assembled and delivered to the Web, or a request could be made for just-in-time printing based on a custom configuration.

Dynamic content is still largely a Web-only solution; product content is only now starting to move to mobile.

Two directions (structure vs. community)

The industry soon began to split into two different directions: one moving towards structured XML-based content for print and user assistance materials while the other moved towards wikis and community interaction.

Structured content using DITA

Realizing that it was still too much work to create and format content for multiple channels, many technical publications teams have adopted structured reusable content using the DITA (Darwin Information Typing Architecture) XML standard. DITA is an open content standard that defines a common structure for content that promotes the consistent creation, sharing, and reuse of content. In addition to the DITA standard, OASIS, the standards organization responsible for the growth and maintenance of DITA, provides a free publishing engine that supports the publishing of DITA-based content to online user assistance and print. For more information on DITA, refer to Chapter 19, "The role of XML."

The basic DITA content model can support a wide range of content requirements, but if the content models you design don't map exactly to DITA, you can customize the DITA model using a process called specialization. However, with the power of DITA comes complexity. The complexity is inherent in the ways in which authors interact with DITA and the power that it provides authors for creating and managing reusable content. OASIS has recognized this issue and is working towards the simplification of DITA. In addition, software vendors have taken on the challenge to create XML editors that hide DITA under a friendly user interface.

One of the challenges of DITA is that the free publishing engine does not publish to channels that support the social Web; however, vendors are filling this gap as well.

Communities, wikis, and the social Web

The task of creating ever-increasing volumes of content to document every possible method in which a customer may use a product is becoming unsustainable. Some technical communicators have moved towards the use of wikis and the social Web. Content begins with the technical communicator but is then opened up to the online community where experts share insights, tips, and best practices.

The wiki provides a better customer experience and increases the breadth and depth of available information, but the content is often locked into the wiki with no easy way to get it out and publish that content to additional formats. This is not unlike the issues of content locked in print or any other format.

Marrying the intelligence of DITA with the social Web

Content does not have to remain locked in wikis and DITA does not have to remain isolated from the social Web; intelligent content (which is not limited to one purpose, technology, or output) can bridge both worlds.

Product content can be developed using DITA best practices:

- Modular, reusable content
- Well-structured content
- Content separate from format (content free of styles, layout, or device-specific information)
- Rapid delivery to multiple channels

After it's created, content can be pushed to the wiki where it can be augmented by customer input. The customer experience is enhanced through:

- Multiple flexible organizations of content (for example, tasks, problems, and solutions)

Case study: The Elekta Group deploys a component CMS with a socially enabled content integration layer

Background

The Elekta Group (Elekta) creates innovative clinical solutions and medical technology for treating cancer and brain disorders. Elekta required accurate, auditable content that would be created and consumed by a fully fledged ecosystem of internal and external stakeholders.

Goals and opportunities

Elekta wanted to stem their increasing translation costs, drive knowledge sharing across teams, and speak with one voice both internally and externally on their various existing, and future, communication channels.

Challenges

With traditional unstructured content tools and proprietary formats, Elekta was unable to keep up with their reuse, production, and delivery goals. Additionally, their rapid growth through acquisitions necessitated the integration of different brands and the information silos in their globally dispersed business units.

Elekta recognized that their technical content went far beyond their technical documentation. They had overlapping sets of operational and reference information with potentially reusable content for internal or external use. The unification and consolidation of content across the entire lifecycle would be vital to realizing the full potential of their technical content as a business asset.

What they did and why

Elekta put together an international project team of internal staff and specialist third-party consultants. As a team, we completed a content and process audit to support the development of a unified content strategy which addressed the challenges with traditional technical documentation and also a wider, long-term vision. We presented the results up the management chain, and put a global proposal with project scope to the Elekta executive committee, who supported it unanimously.

We started with an in-depth user and task analysis, followed by content modeling and information taxonomy workshops, in preparation for the move to DITA XML. Later, in facilitated prototyping workshops, Elekta selected a vendor for the component content management system (CCMS) The team then outlined a modular project that allowed business units and content sets to be included in a phased approach to avoid overstressing teams.

As a forward-looking initiative, Elekta chose to include a socially enabled dynamic delivery prototype in the pilot project. This prototype showed how it would be possible to capture and rank knowledge created by subject matter experts (SMEs), such as field service engineers, as well as link it with technical documentation created in the CCMS. Social features like tagging, commenting, content sharing, and creating customized, user-defined documents will eventually improve access for users. In the longer term, the system will feed knowledge-based articles into a formal editorial lifecycle, and even deliver information directly into software or hardware products that have content display capabilities.

Elekta used a structured XML conversion tool to convert legacy content to DITA XML topics. However, ensuring that the content complied with DITA XML and Simplified Technical English (STE), and then revalidating it after conversion proved time-consuming. We introduced a faster, more automated bulk conversion process.

Continued...

*Case study: The Elekta Group deploys a component CMS with
a socially enabled content integration layer continued*

Benefits

This project demonstrated how a unified content strategy can provide a common denominator for content and branding. This is a strategy that allows everyone, irrespective of geography, language, culture, or business unit, to participate while still meeting specific local needs.

Return on investment

With estimates in the business case indicating potential savings in translation cost between 40 percent and 70 percent through the use of STE, DITA minimalist writing, and XML for the elimination of DTP, it was encouraging to see a £24K ($38,000) saving, or 30 percent saving, on Elekta's first, one-document, 14-language translation project. If this becomes the trend, there is no reason why they should not reach their cost-saving goal, after full implementation, of approximately £400K ($640,000) per year.

Noz Urbina, Content Strategist, Senior Consultant and Trainer at Mekon Ltd

- Search for information based on categories
- Access to rich media (video, simulations, and audio)
- Selecting the best and most useful customer information and sharing it with other customers (curation)

Customer content is not locked in the wiki; the most highly rated or the most frequently viewed customer content can be transferred back into the DITA environment for use in augmenting the core content.

DITA and dynamic personalized content

DITA can also be used to facilitate dynamic delivery of personalized content to provide intelligent content on the back end and specifically targeted customer content on the front end.

Modular DITA-based content can be easily assembled on the fly to meet customer needs. Once the content is extracted from the content management system (CMS), the content is transformed into traditional HTML for ease of customer viewing and use. Or the content could be accessed by a mobile app and similarly rendered on the fly to the mobile device.

Customers can comment on the content, providing feedback loops back into the source content.

Mobile

The explosion of mobile devices is also changing the way technical communicators share content. No longer can they assume that customers will access their product content in a PC-sized browser or in a printed manual. More and more customers want access to content on tablets, smartphones, and other mobile devices.

It's a relatively simple exercise to convert modular structured content for mobile with the addition of stylesheets that optimize the content for a given device.

Augmented reality

Technical communicators are going beyond text and simple graphics by creating three-dimensional renditions of their content. It's no longer necessary to produce manuals or provide a product CD with consumer products. For example, a customer whose printer has a paper jam can point the camera in their smartphone at the printer and have the image overlaid with an interactive display showing how to clear the paper jam.

Augmented reality systems are also being used to create service documentation for cars and large medical devices.

The opportunities are exciting as technical communicators learn how to integrate this form of delivery into their unified content strategy.

The role of a unified content strategy

Technical communicators have a long track record in the creation of a unified content strategy and intelligent content. While their strategies are more complex than most, their content is future-proofed and they can easily adapt their content to new devices yet to be designed.

In addition, enterprise and digital publishers can follow in the footsteps of technical communicators and move into the world of content reuse, secure in the knowledge that the processes and systems are proven and successful.

Summary

Technical communicators have a long track record of multichannel delivery that enterprise and digital publishers can learn from. As the technical communication industry matured, it discovered how to reuse content in different ways:

- Multiple channels, multiple copies
- Single-source publishing
- Customized content
- Dynamic content

The industry soon began to split into two different directions: one moving towards structured XML-based content for print and user assistance materials while the other moved towards wikis and community interaction. However, the two communities are now moving together to marry the intelligence of DITA, XML standard and wikis, communities and the social Web.

Because technical communicators have moved to structured, reusable content, their content is future-proofed and they can easily adapt their content to new devices yet to be designed.

Chapter 6

Learning materials

Learning plays a critical role in most organizations. A workforce that's highly trained is productive and effective; it can adapt to changing market and customer requirements. Many organizations have their own learning development (LD) teams and may also bring in training expertise from outside the organization. Some even use their LD teams as cost centers and hire them out to customize content for customers.

Instructional designers (IDs) are highly skilled at creating learning materials that specifically meet the learner's needs. However, on a tight budget and even tighter timeline, they're hard-pressed to provide multiple types of training materials for multiple learners.

Learning development teams are no strangers to the concept of modular reusable content. In 1997, Advanced Distributed Learning (ADL) began working on a reference model that defined reusable learning content. This model is known as SCORM (Sharable Content Object Reference Model). SCORM is a collection of standards for eLearning materials that facilitates the delivery of eLearning through a learning management system (LMS). Most authoring tools and learning content management systems (LCMS) are SCORM-compliant. However, while SCORM makes it possible to reuse learning modules in a variety of different learning delivery tools, it doesn't truly promote the concept of reusable learning content.

Types of learning materials

Learning development teams develop a wide range of learning materials, and each type of learning poses its own challenges.

Instructor-led training (ILT)

Instructor-led training is still a dominant form of training. Organizations and participants like the face-to-face interaction and the ability to work closely with an instructor. Participants also learn from other participants. Classroom training is typically supported by instructor-led materials and participant materials. The primary vehicle of delivery is the instructor, accompanied by PowerPoint slides and possibly some video.

ILT does, though, pose a number of challenges:

- Synchronization of handouts and slides

  Instructors love to have thumbnail images of the slides in their materials to guide them in their presentation. However, creating a slide, then creating a thumbnail and including it in the instructor's guide takes a lot of manual work. And when the slide changes, the instructor guide needs to change too.

  Some organizations have stopped putting in the thumbnail and instead reference the slide number. But that also presents a problem when the content is reorganized and the slides no longer fall in their original order. So it's a huge manual task to keep the slides and handouts synchronized.

- Synchronization of instructor materials and participant materials

  Instructors like to know what information the participant is getting, and then be guided in what they should do with that information (for example, explain a concept, demonstrate something, or conduct an exercise). Some organizations have created their materials in a two-page-spread format so that the left side of the page contains the instructor materials while the right side contains the participant materials. However, this design again requires a tremendous amount of manual work to create and maintain, and for this reason many organizations have abandoned this format.

- Customization

  Content often needs to be customized to meet specific learner needs. Instructors can perform minor customizations on the fly by changing what they say while, or after, they display a slide or other learning asset. In many cases, however, customization requires actually changing the materials themselves.

Sometimes the changes may be as simple as reorganizing the content, but often, terminology and exercises must be changed too. It's very difficult to customize the materials and still keep these materials synchronized with the standard materials for future updates. Ensuring that customized and standard materials remain synchronized becomes a tedious, error-prone manual process when content is locked in print layouts and when the current toolset doesn't facilitate the creation and management of customized content.

- Cost of travel

  Although both trainers and participants generally appreciate the immediacy of ILT, there's one group of people who isn't enamored of the process: accountants.

  Classroom training is becoming harder to justify for some as companies have become more global and the cost of travel and accommodation to bring learners to the training has skyrocketed. It simply isn't always feasible to move employees to training; training has to come to the learner.

Virtual classroom training

Virtual classroom training has become popular in recent years. Virtual classroom training can be as simple as web-based, instructor-led sessions with traditional PowerPoint slides, or it can be more elaborate, with whiteboard sharing, breakout sessions, and collaboration among students.

Virtual classroom training also poses certain challenges:

- Creation of materials

  Creating materials for the instructor and the participants presents problems similar to those associated with producing ILT training materials.

- Management of materials

  Virtual classroom software is designed for learning to be shared in a virtual classroom. The software often provides a method for uploading learning assets (PowerPoint slides, videos, and so on) but there's no way to actually manage the materials once they are loaded. There's also no way to tell what the most current version of the asset is or even where to find it. Virtual classroom software provides very rudimentary search and retrieval capabilities. Once an organization starts to use the virtual classroom extensively, they lose the ability to keep track of the content.

- Instructor availability

  Despite the fact that this type of training can reach more learners in many different locations, the amount of delivery is still constrained by the availability of instructors, and the fact that there are only so many hours in a day for delivery. Some companies record the presentation so that others can watch it in the future, but these secondary learners lose the live interaction, the collaboration with other participants, and the ability to ask questions. Just listening to sessions can be pretty boring, and learners may lose interest.

eLearning

Many organizations have moved away from classroom-based learning to eLearning. eLearning provides web-based training for self-paced learning. eLearning can be as basic as a "page turner," where content is presented on a screen and the learner clicks the next button to read through the materials, or as high-end as learning with simulations and virtual worlds. Most eLearning offers medium-level interactivity, with some page turning plus video, audio, interactive exercises, and quizzes.

eLearning involves its own challenges:

- Cost

  The biggest issue with eLearning is its cost. It can be significantly more expensive to design medium or high-end learning materials.

  Early proponents of eLearning touted it as a way to combine the immediacy and interactivity of ILT with the low cost of web delivery (compared with the cost of an instructor). But it turns out that "replacing the instructor" is not as easy or inexpensive as it first seemed. To understand what the learners need, to anticipate all the interactivity required at any point in the learning cycle, and then to design and create all the learning assets (text, audio, or video) is very difficult and expensive.

  Although costs can vary, the typical cost of developing ILT is about 30 hours of development for one hour of instruction. Compare that to eLearning, which often takes 100 hours of development for one hour of basic eLearning, 200 hours of development for medium-level interactivity, and 300 hours of development for high-end eLearning. We've known some high-end eLearning to cost millions of dollars. Unless you have a lot of learners, these costs may simply not be justifiable.

- Customization and localization

  The higher the level of eLearning, the more expensive it is to customize. Simulations, videos, and other interactive materials tend to be created as a single "chunk" of content. It isn't easy to switch out language or images, or change interactivity, without redoing the entire set of materials.

- Bandwidth

  If you're accustomed to a high-speed Internet connection, you take it for granted. It's only when you don't have high-speed access for some reason that you realize how important it is. High-end eLearning requires very fast Internet speeds with good throughput. If your learners are in a location where they don't have reliable high-speed access, then high-end eLearning might not be an option. In most cases the files are designed to be streamed (viewed in real time over the Web) rather than downloaded. If the content is being handled by a local server, it may not be too much of a problem, but eLearning that's located on a geographically different server can become unusable because of slow performance issues.

Mobile

Learning has moved from the classroom to the desktop and now to mobile. With mobile, learners can learn wherever they are. Learning materials can be delivered in bite-sized pieces to enable learning whenever people have some downtime, such as in lineups, on the commuter train, or between other activities.

Learning via mobile (mLearning) is still in the early adoption stage but growing quickly. A recent survey of their membership conducted by the eLearning Guild[1] found the following:

- 25.5 percent were engaged in producing mLearning

- 40 percent were exploring mLearning

- 51 percent had seen a positive return on investment (ROI), while another 38.8 percent said it was too early to tell

- 47.4 percent intended to do more mLearning in the next year

In another report, Ambient Insight Research determined that the mobile learning market is growing at a rate of 18.3 percent annually; revenues reached $632.2 million in 2009 and will top $1.4 billion by 2014.[2]

Mobile learning involves the following challenges:

- mLearning versus eLearning

  Mobile's ease of access and the short time periods people typically spend on it are better suited to performance support than to full-scale learning. Typical

---

1   The eLearning Guild. *Mobile Learning: Landscape and Trends,* www.elearningguild.com

2   Ambient Insight Research. www.ambientinsight.com

examples of mobile performance support include job aids, checklists, and access to information we can't easily remember (for example, numbers and details). Mobile can capture activity and provide unique responses based on customer selections.

- Content conversion

  Learning content developed for classrooms, virtual classrooms, or eLearning doesn't convert well to mobile. Learning materials developed for one channel aren't designed to adapt to another. As in other industries, content is tied to format and delivery channels, making it difficult to convert. However, more importantly, content for other learning channels isn't optimized for the unique environment of a mobile device (for example, small screen; short, rapid usage; and lack of integration with enterprise tools).

- Proliferation of devices

  Mobile content has no equivalent to the eBook EPUB standard. There's no single across multiple mobile platforms; material developed for the Android won't work on iOS (Apple), and material developed for webOS won't run on Windows Phone 7. This means that mLearning materials have to be recoded to run on each device platform.

  In addition, the differing capabilities of devices running the same operating system, such as Apple's iOS, are significant—consider the differences between an iPhone and an iPad. What works on one may not work on the other. The combinations of operating system and hardware capabilities mean that the mobile training market is highly fragmented.

- Lack of Adobe Flash

  A lot of learning materials have been built using Adobe Flash. Many devices, notably Apple's iOS-based devices such as iPhones and iPads, don't run Flash. Adobe has ceased the development of Flash for mobile devices. It will be replaced by HTML5-based interactivity. This will require the conversion of existing Flash materials.

- Security

  Organizations are often concerned about the security of their content. Passwords and wiping of stored information can help, but many are concerned about the information being accessed en route.

Case study: Global foodservice retailer

A global foodservice retailer with restaurants in more than 100 countries needed to find a more effective way to create and distribute global learning materials. The worldwide training and development team (WWTD) was responsible for creating and delivering global operational training in nine core languages. They created a broad range of materials including:

- eLearning
- Classroom and self-study materials
- Paper-based performance support tools
- Web-based performance support tools

WWTD was developing a large number of materials. In the past they had created print-based materials for the USA and supplied these same materials to the other regions. In some cases the materials were used unchanged, but in others content required localization to be country and/or market specific. WWTD wanted to:

- Create a core set of operational standards that would be used by all markets
- Provide tools and processes to enable markets to localize materials
- Track the changes being made by markets, incorporate and share content created by the markets among markets, and integrate this content into the corporate core materials
- Make sure that content was easily reusable and retrievable
- Adopt a technology that would let WWTD manage content and deliver to all required learning channels
- Adapt to new learning devices such as mobile
- Provide just-in-time training in the restaurants to communicate critical

information such as hygiene procedures and safety training

WWTD knew there was a lot of reuse (typically done through copy and paste) among the materials, but it was difficult to track; content was becoming inconsistent, translation costs were higher than desired, and there was no way to track common content and update it when necessary. Programmatic analysis of the content identified 85 percent reuse between the operational performance support tools. But different tools were used to create each content type, so reuse was very difficult to manage.

The process

WWTD began the process by analyzing the content set. A unified content strategy was developed to ensure structured content creation and reuse. The content strategy initially focused on developing a core corporate set of materials, then expanded to provide support for global requirements. Corporate didn't want the training to be a one-way street with guidance only coming out of corporate; sharing of learning materials and ideas from the regions was critical.

WWTD also knew that communication with the regions would be important to ensure success. WWTD created a communication plan that helped the regions understand the basics of structure, modeling, reuse, metadata, and workflow. The strategy communicated the decision-making process to the organization at large and served as pre-course homework to put the learning in context.

Project success

The content strategy, LCMS, and new associated processes were rolled out globally over a three-year period. Regions began to share content not only within their own content set but also across regions. Translation costs were significantly reduced.

The role of a unified content strategy

Learning development teams must free themselves from thinking in deliverables (ILT, PowerPoint presentation, eLearning, and mLearning) and think instead in terms of modular reusable content. Some organizations already employ reusable learning objects (RLOs), but the objects are still tied to a particular format. It's time to start thinking about content separate from format and channel. Learning development teams need to adopt a unified content strategy that bridges channels and learning types to deliver just-in-time learning and support for learners wherever they are and on whatever device they're using.

A unified content strategy facilitates learning in these ways:

- Content relationships can be updated when a related component is updated to aid in the synchronization of content.

- Modular RLOs (content) can be mixed and matched to create custom learning experiences.

- Content can be tagged with metadata (for example, Instructor, Objective, Quiz, Concept, and Support) to facilitate the automated assembly and delivery of content.

Summary

Learning plays a critical role in most organizations. IDs are highly skilled at creating learning materials that specifically meet the learner's needs. Learning development teams produce a number of different types of learning materials, including instructor-led training, virtual classroom training, eLearning, and most recently mLearning. However, they're hard-pressed to provide multiple types of training materials for multiple learners on a tight budget and an even tighter timeline.

A unified content strategy can help in the development of learning materials through the use of:

- Modular RLOs (content) that can be mixed and matched to create custom learning experiences and assemblies of different types of learning materials and delivered to different channels.

- Format-free content that can be adapted and delivered to multiple devices.

Part 3

Performing a substantive audit: Determining business requirements

Customers are the reason for your business's existence, your products and services, and your content. You need to understand who your customers are and how well your content meets their needs.

Before content makes its way to your customers, many different hands help to produce it. As a result, there can be duplication of effort and stylistic disparities. By unifying content, you can enhance its usability and consistency, and save your company considerable time and money.

However, unified content requires unified processes. You need to figure out how it's being used, and how it's being created, published, and stored. We call this discovery process the "Substantive Audit." During a substantive audit, you examine who needs and uses what content, how that content currently supports the audience, and how it's produced, as well as the technology that supports your content life-cycle processes. When that's finished, you can identify how your unified content strategy will work.

When implementing a unified content strategy, start with the customer. Your content is for your customers, and if you don't understand them, your unified content strategy will fail. Chapter 7, "What does your customer really need?," helps you determine your customer requirements.

In Chapter 8, "Where does it really hurt?," you'll learn ways to identify the dangers, opportunities, and strengths related to your organization. You'll also learn how to determine the organizational goals you want to achieve.

Just as in a theater production where different processes support the front stage and the back stage, you have front stage processes for your customer and back stage processes for producing your content. Chapter 9, "Analyzing the content lifecycle," helps you identify what's working and what's not so you can address these challenges.

At the heart of your content strategy is the content itself. Chapter 10, "Performing a content audit," helps you analyze your content for appropriateness, completeness, and clarity. In addition, this chapter illustrates how to audit your content to identify opportunities for reuse. Once you determine how your information is being used and reused, you can make decisions about how you might unify it.

Chapter 11, "Envisioning your unified content strategy and lifecycle," shows how you can picture your content strategy working and what processes will be required to support the strategy. It will also help you determine some of the challenges you'll face.

Chapter 7

What does your customer really need?

Before restructuring the content for effective reuse and delivery to customers, you need to determine how well your current content is meeting your customers' needs and identify any gaps in the content. Simply producing a content strategy based on your current practices or improving the way you produce content will not help customers if you are not producing the right content.

Your content is used by many different customers, both internal and external. Internal customers are those within your organization who use content to assist them in doing their jobs, making decisions, and supporting the customer. External customers are those outside your organization (for example, customers and stakeholders) who use content to get information about your company, such as what products and services you provide, how to use your products and services, and how to contact you.

You may not be able to interview your customers directly, but you can interview people in your organization who do have contact with your customers, for example, staff who work in marketing or customer support. However, you should make every attempt to conduct customer research. Creating content without a solid knowledge of your customer requirements results in ineffective and ultimately costly content because you have to substitute for inadequate content with higher customer support and lost sales.

Identifying customer needs

To determine customer requirements you have to understand customers' needs in more depth. You need answers to the following questions:

* Can you group your customers into categories? How many categories? What defines each category?

* What content does each customer use and when?

* Is the content for one customer group different from that for another customer group? How is it different? Where does it differ?

* How do customers access your content?

* How do they want to access your content?

* What content do they need to know? What content is nice to know?

* At what level of detail do customers want to see content? Do they always want to see it at the same level of detail, or do they want to be able to switch from very detailed to top level?

* What are their interests in your content?

* What are their goals in using your content?

Conducting a needs assessment

There are many ways to conduct a needs assessment, ranging from formal to informal. Methods include:

* Interviewing people in your organization who do have contact with your customers: marketing, sales, customer support.

* Analyzing existing customer information.

* Gathering new information, in the following ways:
    * Using a Web survey.
    * Interviewing members of your customer base through a focus group or by telephone or email.
    * Testing a key information product (for example, website) for usability.
    * Reaching out using social media.

Case study: City of Vancouver

The City of Vancouver in British Columbia is committed to providing a content-rich website to communicate with its residents, businesses, tourists, and other website visitors.

Since its inception in the mid-1990s, the City's web presence had grown organically to the point where it was no longer perceived as a useful or reliable primary source of information. The site had become unwieldy, with decades of information contributed by over 100 authors, organized largely by departmental silos. Its search function was thwarted by optical-scan PDFs and lack of metadata. While some web apps worked only with certain browsers, other new mobile apps were being designed as device-specific.

The City created a three-word mandate: fix the website. From this came the vision, which was to create a unified experience for users. This meant presenting content in useful contexts, for example, routing the content to pages by neighbourhood, sorting it by subject matter and date, and so on. Content needed to be sorted and grouped in ways that provided information, encouraged online transactions, and supported citizen engagement. Content also had to be universally available, regardless of accessibility issue, browser, or device.

At the tactical level, the goal was to restructure content according to the mental models of the typical site users. Surveys, and some interviews, of over 5,000 site visitors provided enough insight to create seven personas. Their vision of the City radiated out from their property, with information from property taxes to pet licenses, to their street, then to their neighbourhood, and finally to the City at large. This became the goal for the new site architecture.

In 2010, a dedicated team of web professionals was created to redevelop the website. The content, all 35,000 HTML pages and 25,000 PDFs, was inventoried.

Subsequent analysis identified the high-demand content, allowing for retirement of old pages and a reduction of the site to under 5,000 pages of high-value content and related attachments.

To be handled intelligently by the content management system (CMS), the content needed semantic properties, both in editorial and semantic structure. Each content type, such as news releases, council decisions, and contact information, was codified both structurally and editorially. Content flows were created to demonstrate the paths through the CMS for each content type. A taxonomy was developed, and the team tagged the content so that it could be filtered and grouped by context. The team also set stringent editorial standards so that content across the site would have a consistent tone and voice, even when the content written by multiple authors was recombined for reuse in multiple places on the site.

At the time of writing, the project has not yet launched. Yet the preliminary feedback is already validating the new direction. Testing of the information architecture has demonstrated a remarkable ease of use for site visitors, and internal stakeholders are overwhelmingly supportive of the approach. Even after launch, the project will never be "complete"; the site is a living entity, and will continue to be developed as the City's priorities grow and change.

The organization recognizes that the first step—rework the content and implement a system that could handle content intelligently—is just the beginning of a longer process. The next steps are to integrate the numerous applications that allow residents and visitors to interact with the City online and to find ways to use the new content framework to encourage resident engagement.

Rahel Anne Bailie, Principal of Intentional Design. Courtesy of City of Vancouver, BC.

Analyzing existing customer information

If you already have customers you should already have some customer information, though it may not be as focused or as in depth as you would like. Talk to people with the following roles to gain an understanding of your customers.

Marketing

Marketing staff understand who they are marketing the product or service to. They may not know exactly what content customers need, but they'll have a good idea of who they are. Marketing should be consulted not only on the requirements of customers, but also from the perspective of original equipment manufacturers (OEMs), value-added resellers (VARS), and partners because they're all customers too. Ask marketing:

- Who are the primary customers?
- Where do your customers come from (region/country, referring site, search engine)?
- What platform are they using: Mac, PC, smartphone (OS)?
- Who are the secondary or associated customers?
- What do they know about the customer profile?
- What do customers need to know to make the buying decision?
- What do they think are the most effective ways to reach the customer?

Sales

If you sell a fairly large product or service, salespeople are always in front of pro-spective customers—or at least they sure want to be! Sales staff deal with custom-ers all the time and have firsthand knowledge of where the customers are experiencing pain. Ask sales many of the same questions you ask marketing as well as ones that relate to the kind of content they need in a proposal:

- Who are the primary customers?
- Who are the secondary or associated customers?
- What do they know about the customer profile?
- Where do your customers come from (region/country, referring site, search engine)?
- What platform are they using: Mac, PC, smartphone (OS)?
- What do customers need to know to make the buying decision?
- What do they think are the most effective ways to reach the customer?

- What kind of content do you need for your proposal? How much is unique to the proposal and how much is reusable content?

- What content do they point the customer to (brochures, the Web, product content, other)?

Customer service

Customer service has an incredible amount of knowledge about your customers. Granted, they'll most often hear the complaints or frustrations, but that information is fodder for what needs to change and where the content gaps are, and will tell you about the tasks customers are trying to complete. Ask customer service the following:

- Who do they think are your customers? Their answers may surprise you. You may have an audience you never even thought of before.

- What are the most common questions that people ask? This is going to tell you where people are experiencing problems and give you a good indication of what people are trying to do.

Don't forget to ask customer service about what makes callers happy or what they say "works." Believe us when we say that most customer service people will remember those who mentioned something good!

Web analytics

If your content resides on the Web, then web analytics can be invaluable in providing you with information about your web visitors. Web analytics are becoming more functional all the time, enabling you to gather ongoing information for continual measurement.

Use web analytics to answer these questions:

- Where do your customers come from (region/country, referring site, search engine)?

- What platform are they using—Mac, PC, smartphone (OS)?

- What did they look at and where did they go on your site?

- What landing pages did they land on? What page did they exit from?

- What keywords did they use to search for information?

- How frequently do they visit your site?

- How recent was the visit?

- How much time was spent on site?

Customer satisfaction surveys

Customer satisfaction surveys are another good place to start. Unfortunately many of them focus on just the product or service and not the site's content, but even without specific content questions you can still glean some information. If you have content questions, bonus! If not, make sure you do for next year.

Gathering new information

Even if you have good existing customer information you may need to reach out to your customers to gather more detailed information.

Surveys

Surveys are a great way to get top-level information from your customers.

Ask people to take a survey as they access or exit the site. Or ask people to take a survey after they have searched for and used information to determine if they found it useful or not. Be careful not to launch the survey over and over again or you risk irritating your customers. Nothing is more annoying than a survey that pops up every time they do something.

If you have a customer list, email them a survey. Entice them to respond by giving them an opportunity to win free products or services, or an exciting new gadget. Be sure to have an automated response that thanks people for taking the survey.

Think carefully about the design of your survey; free text questions are more difficult to analyze and score while questions that ask customers to score are easier to measure, chart, and use to illustrate business arguments.

If you have customers with whom you would like to grow or deepen the relationship, call them and ask them directly to participate in a survey. Provide them with a customized URL, and make sure they feel that their answers will help you serve them better.

Interviews or focus groups

You can gain really valuable information from a focus group or one-on-one interviews. User/customer conferences are a great opportunity to gather customers together for a focus group. You don't often get the opportunity to actually talk to "live" customers, so make sure you get the desired results by being fully prepared. Interviews and focus groups let you ask the standard questions, but they then delve down further to expand on the answers to get a rich understanding of customer needs. Be sure to thank all participants afterward for giving you their valuable time.

Customer interviews are critical to understand how the intended audiences use and access your content, and to determine what changes should be made to accommodate them. Customer interviews can help you realize how similar groups of people need similar types of information and if the content they need is there. Customer interviews can also tell you in which format customers prefer to receive information (web static or dynamic, mobile, print).

Refer to Chapter 9, "Analyzing the content lifecycle" for sample questions.

Usability testing

When people think about usability testing, they often think about testing the product. You can test your information products as well (website, mobile site, user guide, help, mobile app, eBook). Define a scenario and tasks that these products need to perform, and then observe their performance. See how they navigate the content, where they get stuck, and what questions aren't answered by the content.

Social media

Reach out to your community and start a conversation. Track your social media responses and see what people are saying on other influential social media sites:

- Write a blog entry asking your customers for feedback.
- Ask a question on Twitter and track the responses.
- Post a question on Facebook and LinkedIn.

Personas

After you have finished identifying customer needs, consider creating a persona for each of your major customer types. A persona is a profile of a typical customer. It is created based on a series of interviews with actual customers. The persona is not impersonal the way a standard customer description is; you write a persona as though you are describing a real person. The persona has a name, a history, and a set of goals. Personas help authors and designers and others within your organization understand who they are designing the content for. When authors and designers satisfy the goals of the persona, they also meet the needs of users with similar goals. It's easier to design when you have real people with real goals in mind. The persona makes the design exercise real and applicable rather than abstract.

Case study: Start with content and context

A construction materials company wanted a new concept and collateral for its annual safety awareness campaign. Past efforts had met with mixed results. No matter how hard the company tried, no one seemed to get very excited about safety. The agency I was working with thought the solution lay with better messaging or better creative.

I wasn't so sure. I decided to dig a little deeper by looking at two things: the content and the users. It turned out that most of the safety problems addressed in the content occurred in areas of the workplace where traditional collateral was pretty useless. Posters were forbidden inside factories (for safety reasons, no less). Few people worked at desks, and even fewer of them had access to the intranet. These folks spent their days on the shop floor, out in stockyards and in vehicles.

That's when the lightbulb went on. Instead of trying to drive employees to the content, why not deliver the content to them in a format that was compatible with their context?

We chunked the key content into bite-sized pieces and then used adhesive stickers to deliver these nuggets of wisdom inside vehicles, on lockers, and on shop floors. The entire effort was supported by a handbook for managers, posters, and a dedicated section on the intranet. These chunks of content also became conversation starters for safety training sessions.

By focusing on the context and the content we were able to find a highly effective delivery platform—one that was about as low-tech as you can get.

Richard Thompson, content strategist and copywriter, Richtext

The concept of a persona was introduced by Alan Cooper in his book *The Inmates Are Running the Asylum*. Since then, personas have been used to create marketing campaigns, software, websites, training, and documentation, and of course products. It makes a lot of sense to use personas to create effective content as well.

To create a persona:

- Determine how many personas you require to effectively address your customer base.

- Give each persona a name and a picture.

- Describe the persona. Include as much detail as possible (likes, dislikes, needs, desires, personality type).

- Define each persona's goals. Design decisions are based on goals, so take great care in preparing the goals.

Living the GI Way: Customer needs analysis

Living the GI Way (LGIW) is a fictitious example, provided to illustrate the concepts in this book.

Living the GI Way specializes in providing information about the glycemic index (GI). The organization grew out of the groundbreaking work done at the University of Toronto by Dr. David Jenkins and colleagues in their research to find out what different types of foods were best for people with diabetes. However, since that time the popularity of the GI has skyrocketed as new research has shown its value in diabetes, weight loss, reactive hypoglycemia, polycystic ovarian syndrome (PCOS), fibromyalgia, and potentially in heart disease.

LGIW started off more as a grassroots organization, founded by an interested diabetic and nutritionist but grew rapidly as the popularity of the index grew. It became an incorporated business in the early 1990s. Now it is considered one of the most authoritative sites on the subject.

LGIW provides the following types of information:

- General description
- Presentation
- Quick reference card
- Interactive GI database
- GI self-help books and recipe books
- Training on GI (accessible after sign-on)
- Monthly newsletter

LGIW has three primary customers:

- Diabetics
- Diabetic educators
- People interested in weight loss

Sample persona

Figure 7.1
Persona image.

Continued...

Living the GI Way: Customer needs analysis continued

Diabetic persona

Sharon Stockla is a thirty-something Human Resource manager and mother of two. She was recently diagnosed with type 2 diabetes. She has a very busy life with a full-time job, two-hour commute every day, and multiple after-school activities with her kids such as dance and soccer. Her husband is great and helps out but he travels a lot for business.

She was told to adjust her diet and was given some guidelines but her blood sugars have been all over the place. Her doctor has told her that if she doesn't get her blood sugars under control with diet, she'll have to start taking medication.

Sharon has tried to watch her diet, but there never seems to be enough time to make a good meal at night before rushing out the door again with the kids, and by the time evening comes she's too tired to make lunch for the next day. On the weekend she was at the semifinal soccer game with her daughter. Her daughter's team won so she ended up playing two more games. However, Sharon hadn't brought enough food with her, and the food at the concession at the game was abysmal. She got up between games and passed out!

She's determined to figure out a way to eat properly and has come to www.LivingTheGIWay.com for inspiration on the recommendation of a friend.

Her goals are to:

- Keep her blood sugars under control, not too high and not too low.
- Lose 10-15 lbs.
- Get her energy back.

Summary

Customers are your reason for being. You need to gain an in-depth understanding of your customer so that you can create and structure the content to meet their needs. Use every avenue open to you to gather information:

- Interview sales, marketing, and customer support.

- Analyze existing customer information.

- Gather new information in these ways:
  - Use a web survey.
  - Interview members of your customer base by telephone or email.
  - Conduct a focus group with members of your customer base.
  - Test a key information product (for example, website) for usability.
  - Reach out using social media.

- Create a persona for each of your major customer categories.

Chapter 8

Where does it really hurt?

You've done your customer needs analysis and you probably have tons of ideas about how to address the needs, so you think you are good to go. Right? Wrong.

You can have the best ideas in the world and highly skilled people to follow them through, but if you don't have a handle on how content is created, managed, and delivered in the organization, your project, and subsequently the content, may never make it out the door.

To build an effective, unified content strategy you need to understand your organization's goals and needs. When implementing a unified content strategy, it's good to start "where it really hurts." Start in areas with the most pain, where processes and tools and technology are failing or inadequate and your organization is feeling the negative results from customers or management. This will help you realize a higher return on investment; it will also show other areas in the organization how a content strategy and a more effective content lifecycle can help them. Change typically occurs when the pain becomes too great—when organizations are held back from meeting ongoing requirements as well as profiting from new opportunities. Deadlines are missed, content is inconsistent, content is missing—and customers complain.

To discover where your organization is hurting the most, you need to understand the dangers and challenges facing your organization, the opportunities that can be realized if change occurs successfully, and the strengths your organization can build on to implement these changes. In most organizations, individual departments know the specific pain they are feeling; they may be frustrated by the inability to find relevant content, by duplication of their efforts, by tight deadlines. Talking to management and groups involved in the content lifecycle is beneficial because it helps to identify where the pain points are throughout the organization and it helps you determine where the focus of your unified content strategy should be. Management has a broad-picture perspective on issues and can assist in determining the key issues and strategic goals that must be addressed. And a mix of management and group feedback will paint a more realistic picture of the organization's issues.

This chapter discusses ways to identify the organizational dangers, opportunities, and strengths, as well as the goals you want to achieve in order to move ahead with a unified content strategy. Identifying these issues helps you figure out where a unified content strategy fits within the big picture, ensuring that you're addressing the real issues and goals of the organization and better positioning you to differentiate your product and service to meet ongoing customer needs. Identifying these issues will also help you define your strategy for helping your organization achieve its goals.

Who to interview

Talking to management or senior stakeholders is key to really understanding the big picture and the organization's overall goals. Interview as high up the organizational structure as you can go, such as directors and C-level management. Remember that these are the people who will ultimately sign off on your content strategy and make the decision about which projects get funded and which don't. But be aware that these are really busy people, and don't ask for more than 30 minutes of their time (you might only get 15 to 20). Make sure they understand the purpose of the interview and the project, but don't ask leading questions or draw any conclusions before you start. Stick to your questions.

Provide the questions in advance. Some won't look at them until the interview, others will have worked through the questions and prepared their answers.

Identifying the D.O.S.®: Dangers, opportunities, and strengths

In a competitive business environment and sometimes difficult economy, every organization faces dangers such as lost customers and lost sales and, subsequently, lost revenue. Yet even in difficult and challenging times, organizations can pursue many opportunities and build on their strengths. In fact, challenging times are often the best times to improve processes. However, before charging ahead, you first need to determine the dangers. Only then can you address them by identifying opportunities and strengths.

The concept of D.O.S.® is a registered trademark, protected by copyright and an integral concept of the Strategic Coach® Program. All rights reserved. Used and modified with written permission from www.strategiccoach.com.

Dangers

At some point, every organization faces danger. This is especially true in a competitive environment in which it is difficult, if not impossible, for organizations to maintain their desired competitive position. After all, someone else is always coming up with a newer and better solution, and customers' needs are always changing. From a business perspective, potential or perceived danger reflects the fear of something: the fear of losing competitive position, the fear of not meeting desired revenues, the fear of missed opportunities, and so on. The dangers to your organization can be enterprise-wide or related to a specific department. The first step in overcoming dangers is to identify them; danger can be a positive impetus to effect change. Once you know what dangers you face, you can define how your strategy can help to overcome them.

To help you identify the dangers specific to your organization, ask key people to identify the three top dangers the organization is facing, or will be facing, if you don't meet your goals.

Opportunities

Even when there is a multitude of dangers, opportunity exists. In fact, opportunity often arises from danger. However, when there are few dangers, there are even greater opportunities available—opportunities that you can pursue without feeling pressured by the need to address dangers and that you can pursue solely with the prospect of success.

With many opportunities available, it's important to focus on key ones. To identify where your best chances for improvement or growth lie, ask key people in your organization to identify the opportunities that they hope to take advantage of with a project like yours.

Strengths

Every organization has its strengths. Recognizing and building on your strengths is important because strengths allow you to realize your opportunities. Sometimes in difficult times it's easy to overlook your strengths and focus on the negatives. Focusing on your strengths provides a positive focus for moving forward and helps you build your content strategy using the strengths of the organization. Ask the key people in your organization to identify what they feel are the organization's greatest strengths and why.

Identifying the goals

All organizations have many goals, often reflected in corporate and department strategic plans. Naturally, goals are based on the opportunities organizations have available to them. While not all corporate goals can be addressed with a unified content strategy, you need to identify which ones can be. Goals may be the same as your opportunities; however, they should be more tangible and measurable.

Determine goals by examining strategic plans, and by asking key people what their specific goals are for the coming year. It's important to have long-term goals as well. You can also ask about two-year, three-year, or even five-year goals. In fact, many organizations have five-year strategic plans, broken down into what they hope to accomplish each year.

If you want to sell your content strategy within the organization, you must tie into the corporate goals. Without alignment to the corporate goals, your content strategy will not gain executive support.

Identifying the challenges

Along with goals come challenges, whether they're challenges of money, time, technology, or people. It's important, before forging ahead with change, to identify challenges the organization may face in successfully moving forward so you can address those challenges during implementation. The best way to identify challenges is to ask key people, and everyone else you interview as you get started on your project, what they perceive as the challenges that may impact your ability to meet the goals. When you know what the potential challenges are, you can put a plan in place to avoid and address these challenges.

Sample questions

- What are the business reasons behind this project?
- What problems do you hope to solve?
- What are the greatest dangers facing the organization right now?
- What do you believe are the opportunities available to the organization?
- What do you think your organization's greatest strengths are?
- What challenges do you think the organization may face bringing this project to success?
- What are the success factors for this project?

Living the GI Way: Where does it hurt?

Business goals of the project

- Develop a digital publishing content strategy to improve productivity and reduce costs.
- Publish effective eBooks.
- Provide better navigation on the website to facilitate content retrieval.

Problems to be solved

- We have started to get more requests for customized content, but the last project was very time-consuming and costly.
- We have published our most popular book on the glycemic index (GI) as an eBook but had huge problems with the GI tables. In the first version, the tables got really messed up, with one column on one screen and the next column below. Got lots of customer complaints. Redid all the tables as images but that didn't work well either because the tables were hard to read. Need to find a better way of displaying tables.
- Content is being manually reused in a number of places (on the Web, in the books, in training) and we are having a really hard time keeping it all up to date. We did a review of one piece of content and found it in 48 different places! Content wasn't consistent in all those places. That's a problem.

Dangers

- As the glycemic index becomes more recognized and is used more, there is starting to be a lot of competition for what we do.
- We are falling behind in technology, people want information in different ways, and we aren't able to provide that yet. They may go elsewhere.

Opportunities

- We think that the new devices give us a lot of opportunity to provide our content in new ways.
- We can provide more customized content.

Strengths

- Our people are amazing. They work really hard and do a lot with a little.
- People are eager to learn about new ways of doing things.
- Diabetes associations and other types of health care organizations trust us to provide the latest, most accurate information on GI.

Continued...

Living the GI Way: Where does it hurt? continued

Challenges

- Time. We are a small organization so it will be hard to implement new processes while still doing our regular activities.
- Money. Again, because we are small we don't have a lot of excess funds. We don't know what this is going to cost us.

Success factors

- Create an effective eBook in a timely and cost-effective manner.
- Be able to sell and support more customization of our content to health care organizations.
- Make customers happy.

Where a unified content strategy won't help

A unified content strategy will not be a solution to all the dangers you identify (for example, employee turnover). Its focus is on helping to solve the problems your organization is experiencing in the area of content creation, management, delivery, and communication with your customers. A unified content strategy is just one piece of your overall corporate strategy to address your dangers, realize your opportunities, and build on your strengths; it's not the whole solution. As you gather your information, ensure that you and the rest of your organization understand what a unified content strategy will help you do and what it won't.

Summary

To successfully move ahead with a unified content strategy, you need to determine where content management and authoring issues are really causing pain in the organization and jeopardizing your organization's ability to support a robust content strategy. You do this by determining the dangers and challenges facing your organization, the opportunities that can be realized if change occurs successfully, the strengths your organization can build on to implement these changes, the goals of the organization, and the challenges you may face while implementing a unified content strategy.

Chapter 9

Analyzing the content lifecycle

Within your organization, content is developed in many different ways by many different people and by many different departments. Development may follow a predefined process or it may not, and if there is an established process, it may differ from department to department.

You're probably asking yourself, "I'm concerned about content strategy—why do I need to be concerned about process?" To implement a unified content strategy, you need unified processes so that everyone involved in creating, developing, storing, and publishing content does it the same way, or at minimum, is able to interact effectively and share content. Without a good handle on your content processes the best content strategy in the world will fail.

Think about a theater production. There is the front of stage that your audience sees. It needs to be an amazing experience that draws them in, keeps them entertained, and provides a fulfilling experience. But if an actor is late getting on stage or forgets his lines, or when the curtain goes up in the second act and a chair that was in the scene in the first act isn't there, or one of the characters now has red hair instead of brown, this is a sure sign of disorganization and your audience is going to begin to question the quality of the presentation. There's a discontinuity and you've introduced uncertainty into the environment you've created. Your content and the way you choose to deliver it (Web, mobile, print) is your front of stage. Your content lifecycle is your back stage. Without a well-controlled back stage, the performance will be flawed.

To understand where you should focus your efforts, though, you need to examine your content lifecycle and any issues associated with it. Where your organization currently has challenges, you need to improve the processes and technology to eliminate these issues. Where processes and technology are working well, you want to see if they will continue to work effectively in the new strategy and if so, incorporate them. Identifying the issues will help you determine the scope and required functionality of your unified content strategy, define the tools selection criteria, and determine which processes you must redesign or create.

Identifying your content lifecycle

Content moves through various phases of development, such as creation, review, management, and delivery. These phases are collectively known as the "content lifecycle" (see Figure 9.1).

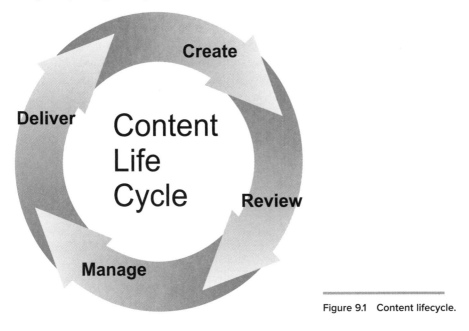

Figure 9.1   Content lifecycle.

Although your organization may have different phases, or call them by different names, these are the most common. To identify the content lifecycle in your organization, look at how content is developed for one area or across the enterprise. Is it the same across all content creation areas, or does it vary from area to area? How effective is the content lifecycle in each area?

This section poses questions about your content lifecycle and its effectiveness. To answer these questions, you'll need to interview all the players (everyone involved in the content lifecycle).

Identifying the players, processes, and issues

The previous section poses many questions that you should ask as you analyze your content lifecycle. To answer these questions, you interview all the players (everyone involved in the content lifecycle). This section provides sample interview questions. Developing content involves not only many different phases, but also many players with differing skills participating in many steps over an extended period of time. These players bring different insights into the issues related to the content lifecycle, so it's important to interview them to learn their different perspectives.

Depending on the area of the organization to be supported (for example, marketing versus product content) or by the type of organization, the players may change.

Typical players include:

- Customers (internal and external)
- Authors or content contributors
- Acquisitions or product development
- Design
- Editors
- Information technology
- Learning development and instructional design
- Production
- Reviewers
- Sales and marketing
- Translation/localization

Customers

Your content is used by many different customers, both internal and external. Internal customers are those within your organization who use content to assist them in doing their jobs, making decisions, and supporting the customer. External customers are those outside your organization (for example, customers, stakeholders) who use content to get information about your company (for example, what products and services you provide, how to use your products or services, how to contact you).

Customer interviews are critical to understanding how the intended audiences use and access your content, and to determining what changes should be made to accommodate them. Customer interviews can help you realize how similar groups of people need similar types of information and whether the content they use contains it or not. Customer interviews can also tell you how they prefer to receive information.

For more information on gathering information about your customers refer to Chapter 7, "What does your customer really need?"

Sample internal customer questions

- What is your role?

- What challenges do you face in getting your job done?

- How do you receive content now? How would you prefer to receive information?

- What content do you use to help you in your job?

- Has the content been designed to help you meet the challenges of your job, that is, can you find and access the right content when you need it? If so, what is it about the content that helps you?

- What types of information do you look for in content? How does that information help you do your job better?

- What do you like best about the content you use? What do you like least? Why?

- What suggestions can you make to improve the content?

Sample external customer questions

- What is your role?

- What content do you use most?

- What content do you use least?

- What is missing from our content?

- What do you like most about the content? What do you like least about the content?

- How do you use our content? Does it help you accomplish your tasks or make decisions?

- How do you receive content now? How would you prefer to receive content?

- What is the most challenging aspect of daily work? Can content help make this easier? If so, how?

- What suggestions can you make to improve the content?

Authors or content contributors questions

Questions related to the authoring processes are critical to uncovering issues related to the writing and management of content, issues that may hinder the usefulness of the content, its timeliness, and its overlap with other content. For example, do authors have the right tools? Are time frames realistic? Where do authors get the information they need? Are your authors also the subject matter experts (SMEs) or do they rely on SMEs to get the right information?

You may have internal authors, external authors, or a combination of both. We sometimes find that there's resistance or pushback when we ask to speak to external authors. If you find this, at minimum make sure you understand what templates and guidelines they're provided with and get an understanding of how well external authors follow those guidelines.

Looking at global authoring requirements is also very important. If you distribute content globally, global authors may have similar or very different requirements and issues.

Sample internal author questions

Questions for internal authors or content contributors might include something like the following:

1. What is your role? What are your responsibilities?

2. What are your current content creation processes? Which processes are effective? Which processes are ineffective? Explain.

3. Who do you work with during the content creation process? How effective are these relationships?

4. How do you collect information to write your content? How well does this work?

5. How do you currently handle sign-off or review?

6. How do you handle document control? Version control? Access control?

7. How do you create content (for example, are there stylesheets or templates)?

8. Do you reuse content? In what way? How effective is it?

9. What tools do you use? How well do they meet your needs?

Sample external author questions

Questions for external authors or content contributors might include something like the following:

- How do you create content (for example, are there stylesheets or templates)?
- What is the process you follow to create your content? How effective is this process?
- How much guidance do you get to help you create your content? Is there too much? Too little? How much guidance would you like?
- What suggestions could you make to improve the process between you and [company X]?
- What tools do you use? How well do they meet your needs?

Sample global author questions

Questions for global authors might include something like the following:

- What is your role? What are your responsibilities?
- What are your current content creation processes? Which processes are effective? Which processes are ineffective? Explain.
- Who do you work with during the content creation process? How effective are these relationships?
- How do you collect information to write your content? How well does this work?
- How do you currently handle sign-off or review?
- How do you handle document control? Version control? Access control?
- How do you create content (for example, are there stylesheets or templates)?
- Do you reuse content? In what way? How effective is it?
- Do you use the same tools as authors in other locations? If so, how well do the tools work for you? If not, which tools do you use? Why don't you use the same tools as other authors?

Acquisitions or product development

If content is your business, you'll have an acquisitions or product development role in your company. It's important to talk to people in your acquisitions or product development department because they start the process by identifying new opportunities, seeking out authors or existing content materials, acquiring the rights to these materials, determining what information products will be produced, and setting the required timeline. They are critical to your content lifecycle.

Sample acquisitions or product development questions

Questions for acquisitions or product development might include something like the following:

• What is your role? What are your responsibilities?

• Please describe your customers and markets, including how your customers want to interact with your content.

• How do you determine what type of product you will acquire and deliver? What factors help to make that decision?

• What are the major challenges you face in your job?

• What impact does the current publishing workflow have on your job?

Design

Design can consist of website visual design, art, photography, and rich media design and creation. Design can also include print, eBooks, mobile, or apps. Design provides the visuals and interaction for your content. Design may be grouped in one area of your organization or spread across multiple areas.

Sample design questions

Questions for design might include something like the following:

• What is your role? What are your responsibilities?

• What types of material do you design?

• At a top level, describe your processes. Which processes are effective? Which processes are ineffective?

• Where or who do you get your requirements from?

• Who determines the format of the asset (photography, line art, video)? What determines the "level of quality" (resolution, scalability) of the asset?

• Is the asset designed or created with reuse in mind (for example, multiple formats for different platforms)?

• How do you currently manage the assets that you've created?

- Do you add metadata to the asset when storing it? Is there a consistent format or rules for adding metadata?
- What tools do you use? How well do they meet your needs?

Editors

You may or may not have an editorial role. If you're developing product content, there's often no formal editorial role, but there should be! If you're responsible for web content you will have an editor, and if you're a publisher you're likely to have a whole slew of editors (acquisition editor, developmental editor, copy editor).

Sample editorial questions

Questions for editors might include something like the following:

- What is your role? What are your responsibilities?
- What is the current editorial process? Which processes are effective? Which processes are ineffective?
- What standards are the materials expected to meet?
- How do you communicate your requirements to authors?
- How do you receive content for edits?
- How do you mark it up?
- How do you return it to authors once reviewed?
- How do you track changes?
- What tools do you use? How well do they meet your needs?

Information technology

The information technology (IT) group plays an important role in selecting, managing, and deploying technology throughout the organization. Sometimes there's friction between the content groups and IT, where each group feels that the other simply doesn't understand them. Maybe that's true, but we suggest that you ignore them at your peril. Ignoring IT can result in the following:

- Technology that is isolated (siloed) from the rest of the company
- The need for your own technical resources to manage your technology
- Increased costs

Our preference is to open up the communication lines to determine if IT can support the technology you are considering using, and if they can what standards they want met. However, there are situations where IT manages only the enterprise-wide tools such as Microsoft Office, and department-specific tools are not supported.

Don't forget to ask everyone in the content lifecycle what tools they use and how effective they are. Tools can be a significant stumbling block for success. If people can't use them, if they slow them down, or if they truly hate them, productivity will be significantly compromised. Questions about tools are included with the sample questions for each type of interview.

Sample IT questions

Questions for IT might include something like the following:

- What is your role? What are your responsibilities?

- Are there existing content management systems in the company? What are they? Who uses them? How well do they work?

- Do you support any department-specific tools?

- Have you developed any custom content management or publishing systems?

- Why was the system developed? What corporate needs was the system designed to meet?

- How well is the current system working? What works well? What problems do you have with the current system(s)?

- What functionality do you require that your current system does not provide?

- Is there a standard for tools and databases? If so, what is it and why is it a standard? What is the process for changing an existing standard where appropriate or adopting a second, alternative standard?

- Are there any specific product requirements (for example, Microsoft versus UNIX server)?

- What is the process for adopting new technology?

Learning development and instructional design

Many organizations develop learning materials to support their products and services. While some organizations develop learning materials exclusively, most develop learning materials in conjunction with documentation and support materials, or possibly books and eBooks. There is often a lot of opportunity to reuse content, either between courses or from materials developed elsewhere in the organization and learning materials.

Sample learning development and instructional design questions

Questions for learning development and instructional design might include something like the following:

- What is your role? What are your responsibilities?

- What type(s) of learning materials do you produce?

- What are your current content creation and management processes? Which processes are effective? Which processes are ineffective?

- How do you currently handle sign-off or review?

- How do you handle document control? Version control? Access control?

- Do you reuse content? In what way? How effective is it?

- What tools do you use? How well do the tools support your development tasks?

- How are your materials created (for example, are there stylesheets or templates)?

- What impact does the current publishing workflow have on your job?

Production

In many organizations, authors are responsible for publishing their own content. In other organizations, there are production staff whose sole task is to publish content to paper or the Web. Production staff may accept content from multiple authors and format the content appropriately for the specified media. In yet others, writers may work with SMEs to publish content.

Sample production questions

Questions for external production might include something like the following:

- What are the current publication processes? Which processes are effective? Which processes are ineffective? Why are these processes effective or ineffective?

- What are the problems or frustrations you face in producing content?

- How do you handle document control? Version control? Access control? Distribution control?

- How are documents created (for example, are there stylesheets or templates)?

- What tools do you use? How well do they meet your needs?

Reviewers

The review and approval process is a phase in the content lifecycle that can be either a roadblock or an enabler for the delivery of content. There are many different types of reviewers, including SMEs, management, quality assurance, customer support, compliance/standards groups, or legal. Each reviewer will look for different things in the content and may have different issues. To cover all the bases, make sure you interview representative reviewers from each type.

Sample reviewer questions

Questions for reviewers might include something like the following:

- What is the current review processes? Which processes are effective? Which processes are ineffective? What kinds of information do you look for when reviewing content?

- What standards are the materials expected to meet?

- How do you communicate your requirements to authors?

- What are the major issues that you identify?

- What tools do you use? How well do they meet your needs?

Sales and marketing

Sales and marketing deal with customers all the time and often use corporate content in the development of their own materials. They are often the first to hear customer requirements.

Sample sales and marketing questions

Questions for sales and marketing might include something like the following:

- What is your role?

- Please describe your customers and markets, including how your customers want to interact with your content.

- Describe at a top level how you develop a marketing and sales campaign for products.

- What are the major challenges you face in your job?

- How do you collaborate with acquisitions or product development on new product ideas and decisions?

- What impact does the current publishing workflow have on your job?

- What tools do you use? How well do they meet your needs?

Translation/localization

Translation/localization involves translating content and modifying it to meet local language and cultural requirements. Questions related to translation/localization are important in understanding how content is provided to translation services, how effective the translation process is, and what issues arise in translating content in a timely and cost-effective manner.

Sample translation/localization questions

Questions for translation/localization might include something like the following:

- What are the current translation/localization processes? Which processes are effective? Which processes are ineffective?

- What are the problems or frustrations you face in translating content?

- Do you have written standards and guidelines for authors to prepare content for translation?

- How do you handle document control? Version control? Access control? Distribution control?

- What tools do you use? How well do they meet your needs?

- Do you use/have a translation memory system?

Living the GI Way: Content lifecycle

The following is just a short example. When you interview multiple groups with multiple challenges, the results of your analysis will be much longer.

- We have a large amount of content. You have to know what the content was published in before you can find it.

- When we change a piece of content we have to manually go through all our content to make sure we change it everywhere. Sometimes we miss one.

- People can't find things on our site. We get a lot of complaints from people who have seen the content before, but now can't find it.

- We did a big project for one of the state-based diabetes associations where we customized some of our content for their diabetes educator training. It was a huge amount of work and we were constantly changing things right up until the end. We missed a few changes and had to reprint some of the supporting information.

- We converted our best-selling book *Living the GI Way* to an eBook using EPUB. It was a disaster! The tables were a mess. Columns didn't match up. There were screens and screens of mismatched content. We had to withdraw it and redo the GI tables with images of the tables. Nobody really liked that either, but customers are living with it.

Summary

The various phases in your content lifecycle need to be identified and detailed to identify areas for improvement. Recognizing the processes and issues will help you plan and define your unified content strategy. For example, where your organization currently has issues, you need to improve the processes and technology to eliminate these issues. Where processes and technology are working well, you want to incorporate them into the new systems and processes where appropriate. Identifying the issues will help you determine the scope and functionality of your unified content strategy, define the criteria for selection of appropriate tools, and define the processes that must be redesigned or created.

Chapter 10

Performing a content audit

Content is at the heart of a unified content strategy. Before you can model your content—and subsequently, unify it—you need to gain an intimate understanding of its nature and structure. During a content audit, you look at your organization's content analytically and critically, which allows you to identify how effective the content is.

In addition, you analyze the content for opportunities for reuse. You look for similar and identical information, as well as for information that could be similar or identical, but is currently distinct. Once you see how your information is being used and reused, you can make decisions about how you might unify it.

This chapter describes what a content audit is and how to perform one; it also provides examples of content audit findings.

What is a content audit?

A content audit, as the name implies, is an accounting of the information in your organization. However, unlike the usual associations with the word *audit*—associations that strike fear into the hearts of many taxpayers—a content audit has positive results that enable your organization to save money if your findings are implemented. The purpose of a content audit is to analyze how content is written, organized, used, reused, and delivered to its various audiences.

Content audit vs. content inventory

Many people refer to a content inventory as a content audit, or sometimes a quantitative audit. For our purposes, when we talk about a content audit we mean the process of actually looking at the content and assessing its value and opportunities for reuse.

What's involved in doing a content audit?

To get started on a content audit within your organization, you first need to identify your scope, and then select representative materials within that scope. The larger the scope, the more work involved, but the greater the return on investment.

Identifying scope

You don't have to start big; doing a content audit within one area of an organization can realize significant returns and illustrate to other areas how, by including their content, the organization can realize even greater returns. It isn't necessary to look at absolutely every piece of information—a representative sample is enough. You'll start to see patterns that can then be extrapolated across your content set.

Selecting representative materials

After you've determined the scope of the audit, you need to select representative materials. Select as much content as you can, representing all the different departments included in your scope, not just the content that you create. Below are examples of content to look at depending on your focus.

Marketing: Look at samples including brochures, website, product packaging, point-of-sale materials, newsletters, press releases, ads, promos, and trade-show materials. Be sure to look at the same content on as many platforms as possible.

Publishing: Look at samples including trade press, textbooks, ancillary learning materials, eBooks, apps, journals, associated marketing materials, and any other content you produce. If you produce customer-branded content, be sure to include this as well.

Product content: Look at samples of help materials, manuals, and wikis. Be sure to select samples where content is or could be reused. If you outsource the manufacturing of your product to an original equipment manufacturer (OEM), include customer-branded content as well. Also look at technical support/customer support and knowledge bases. If you share content with learning materials or cover similar content be sure to include learning materials as well.

Learning materials: If your focus is learning materials, select samples of instructor-led, self-paced eLearning, virtual classroom, mobile learning, and apps.

You want to look at representative samples so you're analyzing the full breadth of materials, and you need to look at like materials to assess content for reuse.

Assessing the quality of the content

Look at your content to determine:

- Is the content appropriate to the customer(s)?
- Does it use the customer's terminology?
- How well is it written?
- Is the tone correct?
- Is the level of detail correct?
- Will it support the customer content scenarios?
- Are there any gaps?
- Does it help customers complete their tasks, make the right decisions, and satisfy their needs?

Assessing the opportunities for content reuse

Typically if authors want to reuse information they:

- Determine which information they want to reuse.

- Find the information in another document/section or even on another server in another area of the company.

- Copy and paste the information from one section of the document to another section, or from one document to another document.

- Rewrite or reformat the reused information to fit the new context.

Reusing content this way isn't really reuse; it's actually copy and paste. This results in multiple instances of the same piece of information occurring in the document or across documents. These instances are not linked or referenced to one another physically within the authoring or publishing tool. If the information needs to be updated, authors must first locate all instances of reuse, and then update each instance separately. This can be an extremely time-consuming process, and introduces much opportunity for error and inconsistency.

More often, content is written and rewritten and rewritten, often with changes or differences for each iteration. This results in inconsistent content and increased costs.

The content audit is intended to illustrate where opportunities to unify content throughout your organization exist; it provides the basis for your reuse strategy and modeling decisions.

Analyzing the content for reuse

After you've gathered together a representative sample of materials, you're ready to start digging into it. This is the fun part and usually involves spreading large amounts of information all over your office, walking around with a highlighter and a stack of sticky notes, highlighting your findings, and taking notes as you go. It's fun because it doesn't involve doing anything beyond really examining your content closely to see what it contains and how it's put together. Analyzing materials in this way is a discovery process about your content, something most organizations don't have the opportunity to do in their day-to-day work. You're not making any decisions at this point; instead, you're seeing what you have and making observations about it.

Analyzing content occurs at two levels, at the top level of your representative samples, followed by a more detailed examination of the content.

Top-level analysis

A top-level analysis involves scanning various information products to find common information (for example, product descriptions, introductory information, procedures, disclaimers, and topics). If you have large documents that include tables of contents, you can compare the tables of contents to find similarities in chapter/section names. Such similarities often indicate similar/identical content within and across a documentation set. Start by spreading your information products out in front of you and highlighting areas that look like they might contain similar information. If all your content is electronic, scan your materials for sample sections you want to look at more closely and print them off. Yes, print! No, don't print everything; we don't want you killing whole forests. But you can't easily mark up content that is electronic despite the functionality of some markup tools.

In-depth analysis

During the in-depth analysis, you examine the repeated information you identified during the top-level analysis. Repeated information can be as simple as copyright notices and warranty information, and as complex as whole sections of detail, particularly for product suites.

Once you've found instances of repeated information to scrutinize more closely, you can lay them out in a tabular format to see them all together at a glance. (See the examples that follow.) As you look at instances of repeated information, identify whether the content is identical or similar. If it is similar (or almost identical), which parts differ? Do the parts that differ need to differ? Are there valid reasons for differences such as product/information uniqueness? If the parts differ and there is no valid reason for the difference, identify this content as something that should be rewritten so it is identical for reuse in the future.

Content audit examples for reuse

The following examples show content audit findings for four fictional companies. Each example includes a top-level analysis showing potential content reuse, as well as a small in-depth analysis showing how the company could select a portion of the content for further analysis and interpret the findings.

Example 1 is for a Shakespearean theater company. They publish their content on the Web and in a print-based guide, but more and more of their customers are using mobile devices to access their site, and they don't have a mobile site.

Example 2 is a publisher of scientific textbooks. They have beautiful textbooks supplemented by online learning materials, but they want to move to eBooks and they aren't sure how to do that with their complex materials.

Example 3 is for a medical devices company that produces blood glucose monitoring meters. Because there are several versions of the meters, the company suspects there may be similarities—or inconsistencies—in the information produced for each version.

Example 4 shows reuse in learning materials. A business college that teaches investment courses receives feedback from students complaining that similar information in different courses (or even in the same course) is inconsistent. The college wants to build a database of reusable learning objects, or (RLOs), so that wherever information is repeated, it's the same. In their audit, the college looks for places where the same information is used (for example, the same topics, but with a different depth or focus), so they can ensure it is consistent.

Example 1: Enterprise content

This example is for a Shakespearean theater company, The Bard. They attract attendees from all over North America. They publish their content in the newspaper and in a theater guide, as well as to the Web, Facebook, YouTube, Flickr, and Twitter. They do a lot of reuse between all the different channels, but it is all manual, time-consuming, and expensive. They are looking at government funding cuts in the next calendar year due to fiscal restraint measures and they have to find a better way of publishing content.

Top-level analysis

The Bard has a well-designed and easy-to-use website for learning about the plays, ordering tickets online, and finding out about all the other activities related to the theater, such as readings, music, and kids' camps.

Photos are reused between:

- Play selector page

- Play page

- Theater guide (print)

- Newspaper ad

- Facebook page

- Flickr

The main image for each play is used over and over again either in its entirety or as a partial image in small display areas.

Figures 10.1–10.3 illustrate the commonality of images and content. The *Hamlet* image was used in the play production selection page, the play description page, and in the playbill.

There's also a lot of textual reuse in areas such as the descriptions of the plays and all the cast information.

Figure 10.1   The Bard play production page.

Figure 10.2   Play detail page *(Hamlet)*.

Figure 10.3   Program *(Hamlet)*.

When you look at their site on a smartphone, it's easy to see why customers are frustrated, because the content is impossible to navigate (see Figure 10.4). In addition, all the features of the desktop site like ticket ordering are disabled on the smartphone.

Figure 10.4   Website on a smartphone.

Interpreting the findings

The Bard has a tremendous opportunity for reuse; however, the print-based materials are farmed out to an agency, so under the current process automated reuse beyond web deliverables is not possible.

In addition, there's no mobile solution. A QR code is included in the print materials, which is a great idea, but it takes customers to the regular site. The regular site is very difficult to view on mobile without a lot of scrolling, and it's impossible to purchase a ticket using a mobile device.

In-depth analysis

If we look closely at the content for a play on the website versus the same information in the program, it's very similar. Web content for the description of the play is virtually identical to that in the theater guide, with the tiny exception of a tagline in the web content.

The newspaper ad uses the name of the play and dates, times, and so on, then only the tagline, not the more detailed description. The newspaper ad also uses quotes from play reviews that are also found on the website.

Interpreting the findings

The content could be identically reused.

Conclusion

There is a tremendous opportunity for reuse of images and text across all the channels. The Bard should consider generating the print materials from the same source content as the web materials to save money rather than going to an outside agency.

A specifically designed mobile site should be created to optimize the content for mobile and to enable ticket purchases.

Example 2: Publishing

Science Publishers, Inc. publishes trade press books, high school and college textbooks, and journals. They currently have four major areas in the organization handling the production of content:

- Web (marketing and business-to-consumer [B2C])
- Trade press and textbooks
- Ancillary learning materials
- Journals

Each of the production areas is isolated (siloed), and much of the work is manual with only the assistance of standard web publishing and desktop publishing tools. Content is shared by passing files back and forth through email and a shared file-server. Science Publishers creates online learning materials to accompany the textbooks but wants to start delivering both content and additional learning materials on eReaders and tablets.

Top-level analysis

A top-level analysis of materials showed:

- Journals didn't really have a lot of reuse other than some quotations incorporated into the textbooks.

- Some reuse between the marketing materials, "back of the book," and B2C product descriptions.

- Significant reuse between the textbooks and additional learning materials:
  - Images
  - Objectives
  - Concepts
  - Terms and definitions
  - Practice exercises
  - Electronic flash cards

- Some reuse between textbooks (for example, a section on the digestive system was used in a basic biology text, in a text on nutrition, and in another on the human body).

Interpreting the findings

There was a great deal of opportunity for reuse.

In-depth analysis

An in-depth analysis showed that while the content was reusable, it was not exactly the same, and it was obviously copied and pasted. There were often tiny differences in images, some small text changes, and different punctuation.

The in-depth analysis on publishing to eReaders and tablets revealed some significant challenges and some exciting opportunities. Based on the functionality of E Ink eReaders (standard, grayscale, linear eReaders) there were a number of potential problems, including:

- Very dense content: a single paragraph could easily take up an entire eReader screen

- Two-column layout

- Complex tables

- Complex illustrations

- Illustrations that stretched across columns or pages
- Footnotes
- Sidebars

Interpreting the findings

Science Publishers would have to do a lot of work to transform their content from print-oriented textbooks to more simplistic layouts for E Ink eReaders and to ensure usability. Doable, but somewhat challenging.

Conclusion

Science Publishers has a tremendous opportunity for reuse between textbooks and additional educational materials. However, the task of transitioning to eReaders will be somewhat challenging. Tablets hold a better opportunity to represent the textbooks in a similar way to print, but more importantly they offer the opportunity to:

- Integrate the additional learning materials into the text so the student can learn by traditional reading and also by clicking out to videos, simulations, and interactive exercises.
- Redesign the textbook as an app with even greater interactivity and rich media.

Example 3: Product content

This example involves a medical devices company that produces blood glucose monitoring meters. Because there are several versions of the meters, the company suspects there may be similarities—or inconsistencies—in the information products created for each version. Their audit focuses on comparing content across information products so they can figure out how to reuse information and ensure consistency.

Interpreting the findings

The top-level analysis shows areas that warrant closer examination. For example, the company logo and contact information are used in every information product, and the product description is used in all but three. In addition, a number of topics related to the setup and use of the product are repeated throughout. This top-level analysis shows the findings for just one product—the blood glucose monitoring meter. Expanding the analysis to look at other products in the same family shows that up to 80 percent of the content could be reused. Looking even further at other related product lines shows additional commonality in conceptual information about the company and its products.

Top-level analysis

Table 10.1 represents the top-level analysis of their materials.

Table 10.1   Top-level analysis of information products

Content	Owner's Guide	Quick Reference Card	Quick Start Guide	Press Release	Website	Brochure	Product Package	Label (Package Insert)
Company logo	X	X	X	X	X	X	X	X
Contact information	X	X	X	X	X	X	X	X
Important (read the Owner's Guide before...)	X	X	X		X		X	X
Product description	X			X	X	X	X	
Setting up the meter	X	X						
Testing the meter	X							
Sampling the blood	X		X					X
Inserting the test strip	X	X	X					X
Interpreting the results	X	X						X
Caring for your meter	X							
Solving problems	X	X						

In-depth analysis

The results of the top-level analysis are used to drive the in-depth analysis. In this case, the in-depth analysis (see Table 10.2) shows similar information in the setup and use of the product.

Table 10.2   In-depth analysis of information products

Owner's Guide	Quick Reference Card	Quick Start Card
Step 1	**Step 1**	**Step 1**
Insert the test strip. Make sure the contact bars go in end first and facing up. The meter will turn on automatically. -- will appear briefly on the display. Note: The bars must be all the way into the meter to avoid an inaccurate result.	Insert the test strip. Once inserted, the meter turns on automatically.	Insert a test strip to turn on the meter.
Step 2	**Step 2**	**Step 2**
Apply the blood sample…	Apply the sample…	-- will appear on the screen.
		Step 3
		Apply the blood sample…

Interpreting the findings

There are subtle differences in the first two samples (Owner's Guide and Quick Reference Card), but the third sample (Quick Start Card) has a different second step. Are the differences necessary or will they confuse users? Quick Reference Cards provide concise information so the shorter steps are appropriate. The same holds true for the Quick Start Guide; however, the second step isn't really a step. The differences in the steps should be reconsidered.

Conclusion

Although this example shows just a small portion of content, it illustrates the seemingly insignificant, yet critical, variations that can occur in content. In this case, the content would benefit from a unified strategy to ensure that it's consistent each time the same information appears.

Example 4: Learning materials

A business college teaches classes in investment strategies, targeted to practitioners seeking further education or accreditation in financial planning, and to people who just want more information about their own investment planning. After receiving a number of student feedback forms complaining about inconsistencies in the course content, the college decided to conduct an audit of their materials in an attempt to unify common information. The college wants to build a database of RLOs so that wherever information is repeated, it's the same. Their audit focuses on looking for places where the same information is used so they can ensure it's consistent.

Top-level analysis

A top-level analysis of four courses (see Table 10.3) shows that a lot of content is repeated in a number of different places.

Table 10.3   Top-level analysis of learning materials

Content	Found in
Income Tax Planning	Course 1 ch. 7
	Course 2 entire course
	Course 3 ch. 4
	Course 4 ch. 5
Investment Strategies	Course 1 ch. 10
	Course 2 ch. 6
	Course 3 ch. 8
	Course 4 entire course
Retirement Planning	Course 1 entire course
	Course 2 ch. 3
	Course 3 ch. 2
	Course 4 ch. 7
Wills and Estates	Course 1 ch. 13
	Course 2 ch. 8
	Course 3 entire course
	Course 4 ch. 8

Interpreting the findings

The top-level analysis indicates that there is much repetition of certain subject areas throughout the different courses. Although the focus and the level of detail may be different from course to course, content should be examined more closely to determine if there are inconsistencies and to see if there are similarities that could potentially be unified.

In-depth analysis

A more in-depth analysis of the topics related to investment strategies (see Table 10.4) shows similarities in the overviews of Course 2, which touches on investment strategies, and Course 4, whose entire focus is investing:

Table 10.4   In-depth analysis of learning materials

Course 2 topics	Course 4 topics
The investment planning process	An overview of investment planning
Taxable and nontaxable investments	High-risk versus low-risk investments
When to invest for optimum tax benefits	Investing to reduce taxes
Tax on investment income	How much to invest and when
	Sources of investment income

Note that many of the topics covered in Course 2 are similar to the topics in Course 4, similar enough that they should be compared to see if they are inconsistent, where they differ, where they should differ, and where they are alike.

Interpreting the findings

Closer examination of each topic shows that much of the content in "Investing to reduce taxes" and "Taxable and nontaxable investments" is similar. This is also the case for "How much to invest and when" and "When to invest for optimum tax benefits." The information on investment planning, though, is inconsistent.

Conclusion

The findings in both the top-level and in-depth analyses show numerous opportunities for the college to reuse content and to correct inconsistencies. Correcting discrepancies is critical in learning materials; students learn information one way, then when they encounter an inconsistency in a future course (or sometimes even in the same course), they have to figure out which version is correct, increasing their cognitive load. If students cannot figure it out, they are left with conflicting information. This is especially critical in an eLearning environment where the materials themselves become the instructor; students often don't have another source to help them figure out what's wrong.

After discrepancies are corrected, information can be chunked into RLOs and reused in whichever course it is applicable. If more detail is required to teach the same topic in a more advanced course or to accommodate different learning objectives, information can be added to the RLO, with each level of detail comprising another RLO. Wherever the core RLO is used, however, it's consistent.

Living the GI Way: Content audit

We started by looking at the most common piece of information, the definition of the glycemic index. The definition appeared on the home page, in every single book, and in presentations, training material, the newsletter, and the introduction to the database.

There were three different variations found across the information set.

"The Glycemic Index (GI) measures the effect of carbohydrates on blood sugar levels. Foods with a high GI break down very easily and release glucose into the bloodstream more rapidly than low GI foods. The Glycemic Index uses a scale of 0 to 100 where pure glucose is 100. Low GI foods range from 0 to 55, medium from 56 to 69, and high from 70 to 100. "

"The Glycemic Index is a scale that measures carbohydrates by how much they raise blood glucose levels."

"The Glycemic index is a ranking of carbohydrates. The glycemic index is calculated by measuring blood glucose levels following the consumption of a carbohydrate."

Notice the capitalization of terms is inconsistent and the use of blood sugar versus blood glucose is also inconsistent. While a definition is just a small piece of information, this definition is a critical one and illustrates some of the issues faced in managing content. Further analysis shows a number of inconsistencies in concepts, explanations, and examples.

Looking at the content in eBook form demonstrates the issues the client faces in presenting GI tables.

The first version of the tables was simply unreadable.

The second version was just an image. Tables could run over several print pages and some ran off the screen, making it difficult to use the tables, especially online. This is an example of a small one (see Figure 10.5).

	Measure	Carbs	GI	Ranking
Arborio risotto rice white boiled	1/3 cup	18.2	69	Med
Basmati white boiled	1/3 cup	18.2	58	Med
Broken Thai white rice cooker	1/3 cup	18.2	86	High
Brown boiled	1/3 cup	19.0	55	Med
Glutinous white steamed	1/3 cup	18.2	98	High
Instant white	1/3 cup	18.2	87	High
Jasmine rice cooker	1/3 cup	18.2	109	High
Wild boiled	1/2 cup	13.3	57	Med
White short grained boiled	1/3 cup	19	83	High

Figure 10.5
Caption Image of a table.

Continued...

Living the GI Way: Content audit continued

The third version was just text, which, while not attractive, was readable and—more importantly—searchable. However, screens and screens of text like this were still not user-friendly.

Arborio risotto rice, white, boiled, 1/3 cup, Carbs =18.2, GI = 69 (Med)

Basmati, white, boiled, 1/3 cup, Carbs =18.2, GI = 58 (Med)

Broken, Thai, white, rice cooker, Carbs =18.2, GI = 86 (High)

Brown, boiled, 1/3 cup, Carbs =19.0, GI = 55 (Med)

Glutinous, white, steamed, 1/3 cup, Carbs =18.2, GI = 98 (High)

Instant, white, 1/3 cup, Carbs =18.2, GI = 87 (High)

Jasmine, rice cooker, 1/3 cup, Carbs = 18.2, GI = 109 (High)

Wild, boiled, 1/2 cup, Carbs = 13.3, GI = 57 (Med)

White, short grained, boiled, 1/3 cup, Carbs = 19, GI = 83 (High)

Summary

Doing a thorough content audit is critical to implementing a reuse strategy because it tells you how content is written and how it's currently being used, how it could be reused, and what needs to be done to create effective unified content.

1. Establish the scope of the audit.

2. Select representative samples of your content based on the scope of your project.

3. Look at the content itself to determine its appropriateness, quality of writing, and "fit" for the channel.

4. Assess the opportunities for content reuse.

5. Analyze the content for reuse.

A content audit can help you determine how to reuse content across a number of different information products. Where content is different, does it have to be different? Can information that is similar be made identical? Are there reasons for it being similar as opposed to identical (product name, for example)? Should content in one medium be identical to most of the content in another medium (for example, Web versus mobile)? How will your information products be used, and are there valid reasons to distinguish them from one another? These are the types of questions to answer as you develop an intimate understanding of your content.

Chapter 11

Envisioning your unified content strategy and lifecycle

Armed with your findings from the substantive audit, you can define a vision for your unified content strategy. Remember that the strategy consists of front stage—the customer-facing unified content strategy—and back stage—the unified content lifecycle (processes and technology) that supports your unified content strategy.

When you envision your unified content strategy, you are identifying:

- What types of content your customer needs.
- What format or media they need it in.
- When they need the content.

Your new content lifecycle describes the processes as you would like to see them implemented.

This chapter describes some of the common challenges uncovered during the initial analyses of the content lifecycle and content, and identifies how those issues should be addressed in a new content lifecycle.

The unified content strategy

You need to determine:

- What information products will you provide?

- Why do you have to provide them?

- What needs will they meet?

- How will they be used?

- How is one information product related to another information product?

A good way to determine your information product requirements is to build scenarios for each of your personas and identify the content requirements at each point in the scenario.

Scenarios

One of the best ways to begin the envisioning process is by creating customer scenarios based on your personas. A scenario is a description of an everyday situation. A scenario needs to answer the following questions:

- Who is the person involved?

- What triggers the experience?

- What happens?

- What is the result?

The scenario helps you determine what types of content your customers will need to reach their goals.

Living the GI Way: Scenario

Sharon has determined that this is the day she's going to take charge of managing her blood sugars. It's Thursday and she wants to get as much information as she can about the glycemic index (GI) so she can plan some menus and do some grocery shopping on the weekend. She heads off to www.LivingTheGIWay.com.

The home page has a definition of the GI but Sharon searches for more. She selects the GI overview. She has a choice of reading the overview or watching a video. She selects the video. After viewing the three-minute video she feels she can handle this, but she's not sure of all the details so she decides to print out the overview to read again later.

She takes a quick look at the books, but she decides she doesn't have time to read a book before the weekend and she really wants to get started. So she moves on to the recipes. She's excited to find a week of recipes for getting started with the GI. Recipes in hand, she signs up for the GI newsletter and exits the site.

The customer content lifecycle and content matrix

Customers go through a variety of stages when they interact with your company and your content. They need different content at different stages. Typical stages (see Figure 11.1) include explore, buy, use, and maintain.

Figure 11.1   Customer content lifecycle.

Living the GI Way: Content lifecycle exploratory phase

In the exploratory phase, Sharon would be looking for information to gain an understanding of the GI in general and what information, products, and services LGIW provides. However, a diabetes educator who already has a basic knowledge of the GI would very quickly move into exploring the products and services.

You need to match the customer content lifecycle phase with the types of content the customer requires to reach the goals of that scenario. This is called a content matrix.

Develop multiple scenarios for all your customer personas to better detail your content matrix.

Living the GI Way: Partial content matrix

Figure 11.2 shows a partial sample of a content matrix for LGIW based on the scenario associated with Sharon.

Lifecycle	Information Product	Description	Links
Explore	Home page	Definition, who LGIW is.	GI overview, video, books, magazine, recipes, GI database
	GI overview	Static page, PDF	Video, books, magazine, recipes, GI database
	Video	GI overview	Your first two week's recipes
	Testimonials	Static page	Books, recipes, GI database
	LGIW newsletter	email linked to web	Books, recipes, GI database
	Need help?	Form	List of available GI coaches
	Special offer	Form	Special offer of the month
	My food tracker	Interactive	Interactive personalized food value tracking
	etc.		
Buy	Books	Book, eBook	GI coach, My food tracker
	Magazine	Magazine, iPad version	QR codes to products on the site
	GI coach	Static	List of available GI coaches
	Membership	Form	Membership benefits
	etc.		
Etc.			

Figure 11.2   Partial content matrix for LGIW.

The unified content lifecycle

The success of a unified content strategy is dependent on the processes you put in place to manage it. Those processes are your unified content lifecycle.

A unified content lifecycle can be implemented in a number of ways, depending on the needs of the organization. No two organizations have the same needs, the same budget, the same goals, or the same culture. Everything you've discovered about your company, your goals, and your issues is used to design a unified content lifecycle that will work for you.

Refer to Chapter 14, "Designing workflow" and Chapter 20, "The role of content management" for more information on the processes for managing your content.

Addressing challenges

Your new content lifecycle should address the challenges in your organization—issues that you identified during your analyses of processes and content. Table 11.1 shows some common issues, their requirements in a unified content lifecycle, and the phase where the challenge should be addressed. Challenges are grouped into categories such as issues related to content use, content authoring, localization, and so on.

Table 11.1   Identifying how issues can be addressed

Issue	Requirements	Phase and process
Content use		
Too much detail/ too little detail	Reevaluate requirements and rewrite materials accordingly	Create (Authoring)
Difficult to understand	Provide customized content (specific to customer needs)	
	Provide dynamic content (specific to customer needs)	
Unable to find content	Categorize content in multiple ways for multiple access points	Create (Authoring)
	Add metadata to all content (aids in retrieval)	

Continued...

Table 11.1   Identifying how issues can be addressed *continued*

Issue	Requirements	Phase and process
Content authoring		
Different authoring tools don't interact well	Consider XML as language of exchange	Create (Authoring)
Hard to reuse content	Ensure all authoring tools use enterprise-wide standard templates, style tags, and metadata (facilitates content interchange)	
Unable to find information	Store content in a single repository or ensure all content can be shared among multiple repositories (simplifies access)	Manage (Workflow) Create (Authoring)
	Consider automatic reuse (system finds the content for the author)	
Localization		
Ongoing changes to content	Implement change management processes (regulates how and when change can occur)	Create (Localization)
	Provide only changed components to the translator (focuses change)	
Insufficient reviewers	Route only changed/new content to reviewers (fewer can do more)	Manage (Workflow)
Incompatible formats	Consider XML as language of exchange	Create (Authoring)
	Ensure all authoring tools use enterprise-wide standard templates, style tags, and metadata (facilitates conversion)	
Global requirements		
Multilanguage requirements	Ensure the CMS can support multiple languages	Create (Authoring) Manage (Workflow)
Authors often have to rework the original materials	Ensure authoring templates reflect global requirements	Create (Design) Manage (Workflow)
	Ensure the CMS supports tracking of content relationships (enables derivative reuse)	

Issue	Requirements	Phase and process
Review		
Changes continue to occur after review and sign-off	Implement change management (regulates how and when changes can occur)	Manage (Workflow)
Repetitive reviews	Implement change management processes (regulates how and when changes can occur)	Manage (Workflow)
	Route only changed/new content to reviewers (ensures approved content is not re-reviewed, reducing workload)	
Inability to verify changes	Provide the ability to look at multiple versions of content and "redlined" content (facilitates comparison of content)	Review
Publication and delivery		
Content must be reformatted for different platforms	Consider using XML as the interchange language (facilitates publishing to multiple media)	Create (Authoring)
	Ensure all authoring tools use enterprise-wide standard templates, style tags, and metadata (facilitates conversion)	

Living the GI Way: Unified content lifecycle

This represents a vision for a unified content lifecycle for Living the GI Way.

Create

The content creation phase consists of planning, authoring, and revision.

Planning

Each of the departments in LGIW works in a silo (for example, press, web, and education). There is little communication about the planned products, yet it's been identified that opportunities exist to build off cross-platform products or take advantage of existing content.

Press, web, and education should meet on a quarterly basis at minimum to share information on projected information products. From the quarterly meeting a complete editorial calendar should be created that identifies the expected products and timelines.

Continued...

Living the GI Way: Unified content lifecycle continued

Reports will be used to track the status of these products on an ongoing basis. This will allow LGIW to have a complete understanding of their upcoming content at any time.

Authoring

Authoring by external authors (for example, for books) will remain largely the same, though templates will be adapted to reflect the required structures for information based on the use and reuse requirements. Templates for external authors will remain in standard Microsoft Word. Content from external authors will be automatically converted to the desired XML structure (for example, web page, workshop, article, and so on) once brought into LGIW.

Internal authors will work in Word, with XML "under the covers." Styles will represent XML structures.

Trade press books will continue to be authored by external authorities on the glycemic index. An internal author will be paired with the expert to assist in developing friendly, easy-to-read content. A core set of content will be designed for reuse into a variety of books for specific health conditions such as diabetes, polycystic ovary syndrome, weight loss, and celiac disease. Authors will be encouraged to write content in a modular way so that the content can be easily structured for reuse.

Workshops will draw on content originally created for a book. Core GI concepts will be supplemented by objectives, exercises, and examples. eLearning will reuse workshop modules and be supplemented by audio and video and, potentially, interactive exercises or simulations. Custom workshops can be created by reusing core workshop materials augmented by customer-specific information. Custom organizations of content can be easily facilitated by reordering modules. Custom workshops can also easily be rebranded because the content has been designed to accommodate rebranding.

Web content will be reused from core content originally created for books and workshops and will be supplemented by marketing materials.

The GI database will be converted to a mobile app to facilitate detailed access to GI values. eBooks will link to the GI values app rather than display unreadable tables.

Edit and review

The review phase consists of editing, reviewing, and approving content.

Edit

Editors can either edit content in the Microsoft Word version before it's imported into the system or edit content in the content management system (CMS).

Review

Through workflow, editors and reviewers will be notified that content is "ready for review." The notification will include a link to the document to be reviewed. Reviewers can annotate the content with comments. Comments are associated with the component so that they can be viewed in the context of the component at any time.

Reviewers can see all review comments from other reviewers for a component to compare the comments.

Reviewers can also review a complete history of the changes that have been made to a component either in the current version or in previous versions.

LGIW should consider having content reviewed by all departments to ensure that it will meet all future reuse requirements.

When review is complete, authors update the content based on compiled review comments.

Review is done on components, not documents.

Approval

Once all comments have been received and merged into the source content, authors will use metadata or the workflow to indicate content that's ready for final approval.

Reviewers will review the content and indicate if it has final approval by selecting the final approval metadata.

Manage

A number of activities are involved in the management of content.

Metadata

Metadata must be added to every content assembly and component before it's stored. Wherever possible, metadata will be automatically applied to the content based on the taxonomy and content structure, relieving the authors of having to manually add it. Metadata applied to a higher level of a document (for example, workshop) will be automatically inherited by (applied to) all the subcomponents (for example, subtopics). As much metadata as possible will be added automatically based on the context of the component, the template, and the subject of the content.

Some metadata will be applied by the author, for example, information about what changed in the content or why it was changed.

To apply metadata to a component, authors will select from a list of predefined values (controlled vocabulary). Some metadata fields will allow authors to enter their own metadata; however, the majority of metadata will be controlled using a specified list of terms.

Continued...

Living the GI Way: Unified content lifecycle continued

Version control

Each time content is saved, a new version will be created. There will be two levels of versioning: draft version and full version. Content will remain in draft version until approved, and then it will be fully versioned.

Through version control, authors will be able to view previous versions of the content or revert to an earlier version if necessary.

Authors and reviewers can see the complete detailed history for each item. The history will indicate who made the change (automatic), when the change was made (automatic), and the reason for the change (authors will complete this information).

Access control

Content will be controlled, meaning no one will be able to create, view, or modify content without the appropriate permissions. Different users of the CMS will have different permissions.

Access control will be defined by the system administrator. Once access control is applied to a document, the same access control will be inherited (applied to) all the components that compose the document. If content is reused in multiple locations, the most restricted level of access will be applied to the element unless it is standard content, such as a logo or disclaimer.

Check in content

At any point in the content creation process, authors will be able to check the content into the CMS. At minimum, authors should check in content daily—it shouldn't reside on their local drive. If the content is ready for review or approval, authors will add the appropriate metadata or use workflow, and reviewers will be automatically notified that it's available for review.

Once the content is checked in, it will be automatically stored in the correct location in the CMS.

Workflow

Workflow begins at authoring. Workflow is used throughout the content lifecycle to control and route content automatically. For example, setting the status of the content to "ready for review" will cause the workflow to automatically route the content to the designated reviewers.

Appropriate times (durations) will be added to each step in the workflow (for example, writing, editing, review) so adequate time is allocated. Recipients of the content in the next task will be informed if content is delayed and will be reminded of upcoming requirements (for example, the review must occur by a specific date).

Reports

Reports will be created to aid in project management and content tracking. A variety of reports can be created, such as:

- Where used (where content is reused)
- Status (status of a project or products)
- Responsible party (who is responsible for each task)
- Project review (for example, what were the durations of a task, how many reviews were required)
- Inactive modules (on hold, archived)
- All content on a particular subject regardless of content type

Multichannel delivery

Content can be published to multiple channels:

- Web (website, mobile site)
- Print (for example, InDesign or QuarkXPress)
- Other (for example, Kindle, EPUB, PPT)

Content delivery consists of publishing to multiple platforms. XML stylesheets reflect the requirements of each medium. Detailed rules can be included that ensure appropriate "page" breaks. XML stylesheets address the issues of consistent formatting in publications.

Web

The Web will become one of many delivery channels. The first priority is to reorganize existing content on the standard website and apply the revised taxonomy for improved access and retrieval.

The second phase involves creating a mobile site.

Print

Stylesheets control the look and feel of the content. Information products are automatically assigned an appropriate publishing format (for example, a book is designated as PDF). When an information product is published, the appropriate stylesheet will be automatically selected for use.

The publishing system can be designed to allow users to request immediate or scheduled publishing. Users can be given permission to publish based on their roles.

Other

Content can be published to a variety of additional platforms such as Kindle, EPUB, PowerPoint, or any new platform as required. Content remains the same; only the stylesheet and publishing rules change.

Summary

Before you can begin the design process, you need to develop a vision for your unified content strategy and supporting lifecycle.

Customers go through a variety of stages when they interact with your company and your content. Each stage can have different requirements. Develop a customer content lifecycle based on your customer requirements. A typical content lifecycle includes the explore phase, the buy phase, the use phase, and the maintain phase.

Develop scenarios to identify a typical customer activity. Each scenario helps you determine what types of content your customer will need in order to reach the goals of that scenario. Develop multiple scenarios to ensure that you understand the complete set of customer content requirements. Match the scenarios to the customer stages and develop a content matrix that identifies what information products are required for each phase for a particular customer.

Develop a vision for your unified content lifecycle, explaining to your stakeholders how content will be managed throughout the content lifecycle.

Part 4

Developing a unified content strategy

Developing a unified content strategy involves creating models for your content, determining how you want to reuse content, defining how people produce content, making it easy to find content, creating usable content, and managing all the change that has to take place in your organization.

In Chapter 12, "Content modeling: Adaptive content design," we discuss the basis of content modeling and how your content must be consistent in writing style and structure. We explain how you must store your content so it can be reused and delivered when and where it's needed.

A unified content strategy is only successful when content can be reused. In Chapter 13, "Reuse strategy," we explore the impact of manual reuse and automatic reuse and what kinds of decisions you have to make to determine how you are going to reuse your content.

Workflow, in the context of a unified content strategy, defines how people and tasks interact to create, update, manage, and deliver content. Without consistent and effective workflow, your unified content strategy will not work. Chapter 14, "Designing workflow," describes the concept of workflow and its benefits, and takes you through the basics of designing a workflow to support your unified content lifecycle.

Finding and labeling your content is also critically important to a successful unified content strategy. In Chapter 15, "Designing metadata," we explore all the descriptive information that's required to manage your content, so people and systems can find content when it's needed.

In Chapter 16, "It's all about the content," we focus on creating the content—why you need to separate format from content, why you need to determine structured writing guidelines, and the advantages of collaborative authoring.

And finally, in Chapter 17, "Change management and governance," we discuss the behavioral changes that are required to keep a unified content strategy on track. For a unified content strategy to be adopted successfully throughout an organization, behavioral change has to occur at an individual level and at an organizational level, all of which requires planning and commitment.

Chapter 12

Content modeling: Adaptive content design

Models formalize the structure of your content in guidelines, templates, and structured frameworks. When you model your content, you identify and document the structure on which your unified content strategy is based.

To ensure that content is reusable and adaptable, it must follow a consistent approach in writing style and structure. In addition, content must be stored in such a way that whoever needs the content can find it, access it, reuse or repurpose it, and deliver it (often dynamically) when and where it's needed.

This chapter discusses the basics of content modeling and adaptive content. We describe granularity, information product and component models, and semantic structure.

What is adaptive content?

Adaptive content is format-free, device-independent, scalable, and filterable content that is transformable for display in different environments and on different devices in an automated or dynamic fashion.

Customers want to access content on the device of their choosing. For example, because they were designed with 13-inch, 15-inch, and 17-inch screens in mind, traditional websites don't display well on mobile devices with small screens. Customers who attempt to access sites that are not optimized for mobile use experience frustration when they try to click on miniscule links or use an interface that was not designed for their device. Developers have done a brisk business developing mobile versions of websites for multiple devices (iPhone, iPad, BlackBerry, and so on). But handcrafting mobile versions for every new device is unsustainable, particularly given the explosion of new devices hitting the market every year. It is not necessary or practical to create countless custom-designed solutions for every new device.

Ethan Marcotte coined the term "responsive web design" and transformed the way websites are visually designed. Responsive web design uses a variety of software techniques to respond to the environment based on screen size, platform, and orientation. This means that content designed for desktop web is automatically resized to the screen size of the device in use.

However, while changing how content is visually displayed is a good start, it's not enough. Customers need adaptive content—content that will scale and adapt to the environment and their purpose.

Adaptive content automatically adjusts to different environments and device capabilities to deliver the best possible customer experience, filtering and layering content for greater or lesser depth of detail. Adaptive content can be displayed in any desired order, made to respond to specific customer interactions, changed based on location, and integrated with content from other sources. Adaptive content is limited only by your design decisions, the functionality of the device being used, and the intelligence of your content.

Content models make it possible to support adaptive content.

Understanding content modeling

Bear with us as we define a number of terms you need to understand for content modeling.

Content modeling is the process of determining the structure and granularity of your content.

Content models define the structure of information products and their constituent content components.

An **information product** is an assembly of content components, for example, a press release, an executive profile, a brochure, or an instructional course.

An **information product model** (IPM) is a hierarchical ordering of components. The IPM can be used over and over again with slight variations for different content.

Components are the building blocks of your content. A component model describes the structure of specific types of content, for example, recipe, value proposition, or overview. Component models can be used over and over again with different content. Components can be reused in different information product models. The structure remains the same; only the content changes. Components break down further into elements.

An **element** is the smallest part of a component that can be semantically defined but not broken out into a separate component.

Content modeling takes place after you've completed your analysis and you know who your customers are, what they need, and what form they need it in.

Content modeling is critical in a unified content strategy because it provides the blueprint on which your content will be built. Content models define the structure of your content.

The content modeling process forces you to consider all content requirements, either for a specific information product, product or service, a specific customer, or a specific device, and to assess what content should be available to fulfill those requirements. And it forces you to design content for a usage you may not have even thought of yet! In a unified content strategy, the content model becomes the catalog of your content.

Content first, not mobile first, eBook first, or any other "first"

As each new device comes out, organizations realize that it's going to be a very painful and time-consuming experience to get their content from its current format to a format that's not only supported by the device, but also actually optimizes the content on the device for the best possible user experience. When intelligence is added to the content, it can be responsive to the people or device. When rules are added to the content, it can adapt to the customer's actions.

When the Web became popular, it quickly became obvious that standard, print-based content wasn't suited for the Web. It was too verbose, formatted for paper presentation, poorly structured for the screen, and designed to be read linearly. Huge numbers of articles, blogs, and books guided authors in writing for the Web. All good things, but all limited to changing the way authors write to optimize their content solely on the Web.

Now that content is increasingly needed in mobile formats, organizations are finding their websites don't work well on mobile devices. Screen size is much smaller, and design-intensive websites are nearly impossible to navigate. Limited bandwidth and costly data plans can limit what you deliver.

Traditional publishers are scrambling to rapidly convert their print books (back catalog) to eBooks. The results are often lacking in quality and sometimes difficult to read. The more complex the content, the harder it is to successfully move it to eBook formats. For example, textbooks typically feature an intensive use of formatting and layout techniques to communicate lessons to students. These learning experiences are difficult to convert to eBooks. You can't just use "file save as" PDF or EPUB and expect it to work without incident. These books contain too many handcrafted layout structures like sidebars, two-page spreads, tables, and columns that sabotage any simple conversion.

Content strategists cannot, and we repeat, cannot, continue to handcraft content for a particular output. If you want your content to be adaptive, you can't think about how it will look and then tweak and tune the content to get that perfect fit. You can't design your content strategy around a particular page or layout. You have to create a content strategy that's only about the content and its purpose, scope, use, and reuse. You need to know what content is required, by whom, when, in what circumstance, and in conjunction with what other content or interactivity.

The only way you'll achieve your goals is with structured models and intelligent content.

Know your constraints

Even though you should write content separate from its eventual output, you must understand the constraints of the device on which your content will be displayed. Then you need to design your models to adapt to those constraints.

The constraints of print and the Web are pretty well known at this point, so we'll just focus on some of the new devices. Note that devices are changing rapidly, so the constraints at the time of writing may be different than when you read this book.

Constraints of mobile

The constraints of mobile include:

- Small screen size

  Customers don't want to have to constantly be scrolling, swiping, or pinching to view content. It's time-consuming and tiring, and it suddenly makes reading a two-handed operation. Create models and associated guidelines that accommodate "bite-sized" pieces of content.

  Put the key information in the first paragraph or sentence of any element of content so that the rest can be filtered out or made accessible with functionality such as Read more. Think of the first paragraph or sentence as a building block. Then each subsequent paragraph can build on the previous one.

  Explore the practical use of images, graphics, and rich media to communicate ideas that don't require words.

- File size

  Customers don't want to wait for content to arrive. They want it now. Large file sizes take a long time to deliver, and that's frustrating—whether it's a web page with animations, high fidelity audio or video files, or a document server delivering content (such as an eBook) designed to be read offline at a later date. Waiting for a large chunk of content to arrive can be irritating.

  Break apart your content and deliver it in smaller chunks. If you're delivering content for offline reading and it must be sent in one piece, consider creating a version for mobile—one that relies less on audio, video, and other rich media and will therefore be smaller to deliver. Design your content to quickly convey information even in a restricted delivery mode.

  If you need to deliver to a mobile device, plan for mobile delivery when you are designing your content. Ask yourself, for a given topic or page of content, if I can only deliver text, what text-based content is needed? Then determine what rich media could be added that would enhance the user experience. Deliver the rich media to the devices or environments that can handle or support it.

- Connection cost

  Large files can be expensive, not for the publisher or deliverer, but for the customer. If your customers use a cellular connection and they're out of their home area, roaming charges can be a significant barrier. Deliver content optimized for mobile. This will help prevent an excessive expense to customers.

- Download or connection speed

  The differences in speed between older model smartphones and newer models can be quite significant.

  Small file sizes are key. Also, depending on the technology used, it's sometimes possible to restrict the use of an application or the downloading of large files based on the connection method or the connection speed.

- Device performance

  Due to memory limitations or processor speed, content may download quickly but take a long time to render on the screen. Once again, it's often possible for the system to determine the device capabilities and provide the content you have defined as being appropriate to the device.

Constraints of eBooks

eBooks involve a number of constraints, and ironically eBooks are more constrained on eReaders (specific eBook devices) than they are in eReader software (software that runs on your desktop, tablet, or smartphone). eBooks aren't good at:

- Complex tables (greater than four or five columns and rows)
- Images:
  - Images with captions and callouts
  - Multiple images related to a single callout
  - Large, complex images, especially those spanning most of a page or across pages
  - Images not referenced from the text
  - Images embedded in text
  - Images that are pretty but serve no specific purpose (for example, images at the beginning of a chapter)

- Layout-specific content:
  - Columns
  - Sidebars
  - Margin notes
  - Margin icons
  - Icons associated with text
  - Use of shading or color to highlight information
  - Text that wraps around images
  - Equations and math symbols
  - Long, dense paragraphs

eBooks really exemplify the need to separate content from format. An eBook is not a print book. If you're publishing to both print and eBooks, structured components are critical so you can define how the content will be handled in a given situation. For example, sidebars should be placed after the content they're logically related to.

More information on designing for eBooks can be found in *eBooks 101: The Digital Content Strategy for Reaching Customers Anywhere, Anytime, on Any Device* by Ann Rockley and Charles Cooper.

Creating models

There are two levels of content modeling required: modeling at the information product level and modeling at the component level.

Information product models

When you model an information product (such as a press release, an instructor guide, a website, or a brochure), you determine the structure of the product. The structure is a hierarchy or collection of content components. Later, in component modeling, you will determine the structure of those individual components.

Authors follow the model to create and compile information products consistently. If you automate content assembly, the system uses the models to determine what content is valid in what context.

Living the GI Way: Marketing and sales information product models

Living the GI Way has a number of marketing and sales materials to develop information product models for, including:

- Product overview pages on the website
- An elevator pitch to help teams evangelize the product and services when they're in situations where they might meet likely customers, such as at the yoga studio or the health food store
- A brochure for use in their booth at tradeshows
- Sales training materials for use by their partners who also help to market the products and services

They begin by creating a series of information product models for each type of desired information. See Figure 12.1 for the information product models.

Product Overview	Elevator Pitch	Brochure	Sales Training
Overview	Value Proposition	Takeaway	Market Opportunity
Value Proposition	Challenges	Challenges	Market Drivers
Features & Benefits	Overview	Value Proposition	Challenges
FAQ	Features & Benefits	Overview	Overview
	Next Steps	Features & Benefits	Features & Benefits
		Summary	Qualifying Customers
			Value Proposition
			Objection Handlers
			Cross-Selling Opportunities

Figure 12.1   Living the GI Way marketing and sales information product models.

Component models

In addition to product models, you need to create component models. A component model breaks down the information product model even further. It describes the element structure of the components that are assembled to create the information product.

Living the GI Way: Component models

Each component must be modeled to determine the structure of the elements. A number of common components appear across the information products, and one of the most important is the Value Proposition. Figure 12.2 illustrates a component model for the Value Proposition.

Value Proposition
The Value
Competitive Differentiators
Cost of Offering

Figure 12.2   Component model for the Value Proposition.

Understanding granularity

A content model reflects all the components that make up each information product; the level of detail in the model depends on the granularity. Granularity determines the smallest piece of information that's defined by your structure.

There are two types of granularity:

* The granularity of reuse (components)
* The granularity of structure

Granularity of reuse

The granularity of reuse identifies the size of your components. Components can be reused in multiple information products. Having content chunked into components makes it easy to select a component for reuse.

A number of components are reused across the information products, including the following:

* Overview
* Challenges
* Features & Benefits
* Value Proposition

You create components when:

- Content is a logically self-contained chunk of information.
- Content can be reused across and within information products.

The granularity of structure

The granularity of structure defines the semantic structure within a component. The semantic structure guides authors so that they can see exactly what to include as they write. The semantic structure can also be filtered and acted on using system rules. When we looked at the value proposition, we could have chosen to have a component (for example, no semantic element structure) called Value Proposition. Certainly an author understands what a value proposition is, and in many cases could write a pretty good value proposition, but there would always be variations in the way the value propositions of your organization get written. A more granular semantic structure, as shown in Figure 12.2, can be used in a number of ways:

- The elements of the Value Proposition component can clearly guide authors in writing consistent and effective value propositions.
- If the Cost of Offering is a complex table, it could be excluded from mobile.
- If the Value Proposition is written clearly and succinctly and is restricted to 140 characters, this element could be automatically delivered through Twitter.

You don't need to chunk content out into its component parts to gain the value of reuse and automated delivery. The semantic structure of the elements is accessible to the software that manages the content.

Although granularity must be reflected in the content model, the level of granularity can change throughout your content. In one instance you may decide to define a very detailed semantic structure; in others, you may decide to break content out into its component parts.

However, care should be exercised when determining the level of granularity. The more granular the content, the greater the complexity of modeling, authoring, and managing the content. Yet if the content isn't granular enough, you compromise your ability to support adaptive content and lose the authoring guidance that detailed structure provides.

Weigh the benefits and reasons for very granular content before modeling and implementing it. You also need to consider that the meaning of an element may change if it's used out of context. If an element relies on surrounding information to make its meaning clear, the surrounding information may need to be included as part of the element. At first, you may find it necessary to model very granular information. Then, before you implement it, you will need to review the model in the context of how information will actually be authored, reused, and manipulated. Note, for example, that we don't typically recommend granularity at the word level. It's extremely difficult to model and maintain, and can impede the writing and maintenance process. In cases where you have word variations, you can use meta-data to define variables that are inserted as required.

Keep in mind, too, that regardless of the level of granularity, authors still write coherent content, not elements. They may write full "documents," sections, or other recognizable topics of information, but they don't write separate sentences. Rather, authors write content, assigning the required granularity to elements (as defined by the content model) as they write. The granularity defines how the completed document is broken down, tagged, and stored for reuse. Refer to Chapter 13, "Reuse strategy" for more information on granularity.

How are models used?

Models support your content strategy in a number of ways. Models:

- Guide authors in content creation.
- Facilitate reuse.
- Support adaptive content.

Models support authors

Authors use content models to determine what information goes in which information product, as well as how to structure each component. For example, by referring to the content model, authors can determine that an information product requires an overview and what the structure of that overview should be. In addition, they can get hints or rules (guided authoring) about how to write certain components and their associated elements. You can provide detailed writing guidelines, and depending on your tools, embed the writing guidance in each element. For more information on structured writing guidelines refer to Chapter 16, "It's all about the content."

Living the GI Way: Using models to support authors

Living the GI Way has created very detailed writing guidelines for all their models. The writing guidelines for the Value Proposition look like the following.

Value Proposition

Value propositions must be written to a specific target audience; generalized value propositions have no value. Because the customer is always the first priority, always write content with the customer in mind. As far as possible, use the second person when writing for the customer—any content written for the customer can also be used by salespeople. The value proposition should be written in a tone that captures the customer's attention, using words that are active and strong wherever possible. The value proposition also needs to be scannable so that a customer can quickly skim through the information and find the key points that are of interest.

An effective value proposition is:

- Unique, built around why someone would buy the product or trust LGIW
- Simple and easy to understand
- Brief
- Believable
- Memorable
- Backed by statements of strength

The Value

Explain the compelling reason(s) why the customer will buy the product or service. Communicate the key benefit(s) the customer will realize from purchasing the product/service.

Competitive Differentiators

Highlight LGIW's product's competitive advantage(s) versus one or multiple competitive alternatives, or describe what makes the LGIW product better, different, and/or special versus competitive options.

Cost of Offering

Identify the overall cost to the customer. Where possible, be specific. However, generalized statements are acceptable.

Models support manual reuse

Information product models identify the components that are required to create the information product. Authors write content to ensure that reusable content is appropriate wherever it appears. Reusable components can be opportunistically reused (authors specifically select components to reuse) or automatically reused (the system automatically populates the reusable content in the appropriate areas as defined by your reuse strategy).

Living the GI Way: Value proposition reuse

The value proposition is reused across a number of information products as shown in Figure 12.3.

Product Overview	Elevator Pitch	Brochure	Sales Training
Overview	Value Proposition	Takeaway	Market Opportunity
Value Proposition	Challenges	Challenges	Market Drivers
Features & Benefits	Overview	Value Proposition	Challenges
FAQ	Features & Benefits	Overview	Overview
	Next Steps	Features & Benefits	Features & Benefits
		Summary	Qualifying Customers
			Value Proposition
			Objection Handlers
			Cross-Selling Opportunities

Figure 12.3   Reuse across information products.

Models support automatic reuse and adaptive content

Models provide the specification for the structure of your content. Adaptive content uses the structure to determine how to display, organize, and order content. Content strategists define the models and the rules for how content should be displayed in a given context.

Living the GI Way: Automated device adaptation

Recipes are a key part of helping customers live the GI way. Recipes are automatically published in multiple channels.

LGIW expands the model to include information such as preparation, cooking time, servings, and GI ranking (see Figure 12.4).

Recipe
Title
GI ranking
Prep time
Cooking time
Servings
Description
Ingredients
Directions
Suggestion

Figure 12.4   Recipe model.

LGIW identifies some of the constraints associated with each of the channels. Note that a mock-up of how this content could potentially look is provided to show you, the reader of this book, how the semantic content could be displayed for each channel. You wouldn't normally have this mock-up when you're doing your content strategy, but you should be envisioning it.

Book

They'd like to work towards an image followed by the recipe (see Figure 12.5). Decision: Recipes have to be simple and short.

Figure 12.5   Recipe in a print book.

Continued...

Living the GI Way: Automated device adaptation continued

eBook

You can't control where a recipe starts or ends. The customer can change the font size so you can't control where the titles appear. The customer may have to go back and forth on a screen to see the whole recipe. Decision: The Ingredients and Instructions subtitles will not be used so the text will be more compact. Layout will identify the ingredients and steps instead (see Figure 12.6).

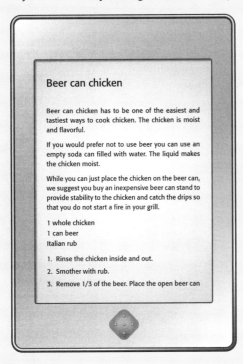

Beer can chicken

Beer can chicken has to be one of the easiest and tastiest ways to cook chicken. The chicken is moist and flavorful.

If you would prefer not to use beer you can use an empty soda can filled with water. The liquid makes the chicken moist.

While you can just place the chicken on the beer can, we suggest you buy an inexpensive beer can stand to provide stability to the chicken and catch the drips so that you do not start a fire in your grill.

1 whole chicken
1 can beer
Italian rub

1. Rinse the chicken inside and out.
2. Smother with rub.
3. Remove 1/3 of the beer. Place the open beer can

Figure 12.6   Recipe in an eBook on an eReader.

Continued...

Living the GI Way: Automated device adaptation continued

Website

The recipe will be fighting for attention with all the surrounding links and ads. Decision: A photo of the finished dish will be included. Subtitles for the subsections will be used to provide easily scannable content for the eye when the cook comes back to check the recipe (see Figure 12.7).

Figure 12.7   Recipe web page.

Continued...

Living the GI Way: Automated device adaptation continued

Mobile recipe app

Screen real estate is very limited. The content will be displayed automatically in three separate screens: the recipe landing page that provides the photo of the finished dish and description of the dish, the Ingredients page, and the Directions page (see Figure 12.8). If necessary, the Ingredients and Directions pages can be scrolled or swiped. The system will automatically display the content on the relevant pages based on the semantic structure.

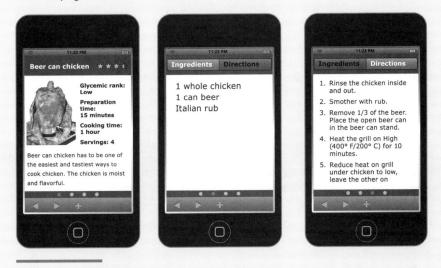

Figure 12.8   Recipe mobile app.

How are models implemented?

Models become the specification for the structure of your content.

Information technologists use models to guide them in creating:

* Authoring templates
* XML document type definitions (DTDs) or schemas
* Forms

- Software structures that enforce the models
- Configuration plans for the content management system
- Delivery stylesheets
- Intelligent content to support adaptive delivery

Summary

Content modeling is the process of determining the structure and granularity of your content. Content models define the structure of information products and components.

Adaptive content automatically adjusts to different environments and device capabilities to deliver the best possible customer experience by filtering and layering content for greater or lesser depth of detail.

Content strategists can't continue to handcraft content for a particular output. You can't think about how content will look and tweak it until you get that perfect fit, and you can't design your content strategy around a particular page or layout. You have to create a content strategy that's all about the content, its purpose, scope, use, and reuse. You need to know what content is required, by whom, when, in what circumstance, and in conjunction with what other content or interactivity. And the only way you'll achieve your goals is with structured models and intelligent content.

A content model reflects all the components that make up each information product; the level of detail in the model depends on the granularity. Granularity identifies the smallest piece of information that's defined by your structure.

Models guide authors in content creation, facilitate reuse, and support adaptive content.

Chapter 13

Reuse strategy

A unified content strategy is dependent on the effectiveness of your reuse strategy, including both manual reuse and automatic reuse.

Content can be reused in many ways, and this chapter identifies the different methods and types of reuse. Note that support for the different types of reuse is dependent on the content management system (CMS).

Structural reuse vs. content reuse

Content reuse is the process of reusing specific pieces of content.

For example, the structural component known as the Value Proposition can be structurally reused in a variety of different information product models, but you'd reuse the content of the Value Proposition for Product X in the brochure for Product X, not in the brochure for Product Y.

Structural reuse is the process of reusing common structures across a variety of information products. Structural reuse is defined in your content models. Structural reuse facilitates content reuse.

Creating a reuse strategy

A reuse strategy defines:

- The way content will be reused (manual versus automated)
- The way you'll secure reusable content
- The types of reuse: identical, section, component, conditional, fragment, or variable
- The level of granularity: how small your content should be chunked (refer to Chapter 12, "Content modeling: Adaptive content design")
- The reuse governance strategy: business rules that apply to ownership, derivatives, and change of reusable content (refer to Chapter 17, "Change management and governance")

Reuse methods

There are two methods for reuse: manual reuse and automated reuse. Each method of reuse offers six options:

- Identical reuse (reuse without change)
- Section-based reuse (reuse of a whole section or series of components)
- Component-based reuse (individual components)
- Conditional/filtered reuse (multiple versions of the content contained within the same component)

- Fragment-based reuse (reuse of a portion of a component)
- Variable reuse (small pieces of content with different values in different situations, for example, weights and measures)

Manual reuse

In manual reuse—the most common form of reuse—authors manually find a component, retrieve it, and reuse it. Manual reuse doesn't rely on specific technology; although it can be done without a content management system, a CMS is advisable.

Any content can be used in a manual reuse situation. In some ways, manual reuse is a replacement for the "copy and paste" that many organizations use. However, manual reuse is not copy and paste; it's simply a "pointer" to the source content. At the reuse location, a link is inserted that points to the reusable content (source). The reused content is visually displayed but it does not actually reside in the "document."

Many organizations use manual reuse when they need to rapidly reconfigure their information products to meet new product or customer requirements. Translating reusable content creates new possibilities. One organization found that just as they could create new documents by assembling reusable English content, they could create new French documents by assembling the already translated French versions of the same reusable content.

Manual reuse provides authors with the greatest flexibility because it gives them the choice to reuse content and the choice to determine which reusable content is appropriate. However, manual reuse results in the lowest incidence of reuse because it puts the burden on authors to want to reuse content, to know that potential reusable content exists, and to find the content they want to reuse. If authors lack motivation, if they're not aware that a suitable reusable component exists or might exist, or if they have trouble finding the appropriate component, reuse may not occur.

To make manual reuse more effective, organizations can optimize retrievability, provide guidelines, and ensure that authors are well trained.

Retrievability can be optimized through the use of content management systems, effective categorization of content, and rich metadata (refer to Chapter 15, "Designing metadata").

Guidelines provide authors with clear information on the models to be used (refer to Chapter 16, "It's all about the content"). Information product models help authors identify where content should be reused (refer to Chapter 12, "Content modeling: Adaptive content design"). Training ensures that authors know how to use the models and the content management system, and that they follow guidelines for reuse.

Automated reuse

In automated reuse the system decides how to reuse content based on information product models, metadata, and business rules.

Once specific content has been identified as reusable in a specific location, the reusable content is automatically inserted (autopopulated) into the appropriate locations. The author doesn't have to determine if the reusable content exists or search for and retrieve it. Automated reuse ensures that content is reused and reduces the burden on the author to know that reusable content exists, to find the reusable content, and to insert it appropriately.

The CMS uses your information product models to identify where content can be reused. If a component exists and matches the author's specific content requirements, the reusable components are automatically inserted into appropriate spots in the "document" (that is, the document is prepopulated with content).

For example, in the case of the Value Proposition, the information product models identify that it should be included in the product overview, elevator pitch, brochure, and sales training. Figure 13.1 repeats the information product model for your reference.

Product Overview	Elevator Pitch	Brochure	Sales Training
Overview	Value Proposition	Takeaway	Market Opportunity
Value Proposition	Challenges	Challenges	Market Drivers
Features & Benefits	Overview	Value Proposition	Challenges
FAQ	Features & Benefits	Overview	Overview
	Next Steps	Features & Benefits	Features & Benefits
		Summary	Qualifying Customers
			Value Proposition
			Objection Handlers
			Cross-Selling Opportunities

Figure 13.1   Reuse across information products.

The marketing author who is responsible for the value proposition completes the Value Proposition component and checks it into the CMS.

Based on the information product model, the system knows what the reusable content components are and checks to see if they are complete. If they are complete, the system automatically populates the product overview, elevator pitch, brochure, and sales training with the reusable content components.

A second marketing author, who is tasked with writing the brochure, opens the brochure template and sees that the reusable content components are complete and in place. The author then completes the content that is unique to this brochure. The other information products are completed by different marketing authors.

Automated reuse is the most costly system to implement because it requires very detailed models, metadata, and business rules. On the other hand, automated reuse provides the greatest return on investment, achieved through guaranteed reuse (guaranteed because reuse isn't dependent on author motivation and knowledge of existing content).

Automated reuse can be perceived as overly restrictive by authors (for example, it doesn't provide flexibility and opportunities to be creative). This perception can be reduced by allowing authors to modify reusable content where appropriate (derivative reuse) and to choose not to use reusable components when they're not appropriate in a particular instance. But make sure that increased flexibility doesn't diminish the effectiveness of automated reuse. For automated reuse to work effectively, authors can't be allowed to remove required content or to edit that content.

Use automated reuse when your content is very structured and you can explicitly identify where content is to be reused, and where you want to ensure that specific content is reused.

Securing reusable content

You can secure your content to ensure that it can't be changed by anyone other than the owner (locked reuse), or you can make it editable (derivative reuse) so that authors can make necessary changes while still reusing most of the component.

Locked reuse

Locked reuse is reuse where the content cannot be changed; only the owner may change the source content of a locked component.

Examples of commonly used "locked reuse" content are legal information, cautionary information, standard statements of disclaimer, and branding information. Any content that you don't want changed by others can be locked. However, don't lock all content because you may limit its effectiveness. We find that companies typically lock only 10 to 15 percent of their content.

Use locked reuse when you want to ensure content isn't changed when reused.

Derivative reuse

Derivative reuse is reuse with change. Derivative reuse is very valuable in an effective reuse strategy. Not all content can be reused identically, so if it can be reused derivatively, it's still possible to track the reuse to ensure that content stays as consistent as possible. However, authors need to receive training to persuade them to employ derivative reuse only when absolutely necessary. Your content repository can become very unmanageable with excessive derivative reuse.

The derivative component is a "child" of the "parent" (source) component. When the source component changes, the owner of the derivative is notified so the author of the derivative component can review the changes to the source component and determine if any changes need to be made to the derivative. This ensures that content remains as similar as possible.

The relationship between derivative content and its original source content is useful when content changes, because it ensures that the source and related content stay synchronized. Care should be taken, though, when deciding to create a derivative version of content. The more derivatives you create, the more variations of the content will exist, and the more work it will take to manage it. Use it, just don't abuse it.

Marketing materials are a good example of an area where derivative content makes a lot of sense. You may have the same product and the same message but you're reaching out to a different audience, possibly with a different offering. Consider creating a common message, then creating a series of derivative components for each of the audience variations. This way, when the message changes, all the authors of derivative versions are notified, which means that your message remains consistent across the derivative content.

Types of reuse

Earlier we listed six types of reuse. Below is a more detailed look at them.

Identical

Identical reuse involves content that's reused without change.

Section

Section-based reuse enables you to reuse an entire section or grouping of components at once.

Section-based reuse is very useful when you're building new information products from existing content. For example, if you customize courses for customers, you can reuse entire sections from your standard materials, then add and augment as required to meet the customer's specific needs.

You can reuse an entire section or grouping of components. Your definition of the "section" grouping will depend on your content and business requirements.

Living the GI Way: Section-based reuse

LGIW has a lot of opportunities for section-based reuse. For example, their chapter on understanding the glycemic index (GI) can be reused across books and eBooks, in the customized diabetes association materials, and on the website. Other sections such as sections on protein, fats, and carbohydrates can also be reused.

Component

Component-based reuse enables you to reuse components of content. A component is a discrete piece of content that is about a specific subject, has an identifiable purpose, and can stand alone.

Components can be reused multiple times in multiple information products.

Living the GI Way: Component-based reuse

As illustrated previously with the Value Proposition, LGIW can use components across a huge range of information products. In fact, very few components can't be reused. However, LGIW may need to employ a secondary type of reuse, such as conditional reuse, so the component can be filtered for a specific situation.

Conditional

In conditional reuse, authors provide variants for content in a single component, with the variations identified by conditional tags or metadata. When the component is "published," the different variations are published as required. Conditional reuse is often called "filtered" reuse because the content that isn't required (for example, for the audience, device, and channel) is filtered out when the content is published.

Conditional reuse is very valuable in multichannel publishing, audience variants, product variants, regional variants, and so on. It's an intuitive way for authors to keep all variations together for ease of writing and review. For example, some content could include a traditional table and an image of the table. The traditional table could be tagged with "print" and the table image "eBook." When the content is published to an eBook, the traditional table would be filtered out.

Conditional reuse has a core set of content that's applicable in all uses, and variant content that builds on the core content and is only applicable in certain situations. To create content for conditional reuse:

- Identify the core content (the content that's identical for all uses).

- Identify unique content to meet other needs.

- Make sure that when the content is filtered (for example, the unrelated content is filtered out), the content still flows (is readable and understandable).

- Tag the elements, indicating where they're valid.

Use of the building block approach allows authors to create all the content for a reusable component at the same time; in this way, all reusable content for a component resides together and can be reused in its entirety. This makes it easier for reviewers as well because they only need to review the single component, not bits of information all over the place.

Living the GI Way: Conditional reuse

LGIW has identified that they need different levels of detail in their content. For example, in their definitions of terms they sometimes need just a very short definition, while in others they need more detail. Take, for example, the definition for the GI.

Glycemic index

The GI measures the effect of carbohydrates on blood sugar levels. Foods with a high GI break down very easily and release glucose into the bloodstream more rapidly than low GI foods. The GI uses a scale of 0 to 100, where pure glucose is 100. Low GI foods range from 0 to 55, medium from 56 to 69, and high from 70 and above.

Sometimes it's preferable to just use the first sentence of the definition, such as in a paragraph or in the app. You could set it up so that the system automatically takes just the first sentence in the term when a shorter version is required, but it would be safer to designate a short version of the term, which may or may not contain more than one sentence. For example, for the definition of insulin resistance, the first two sentences are required for the short definition:

Continued...

Living the GI Way: Conditional reuse continued

Insulin resistance

Insulin resistance occurs when your cells stop responding to the insulin. This results in glucose staying in the blood and not getting into the cells. The body produces more insulin to try and get the cells to respond, which results in hyperinsulinemia.

Figure 13.2 shows what the component model and associated content would look like.

```
Term
  Title
  Definition
    Definition Short
    Definition Detail

Term
  Title             Glycemic Index
  Definition
    Definition Short    The glycemic index (GI) measures the effect of
                        carbohydrates on blood sugar levels.
    Definition Detail   Foods with a high GI break down very easily and release
                        glucose into the bloodstream more rapidly than low GI
                        foods. The glycemic index uses a scale of 0 to 100 where
                        pure glucose is 100. Low GI foods range from 0 to 55,
                        medium from 56 to 69, and high from 70 and above.]

Term
  Title             Insulin resistance
  Definition
    Definition Short    Insulin resistance occurs when your cells stop responding to
                        the insulin. This results in glucose staying in the blood and
                        not getting into the cells.
    Definition Detail   The body produces more insulin to try and get the cells to
                        respond, which results in hyperinsulinemia.
```

Figure 13.2   Component model and associated content.

Imagine that the content is authored in a form or template, not as we've shown it here with the model. Also, even if the content is written in different elements, the content doesn't have to be displayed as separate sentences or paragraphs; the stylesheet can display them as a single paragraph. For example, the sentences Definition Short and Definition Detail can be displayed as a single paragraph.

Fragment

In fragment-based reuse a piece of a component such as a paragraph or a bullet is reused.

While any element in any component can be pointed to and identified for reuse, it makes a lot of sense to group together content fragments for reuse. For example, if an author wants to reuse a term, the author could point to it in the component that includes it, but the next author who wants to reuse that term would have a very difficult time knowing where that term is located. It makes more sense to group together commonly reused content fragments into a single component for ease of search and retrieval.

However, you can also decide to reuse something such as a step, a bullet, or any other piece of information. If others are likely to want to reuse the content, it makes more sense to group it together in a "warehouse" component. The warehouse component holds fragments of content for ease of retrieval but the warehouse component is never reused as a whole component. When you reuse a fragment in a one-off situation, you can simply point to the element and reuse it.

Living the GI Way: Fragment-based reuse

LGIW doesn't envision reusing content at the sentence or bullet level, but does identify that they need to reuse terms in a number of places. They decide to reuse the Definition Short into their content as required.

Variable

Variable reuse enables you to set up a variable that can have a different value in different situations.

Variable reuse is useful when there are only slight variations in content (such as product names in different regions), but otherwise the rest of the content is identical.

Living the GI Way: Variable reuse

LGIW has customers all over the world. This means that they need to change their content to reflect differences in measures such as time (12 hour versus 24 hour), and temperatures (Fahrenheit versus Celsius), and in terminology (blood sugar versus blood glucose). LGIW uses variables to allow these terms to change based on the customer's region.

Supporting adaptive design through reuse

All your content could be published to each of the desired channels, but does it make sense to do so? You need to revisit your models and decide what bits of information make sense in which situations so you can determine what content should be reused for each channel.

In Chapter 12, "Content modeling: Adaptive content design," we identified that you needed to understand the constraints of various devices in order to be able to design appropriate models. When you identify reuse, you determine how the channel impacts the type of content as well as the level of content to be delivered.

For example, a smartphone is often used to:

- Look up or find information. This is often related to the current location of the owner, or simply a reminder of something.

- Read or explore. This typically happens when the owner has some time to kill, perhaps standing in a lineup or waiting for someone, and accesses an app, an eBook, or a website.

- Check what's happening. What's happening on Twitter, Facebook, around the world?

Whatever people do on the smartphone, it tends to be sporadic, short, and frequent. So you need to determine what bits of your information make sense to deliver in the mobile device.

For adaptive content it's a lot easier to determine the reuse for a channel based on the component type or the elements within the component, rather than meticulously identifying each and every piece of information to be reused.

Living the GI Way: Adaptive content

Using the persona of the young female diabetic, Sharon, and the scenario where she's in a rush to get some groceries on her way home, some of the questions she might ask are:

- What's a good recipe I can make quickly and what do I need to make it?
- What should I be looking for again?
- What types of food should I buy?
- What types of food should I avoid?

Looking at these questions, what kind of information might she be looking for? She could be reading the eBook at lunch or on the commuter train, but more likely she's asking these questions as she stands in a grocery store. Potential component types include:

- Recipes (based on glycemic rank: low, medium, high)
- Tips
- Top ten to enjoy (foods in a food category)
- Top ten to avoid (foods in a food category)
- Definitions (for example, what is low GI?)

These and other designated components can be automatically served to the customer based on the device in use. Remember, though, to let your customers select more information if they want it.

When doesn't reuse make sense?

While every effort should be made to reuse as much content as possible, sometimes reuse doesn't make sense. Not every piece of content is reusable, nor should content be reused when it's inappropriate in a given context.

Sentence fragments and individual words may not be appropriate for reuse. If the difference is at the sentence level, consider using conditions to identify the variant sentence. The smaller you break down your content components for reuse, the more complex it is to reuse and manage the content. If individual words are the only component of information that changes, consider using variables that can have a different value depending on the instance. This keeps the component the same, but allows for variation.

You may find that content needs to change to address a different audience. Sometimes the tone or style of the writing is different and the specifics are different, but the message is the same.

To ensure that a component is reusable in many instances, you may contemplate writing very generic components. The generic reusable component may serve the reuse requirement, but may compromise the usability and comprehensibility of the content. Never compromise the quality of the content in order to reuse it. Consider not reusing the content, or use derivative reuse so the content can be adapted to meet the needs of the specific reuse instance.

As you perform your analysis and build your models, consider the value of the reuse. Reuse content where appropriate and effective, and always make sure that the reuse won't compromise the quality and usability of your materials or make the reusable content difficult to create, find, or manage.

Summary

A reuse strategy defines the following:

- The way content will be reused (manual versus automated)
- The types of reuse (identical, section, component, conditional, fragment, or variable)
- The way you'll secure reusable content
- The level of granularity (how small your content should be chunked)
- The reuse governance strategy (business rules that apply to ownership, derivatives, and change of reusable content)

There are two methods for reuse: manual reuse and automated reuse. In manual reuse authors manually find a component, retrieve it, and reuse it. In automated reuse the system decides how to reuse content based on information product models, metadata, and business rules.

You can secure your content to ensure that it can't be changed by anyone other than the owner (locked reuse), or you can make it editable (derivative reuse). Locked reuse is reuse where the content cannot be changed; only the owner may change the content of a locked component. Derivative reuse occurs when a reusable element is modified.

There are a number of different types of reuse:

- Identical reuse is content that's reused without change. The content could be locked or editable, but the author has chosen to use the component unchanged.

- Section-based reuse enables you to reuse an entire section or grouping of components at once.

- Component-based reuse enables you to reuse a component of information.

- In conditional reuse authors provide variants for content in a single component.

- In fragment-based reuse a piece of a component such as a paragraph or a bullet is reused.

- In variable-based reuse small pieces of content with different values in different situations are reused.

While every effort should be made to reuse as much content as possible, not every piece of content is reusable, and sometimes reuse is inappropriate.

Chapter 14

Designing workflow

Workflow, in the context of a unified content strategy, defines how people and tasks interact to create, update, manage, and deliver content. It is the embodiment of the content lifecycle discussed in Chapter 1, "Content: The lifeblood of an organization." Workflow moves content from task to task, ensuring that the business rules specific to your organization are followed, for example, having sign-off occur at the appropriate levels. This chapter describes the concept of workflow and its benefits, and takes you through the basics of designing workflow to support your unified content lifecycle.

Once you've determined what your workflow processes should be, you can select tools to support and automate them.

What is workflow?

Workflow, as its name implies, is the way work or tasks flow through a cycle on their way to getting a job done. Workflow helps organizations perform tasks in an efficient and repeatable manner.

When a workflow is used on a small scale, it does not need to be automated. However, when numerous people and activities are involved in a process, human-controlled workflows can be problematic; steps can be missed, work forgotten or misplaced, and approvals omitted, all delaying the finished product. With automated workflow, organizations can create repeatable processes to ensure that all stages of a project are completed in the proper order. But before automating a workflow, you must first design and test it to ensure that its processes are consistent with your unified content lifecycle.

When designing workflow, you represent it in a diagram, showing the various tasks involved in a project. Your workflow representation not only illustrates all the tasks and people who perform them, it also shows where your processes need to be simplified before you automate them. Just as you're improving the way you create and manage content, you're also improving the processes involved through the content lifecycle.

Components of workflow

- Roles (players): the people who do the tasks, identified by their roles
- Responsibilities (tasks): the steps to complete a particular piece of work; everything that must get done within a process
- Processes: the flow of tasks, as performed by the various players, showing the interactions and interdependencies among players

These components are described in more detail further in this chapter.

Benefits of workflow

We can compare building information products to building a house. Houses are constructed according to blueprints, and information products are constructed according to the information models that define them. After the blueprint is completed and signed off, the builders follow processes to make sure all the construction tasks happen in the correct order. Some tasks are dependent on others, some are concurrent, and at some stages the building inspectors, the architects, and the home owners review the completed work before construction of the next stage can proceed. In the construction industry, timing and planning are critical. The blueprint simply lays out the plan; the workflow ensures that it gets done properly. Accordingly, workflow is tracked throughout construction, ensuring that:

- Materials are delivered in the order they are used (for example, concrete before shingles, framing materials before windows).

- Other players (sub-trades) come in when they're supposed to (for example, electricians can't do their part before the frame is up), and concurrent jobs are scheduled appropriately so that time isn't wasted.

- Approvals are done at the right time and in the correct order (for example, inspection of the electrical work has to be done before the walls are up, which would obscure the wiring).

Workflow in a unified content lifecycle is similar to the workflow that builders follow. Creating information products should progress in a logical, well-designed flow to ensure that tasks and approvals are completed in the right order, by the right people. In the content management world, good workflow design ensures that:

- Departments that should be creating content—or that should at least know about it—aren't left out.

- Content and all other supporting elements, such as graphics, are created in the right order (for example, content is written before graphics are created, ensuring the graphics support the content).

- Content is reviewed at the right time, by the right people, eliminating reviews and approvals that have to be redone if additional changes are made.

- Departments are notified when content is published (for example, customer service staff are notified when a new brochure is published so that they can familiarize themselves with the new information in preparation for phone inquiries).

- Efforts aren't duplicated, and content is consistent (for example, different departments don't end up creating different versions of the same content).

- Work isn't held up at any given stage of the workflow.

- Content is stored in the right place after it's written, reviewed, approved, and delivered.

An effective workflow is really the organized and managed application of common sense, as governed by the business rules of your organization.

Improving and simplifying processes

Workflows have a tendency to get more complicated over time, as people and departments ask for changes and additions to the workflows to meet needs that occasionally crop up. For example, a problem with a description may have occurred in the past, so a department asked for an extra check to be built into the process. Rather than handling this as an exception, the organization made a change, and forever after, all other content elements have been subjected to the same check. Or you may be sending information to a department for approval even though they don't need to approve the information; they just need to know that a change is taking place. A notification is all they need, but you're including them in the approval workflow, adding an unnecessary step (and delay) to the process.

As you diagram your current process, work with all the players to simplify it. Cut out the extra steps, streamline what has to happen, and identify who needs to deal with the information. You only want to implement the best practice, most efficient, and streamlined workflows. Like the information modeling process, where you need to understand what your current models are so you can develop new ones, the workflow process is forward looking. You look back to understand and document your existing processes so you can develop new and better ones.

So identify what the new process needs to do, not what your old workflow did, and strip away all the superfluous paths that have accumulated over time.

To improve or simplify a process, you analyze and change the tasks, and then test the process to make sure the work will flow properly. Tasks may be eliminated or combined, and their sequence and the location where they're performed may be changed, as can the person who performs the task. Benefits of such change include higher efficiency and lower costs.

Higher efficiency

With a well-designed workflow, the work is easier and faster, and the tasks require fewer steps to complete. Tasks are handled concurrently wherever possible, and "what ifs" are built into the processes, eliminating delays.

Lower costs

Costs are lowered in a variety of ways:

- Eliminating duplicate effort saves time and money.
- Ensuring that content is consistent and accurate lowers rework costs.
- Ensuring that content is ready when needed streamlines the process and reduces or eliminates costly delays.

Depicting workflow

A good workflow system must be capable of supporting your business needs. And although it seems self-evident, you must first determine what you need your workflow to do before attempting to implement it. Ad hoc system design is a bad idea, although we've seen it attempted time and again! You need to figure out (given certain business situations) how tasks such as authoring, editing, reviewing, approval, publishing, and distribution should flow throughout your organization, and what should happen if, at any given stage, a task cannot be completed as dictated by the workflow.

Workflow can be designed within a CMS or outside it. In the best case, the analysis and upfront design takes place before a CMS is chosen. In addition, each CMS has its own method of defining and diagramming the workflow within itself. These systems are powerful, but they tend to be somewhat complicated and are really designed for implementers rather than subject matter experts (SMEs). We don't advocate using the built-in workflow within any particular system during the investigation and design phase.

We find that using simpler tools helps separate the ideas from the eventual implementation and makes it easier for nonspecialists (non-workflow specialists, that is) to be involved in the definition and design in a significant way.

Because workflow describes the flow of tasks, we like to depict them diagrammatically in a linear flowchart or swimlane diagram (see Figure 14.1).

Flowcharts

Linear flowcharts depict a process from beginning to end, often using flowcharting symbols to indicate the type of tasks in the process. Flowcharting symbols illustrate such things as which task is a process, which task is a decision, which task is a predefined process, which task is a manual operation, and so on. Many people become frustrated trying to remember what the many different symbols mean, and their frustration is compounded if there are no clear task descriptions accompanying the symbols. Therefore, we recommend a simpler approach: boxes with clear task descriptions written in them. This technique is especially effective when using swimlane diagrams (the method we prefer).

Figure 14.1
Flowchart process shapes.

Swimlane diagrams

Swimlane diagrams show processes in "lanes" (like the lanes you swim laps in) to depict tasks that occur concurrently, illustrating who does what and when. Swimlane diagrams are known by many other names, among them process maps, business process maps, process responsibility diagrams, and LOV (line of visibility) charts. As in a pool, where swimmers are expected to stay in their own lanes, the people or groups responsible for doing the work—the players—stay in their process lanes. By showing each lane, these diagrams allow the players to see how what they do depends on what others do, and vice versa. Arrows connect tasks and show the flow of work. When work changes hands from one role to another, the arrows cross from one lane to the other. Figure 14.2 illustrates the manual reuse process using a swimlane diagram. (Note that players are shown by their role, followed by the name of their department in parentheses.)

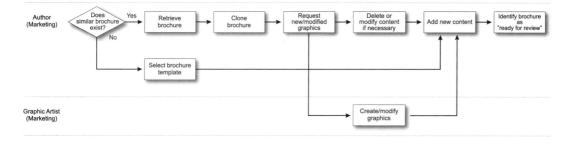

Figure 14.2   Manual reuse workflow.

Figure 14.3 illustrates the automatic reuse process. Note the similarities and the dissimilarities in the process compared with the manual reuse process.

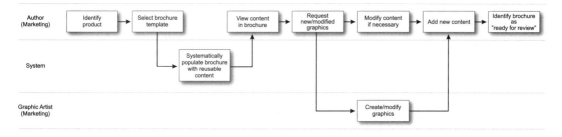

Figure 14.3   Automatic reuse workflow.

Swimlane diagrams or flowcharts?

How should you depict your workflow? It really depends on what you want to depict.

Linear flowcharts are useful if you want to show all the tasks within a process with a view to simplifying them. This technique can be effective when you need buy-in from others in your organization. However, linear flowcharts that detail every step, including handoffs and wait tasks, may end up being many feet long. Their size alone may convince others that the process should be simplified.

We like to use swimlane diagrams because they show the interdependencies of tasks. They help players understand the existing processes and they help define the "to be" workflow. A swimlane diagram shows all roles and all tasks as they relate to each other, which is critical in a unified content strategy.

Nevertheless, you should always attempt to simplify the workflow prior to its automation, whatever type of diagram you use to document it.

Roles, responsibilities, and processes

Workflow consists of roles (the players who participate in the process), responsibilities (the tasks the players are responsible for), and processes (the workflows that connect all the players and tasks together and define the path that each task must take).

Developing, managing, and delivering content involves many people with different skills, and spans many tasks over an extended period of time. Content comprises many elements: text, images (and potentially video and sound), layout and design, and so on. This multifaceted nature of content introduces complexity into its development process. Many different departments create content in a number of different formats for a number of different audiences; after content is created and delivered, it must be stored so it can be accessed later on.

Who is a player?

Generally, a player is any person or group that handles the work between the initial event and the completion of the process. Players and roles sound similar, but they are not the same. The "player" identifies an individual or individual job function (such as engineer) within the organization. In terms of workflow this is not the same as a "role". An individual player may have more than one role in the workflow.

Take an engineer for example. She may "wear more than one hat" during a product lifecycle. She may be a part of the design team, an SME for the training department, a resource for the sales department, and an SME and reviewer for the documentation department.

We can see that the engineer, although a player, is not an individual role in terms of workflow. Instead we see:

Player = Engineer

Role   = Designer or

        SME or

        Test Engineer or

        Reviewer

This means that we don't describe the Player as "engineer" in the workflow. Instead we identify the roles as SME, Reviewer, and so on. The CMS is also a player; it performs tasks, just as people do. The role of a player may be very complex or as simple as being notified that a new product or new information is available. Regardless of the complexity—or simplicity—of each role, the workflow must accommodate all roles. If you leave out roles, you will not have an accurate depiction of all the project phases, which could unnecessarily delay your project.

Some common roles include:

Authors

Authors are anyone involved with creating content of any type (for example, text or graphics). Authors should have full permission to create, modify, and delete their own content, but not anyone else's.

Reviewers

Reviewers check content for such things as accuracy, completeness, and appropriateness. Reviewers are usually limited to making comments about the content without changing it.

Editors

Editors review and make changes to content; the scope of their changes depends on their role as either substantive or copy editors. Editors can also be reviewers, but unlike reviewers, their permissions allow them to modify the content.

Approvers

Approvers provide the final sign-off for content before it is "posted" or published. Approvers can also be reviewers, and while their permissions are similar to the reviewers' permissions, approvers have the final authority to determine if the content is ready to go to the public.

The workflow doesn't tell the players how to do their part; it tells them that they have a part, what that part is, and when it must be done. The workflow must also allow for alternatives if players aren't available when they're required.

Depicting roles

In a swimlane diagram, we depict the "swimmer," that is, the person or department performing the tasks, at the beginning of the swimlane. We use the name of the role, for example, Information Architect or the Publications Department, rather than the individual employee's name. If a department has more than one function, and if, for the sake of clarity, you need to identify the portion of the department that's involved in the workflow, ensure that you do so when naming the role on the swimlane. For example, in some companies, the functions of Marketing and Sales are in one department. But these functions, while related, are quite different. You probably don't want to get marketing input from a salesperson or vice versa. In this case, you'd want to make very clear which part of the department you want to perform the specified task.

Responsibilities (tasks)

Two of the most common questions people ask us when charting their workflows are "What is a task? And how do I know what to include?" A task is a particular series of actions that accomplish a particular goal. Our rule of thumb is if it must "get done," then it's a task and you need to show it. To determine all the tasks within a workflow, you need to talk to the various players about their responsibilities, keeping the discussion focused on one particular process, not on all the activities of the player or their department.

When discussing the task with the players, try to keep in mind the content that the task is related to. The content is the thing that must be created and reviewed. It must move from one state to another. Think about what must be done to move it from its initial state to its final state. It's a way of thinking that could result in a group saying, "We need X done on the content and X is not currently done by any of our current roles. We need a new role."

Types of tasks

You can categorize tasks into four types:

1. Tasks that add value (work tasks)

   When value is added to a task, the work is changed in some way. Content may be written, approved, revised, returned for correction, have metadata added to it, and so on. Work is being performed on a work item, including inspection or validation activities. This is also known as "work time," and it advances the progress of the workflow as a whole.

2. Tasks that move the work along (transport tasks)

   A transport task is one that moves the work along but does not change a work item (for example, content isn't written or edited); instead, it moves the work item from task to task in the workflow. People tend to exclude these tasks from their workflow, but transport tasks are critical to include because they illustrate important parts of the process, such as how a work item gets to the next person. Also, a transport task that moves information to a different location may take longer. In a transport task, include information on how the work item is transported, for example, "route first draft by email to supervisor in head office" or "courier original artwork to ad agency."

3. Notification tasks

   At many stages of the process, the system must notify various players that the content has changed state. The most important of these is when the content has been changed and is now ready for players to interact with. For example, they must review, edit, comment on, or approve it.

   It's crucial to define these notifications (including when they are sent, to whom, and what that player's reaction should be), so the implementers can program them into the system.

4. Tasks that introduce a delay (wait tasks)

   When a task introduces a delay, the subsequent task cannot proceed until the previous one is finished. A task that introduces a delay may not actually do anything to the work item; instead, it pauses the process temporarily. Most tasks introduce a delay simply by their nature; after all, it takes time for work to get done or transported. Sometimes when a delay is introduced, the next task may still be able to proceed. For example, while waiting for graphics, an author may still be able to complete a draft, and then insert the graphics when they arrive. However, a delay-introducing task means that the next task has to wait for a prerequisite task to be done. An example of this might be "wait for content from marketing before completing draft." While waiting, the author can do other work, but not work that moves this process along. It's important to include these types of delays because they give you a more accurate depiction of how long a process will take.

Writing task descriptions

Regardless of the type of task, we recommend writing tasks consistently in a verb-noun format. Anyone who reads a workflow diagram should be able to understand it, so you make it a practice to avoid cryptic descriptions such as "Form CP-13." A task is something that is performed and, accordingly, should be written as an action. Don't write "Form CP-13" as a task, because it might mean nothing to anyone other than the person who created the description. Worse still, it might mean totally different things to different people in different departments. It's better to define the task as "submit graphics request on Form CP-13." Optionally, you can include "how" information in your step, for example, "sort graphics requests" could become "sort graphics requests by due date," which provides additional information on how the task should be completed. You can also use qualifiers to modify the noun, for example, "sort graphics requests from marketing by their due date."

The more descriptive you can make your task, the better. Tasks must never be open to interpretation.

Although the task name must convey its result (the result of "sort graphics request by due date" is that graphics requests are sorted by due date), don't write the task by focusing on the result, for example, "graphics requests are sorted." That's not a task description, that's the definition of an output, or task result. The task name should focus on, and begin with, the verb—the action of performing the task.

It's not necessary to include players in the task description because they're indicated in the swimlane diagram, and all the tasks belonging to a particular role are put in the lane for that role (see Figure 14.4).

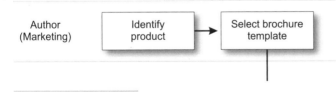

Figure 14.4   The Author (Marketing) lane.

The system can have tasks as well. It can do such things as publish content to PDF, post content to the website, and notify a reviewer that content is ready to review. These tasks are programmed by a system developer or integrator, and to be included in workflow they must be available in your system.

Depicting tasks

In a swimlane diagram, tasks are shown in the swimlane of the player who does the task, using descriptive text to depict each task.

Processes (flow)

A process has a start point and an end point between which various tasks are performed, usually by a number of different people located in different places, often using different equipment or systems. A process comprises the tasks and responsibilities as performed by the various players, and the workflow must illustrate the entire process from beginning to end.

So, where to start? First, you need to decide where your process begins and where it ends. Then start examining and eventually charting everything that happens in between.

Processes may start outside the system, but the automated workflow starts when a task can be managed by the system. For example, the process to create a web product page may start with a meeting to discuss the requirements for the page. But the meeting may occur long before the system takes the content and routes it. This isn't to say that you might not capture the meeting in a set of minutes with action items. In fact, you can store the meeting minutes in the content management system, designating them as "content of record" for access by team members. When you're depicting workflow, you may also include such tasks as "determine project requirements" and "hold meetings." Even though they're not managed by the workflow system, it's a good idea to include such tasks; they form part of the entire process and may be overlooked if not described. However, the automated workflow starts when work begins on the action items, such as when the specification is created or when the marketing writer begins to write. At whichever point the process must be managed automatically, workflow begins. If you include project management, requirement definition tasks, or any tasks that aren't managed through the system in your swimlane diagrams, you should indicate where the automated workflow begins; the automated tasks form your requirements for selecting and configuring a workflow system.

It can also be difficult to determine the end of the workflow. For example, a web product page is posted to the Web or an eBook has been released, but it's modified over time to remain current. You could include the updates in the initial creation workflow, but it probably makes sense to end the workflow when the page has been posted or the eBook is released. Then you could create an additional workflow that handles the content when it needs to be updated, modified, or corrected.

In a sense, the entire workflow process is like a virtual assembly line on which the various players perform various tasks to support the unified content lifecycle. For example, research and development develops a new version of a software package, marketing gets the word out to potential customers, SMEs review the existing documentation to determine which elements can be used as is and which should be revised, technical publications makes the necessary changes, and so on. After all the tasks on the assembly line are complete, the last task is to notify the person who started the process, thus ending it.

Your company may also have specific processes for different types of projects. For example, you could develop workflows to support the content lifecycle for:

- New products/services

- Updates to existing products/services

- Discontinued products/services (for service and support issues)

You may also need to develop workflows for special situations, such as emergency notification of changes to your products. Depending on how complex they are, each of your workflows may also be broken down into various supporting workflows, but they must all relate to the common goal. That is, don't have separate workflows for the various tasks in individual departments unless you can link them to a top-level content lifecycle workflow. For example, in the construction industry, there are workflows for the framing, the electrical work, and the plumbing, but they all relate to the master plan and depend on one another. Likewise, in a unified content strategy there may be workflows for writing user documentation, for developing collateral and graphics, and for creating training materials. All the processes form part of an overall project and are dependent on one another.

Business rules often govern workflow

Usually, processes are also governed by business rules specific to your organization. Business rules include such things as:

- Budgets that dictate how much can be spent on any given task

- Hours of work in which tasks can be completed

- Union (or other association) job descriptions that govern who can perform a certain task and under which conditions

- Physical location of the company that dictates where a task is performed (physical location can affect such things as handoffs and transport tasks, as well as translation and localization)

- Suppliers that your company does business with and their particular constraints

When determining your workflow, you need to consider the business rules specific to your environment.

Depicting processes

Processes are shown in swimlane diagrams with specific start and end points, and with all lanes completed with all relevant tasks, including such things as handoffs and delays. Where a task is performed by two players at the same time you can use various methods to indicate that they're taking place in parallel. You can stack the images as we've done with Review and Final Approval in Figure 14.5. You can also draw a box around or shade parallel tasks to make it clear that they're happening at the same time. Use arrows to connect the flow of tasks and to show when they transfer to another role or lane.

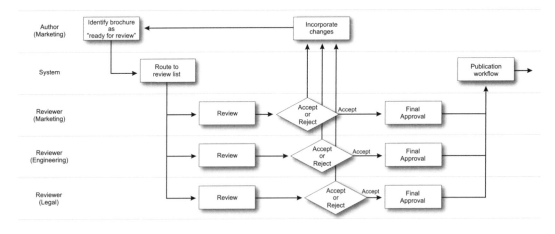

Figure 14.5 Sample review and approval workflow.

Documenting your existing workflow can be a great first step toward an effective unified content strategy, but your ultimate goal is to try to improve—or simplify— your current processes. Accordingly, your first draft flowcharts may show processes in their current state, but your unified content lifecycle workflows could show your processes as they will support your unified content strategy.

Designing effective workflow

The components of an effective workflow are players, their responsibilities (or tasks), and the processes they all follow. Designing an effective workflow involves analysis of players and their tasks, as well as identification of patterns and interactions, then documenting of detailed tasks, followed by testing.

To design effective workflow, follow these steps, referring to your content lifecycle:

- Understand your current workflow. In most cases organizations have only a vague idea of how their content is created and managed. We recommend that before you design your new workflow, you examine, and if necessary, document your current workflow. It's hard to know where you want to go if you don't know where you are. You need to ensure you understand your current workflow and learn what doesn't work, what works but could be better, and what works really well. Only when you have a solid understanding of what your current problems and successes are should you attempt to develop a new workflow.

- Determine a starting point for your new workflow. Usually a process starts with an incoming event, such as a new eBook or app coming to the market, or a request to update existing documentation. A starting point can also be a crisis that you need to respond to. If you include tasks that are not part of the auto-mated workflow, indicate where automated workflow begins.

- Figure out a logical place for the workflow to end. This is typically when the incoming event that triggered the beginning has been handled satisfactorily. In a unified content lifecycle, content must be stored in the repository for the event to be considered complete.

- Identify all players from the beginning to the end of the workflow. Identify players by their roles rather than by their names. A task should be associated with a role to accommodate people moving in and out of jobs. If tasks are assigned to roles, then the task stays with the role regardless of where particu-lar people move in your organization. If you assign tasks to people, you'll need to go into your workflow system and make changes every time those people change jobs.

- Remember that your CMS is a player too. It will handle notifications, reports, and all of the bothersome tracking that we hate doing. If you don't define what you want the system to do, employees will end up tracking files and sending notifications—exactly what we don't want to happen.

- Sketch the tasks. Start by identifying all the tasks that belong to each player, including when they're waiting for something else to happen, or when they're handing off work to someone else. Remember to write tasks clearly so that everyone who looks at the flow knows exactly what the task is about. (You may omit notification in your first iteration, allowing you to focus more clearly on the tasks themselves. However, notification must be included before your workflow can be considered complete.) Look for potential bottlenecks that may slow your workflow down, such as one player having too many tasks at a certain stage, while other players wait for those tasks to be done so they can contribute theirs. Can tasks be delegated to other roles? Can tasks be completed concurrently?

- Identify interaction patterns among players and tasks. When are players working alone and when are they working with others? A critical component of workflow involves designing the interactions among players and their tasks. Who relies on whom or on what information? When there are numerous interactions, there may also be bottlenecks; look for potential bottlenecks that may slow down your workflow, such as information not being ready so one player is delayed in performing a task. Can you build in an alternative?

- Allocate time frames for tasks. In addition to selecting a start and end for the entire workflow, you should allocate start and end times for each task. When is each task complete, and how much time should you allow from the time a task is assigned until it is completed? How much leeway should you build into the time frame?

- Identify notification patterns—determine who needs to know what at any given stage of the workflow.

- Identify approval patterns. Who's responsible for reviewing work items throughout the workflow? It's important to distinguish approval from notification. Sometimes a department only needs to know about what you're doing; they don't necessarily have to approve it. Make sure all your approvals are valid.

- Determine all the "what ifs" that may knock your workflow off its path. Try to think of everything that could derail your workflow. For example, what happens if an approver is away? Can work be routed to someone else for approval? What happens to other tasks if a deadline is missed?

- Once all roles are identified, tasks are sketched, and notification and approval patterns are identified, examine your workflow to see if it can be simplified.

- Repeat these steps for all the workflow processes you need to support your unified content lifecycle, for example, workflow for new projects, workflow for different types of new products, and workflow for updates to existing content.

Now that your workflow is documented, you can focus on selecting a workflow system to support your design. It's important to design your workflow before selecting a workflow system because you need to make sure the system will do what you need it to do. For example, if notification is important to keep your workflow moving, you want to make sure that a workflow system will send notifications automatically.

Living the GI Way: Workflow

LGIW is a multifaceted company. It produces books, a monthly newsletter, training products, an interactive glycemic index (GI) database, and apps for smartphones and tablets, and ties it all together with a website.

Creating new content, responding to customer needs and keeping all this up and running does not happen by accident. It's a well-tuned set of processes, all driven by workflows that allow it to operate smoothly. Each person has a role, and the tasks of each role, and how they interact, are well defined.

Early decisions were taken to define what the products were, which groups were involved in creating them, what they needed to do their jobs, which groups needed to be involved in the review process, and what each group expected from the others—and when.

Summary

A unified content strategy requires unified processes that are supported by a well-designed workflow. A workflow representation shows how tasks are assigned to the appropriate players and how tasks and players interact. It also shows the dependencies within the workflow. A well-designed workflow saves time and reduces duplicate work and potential errors. To design an effective workflow:

- Select start and end points.

- Determine everything that has to happen in between, assigning tasks to roles. Remember to accommodate business rules specific to your organization.

- Identify all the interactions, dependencies, notifications, and approvals.

- Determine what you want the system to do for you.

- Incorporate the "what ifs."

- Document your workflow in swimlane diagrams that show players' roles in the appropriate swimlanes.

- Review and simplify your documented workflow where possible.

Chapter 15

Designing metadata

As you've no doubt noticed, more information is available than ever before—on the Web, on your company intranet, in your content management repository, and elsewhere. This is exciting and a problem, as well as extremely frustrating when you can't find what you're looking for.

What's missing is information about the information—that is, labeling, cataloging, and descriptive information—that enables a computer to properly process and search the content components. This information about information is known as *metadata*.

Although metadata has been a buzzword in information technology and data warehousing, it has recently emerged as an important concept for those developing search and retrieval strategies in reference databases or on the Web, for authors of structured content, and for developers of enterprise content management and web publishing solutions. With more complex authoring processes and information delivery requirements, you need to classify and identify all the information or content "bits" so they can be retrieved and combined in meaningful ways. Well-designed metadata can provide the classification and identification you need.

This chapter introduces the levels and types of metadata that will be appropriate to your unified content strategy. It also describes methods for defining metadata.

What is metadata?

Traditionally, metadata has been defined as "data about data." Although this is true, metadata is actually much more. Metadata is the encoded knowledge of your organization, described by David Marco as

> all physical data (contained in software and other media) and knowledge (contained in employees and various media) from inside and outside an organization, including information about the physical data, technical and business processes, rules and constraints of the data, and structures of the data used by a corporation.[1]

This definition is significant because it includes the often-overlooked idea that metadata can be used to describe the data's behavior, processes, rules, and structure. Describing information in this way is important when developing a sound metadata strategy for content search and retrieval, reuse, and dynamic content delivery, because you can determine not only what the content is, but also who uses it, how it will be used, how it will be delivered, and when.

Metadata is the glue that enables the system (and by extension, you) to find the information you need. It's the "stuff" that allows computers to be "smart." It's the stuff that makes "intelligent content" intelligent. And when it's missing or poorly implemented, it's what makes us slap the side of the computer in frustration when we can't find what we're looking for.

Let's take a look at the most common metadata that most people are familiar with, at least at a superficial level: the metadata used by Microsoft Office.

Open a Microsoft Word file and go to the Office Button > Prepare > Properties > Document Properties > Advanced screen. Click on the General tab and a box like the one shown in Figure 15.1 appears.

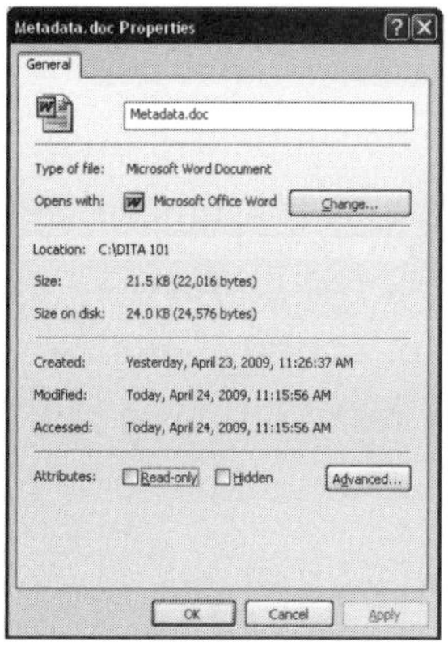

Figure 15.1   Metadata properties General tab.

---

1   Marco, David. *Building and Managing the Meta Data Repository: A Full Lifecycle Guide.* New York: John Wiley & Sons, Inc., 2000, p. 5.

It contains information about the file just opened, such as its name, when it was created, where it is located, and so on. Now, close the file and hover over the name in the File Manager (see Figure 15.2). Some of that same information (name, date modified, and size) will be displayed in the hover box.

Figure 15.2   Hover box showing metadata.

Right click on the filename and select Properties from the options presented. More information is displayed, such as where the file is located, when it was created (in addition to its last modification), and other details (see Figure 15.3).

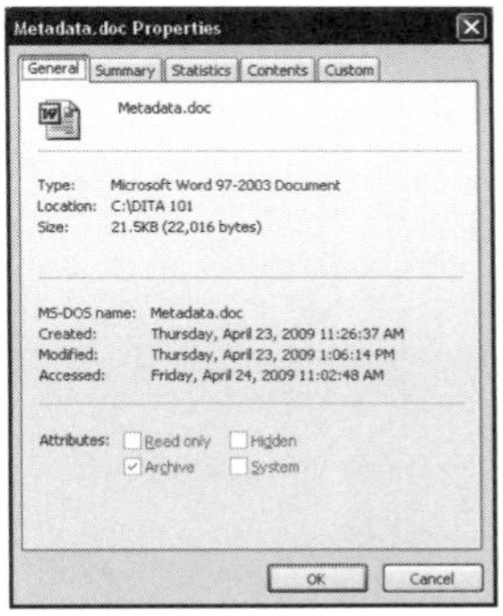

Figure 15.3   Properties box from File Manager, showing metadata.

All this information is metadata, which allows you to know more about the file in question. On a Windows system, the metadata helps the search tool find particular files. This information is very generic though; by adding your own metadata to a file, it becomes more useful to you.

Reopen that Word file and once again navigate to the Properties dialog box. Select the Summary tab this time and you'll see a window where you can enter your own information (see Figure 15.4).

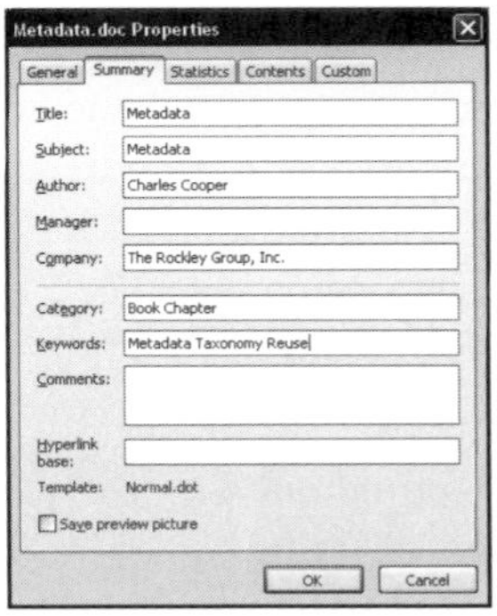

Figure 15.4   Metadata properties, Summary tab.

Enter some information there (the Author, Subject, Keywords, and other information are entered in the example) and close the file. Once again, hover over the file name in Explorer to see a bit more information about what's contained in the file—even without opening it (see Figure 15.5).

Figure 15.5   Hover box showing additional metadata.

In Microsoft Word, though, it's the Custom tab that shows the power of metadata. In the Properties dialog box, select the Custom tab to open the scroll box containing a number of possible types of metadata, including Checked by, Department, Disposition, and so on (see Figure 15.6). Any of these can be selected and relevant information entered there. In content management, this is known as "tagging."

Figure 15.6   Metadata properties, Custom tab.

The file can be tagged with the name of the reviewer (in this case, Joe Bloggs), the date the file was reviewed, and a host of other information. Any program that can read this information can use it to narrow searches and help find information. For example, if you're looking for a particular file and you know that Joe Bloggs reviewed it, you can search for any Word file reviewed by Joe, and that's all the search engine will look for.

The real strength of metadata is realized only when all the information available is tagged in a similar manner. If all members of an organization tag information in the same way, then they can build on that shared knowledge and find information across the organization with the help of the embedded metadata. Microsoft Word files, spreadsheets, images, movies, and more can be tagged for retrieval.

However, it's when the contents of those files (the components that comprise them) are tagged that information can be found and reused throughout a department or organization. For example, content creators can now find individual components and reuse them rather than rewriting them.

Imagine a number of product lines for audio components in which all the brochures (across the product lines) are supposed to contain standard information about the company. If an audit were conducted, the findings would probably show that the "standard" content differs from brochure to brochure. And if each line is supposed to have a common description of the product, the findings would show that those "common" descriptions vary as well. However, if you were using a content management system to manage the content, you could identify that common company information with a tag, ensure that it's "built into" all the documents, and ensure that the product-line-specific common descriptions are built into each of the product lines. And because of the tagging, the correct product line descriptions could be matched with the product lines. For example, the headphone descriptions would be built into the headphone materials, and the loudspeaker descriptions would be made available in the speaker materials—and not vice versa.

Benefits of metadata to a unified content strategy

In a unified content strategy, metadata enables content to be retrieved, tracked, and assembled automatically. Metadata enables:

- Effective retrieval
- Automatic reuse
- Automatic routing based on workflow status
- Tracking of status
- Reporting

Properly defining and categorizing the types of metadata you want to use is extremely important to the success of your unified content strategy. Improperly identified metadata, or missed categories, can cause problems ranging from misfiled and therefore inaccessible content to more serious problems such as those encountered by the National Aeronautics and Space Administration's (NASA's) 1999 Mars Climate Orbiter mission, in which misidentified metadata resulted in the loss of the spacecraft, at a cost of $300 million![2]

Using metadata for retrieval and content management results in the following benefits.

---

2   Marco, David. *Building and Managing the Meta Data Repository: A Full Lifecycle Guide.* New York: John Wiley & Sons, Inc., 2000.

Reduction of redundant content

If content is consistently labeled with metadata, authors can easily retrieve existing reusable content, and if multiple authors accidentally create the same piece of content, your content management system identifies that multiple versions of the same content exist. With automatic reuse, the system assembles a document with the appropriate reusable content. If the content is already in place when authors start to write, they are aware that they do not need to create it again.

Improved workflow

When you tag content with metadata that identifies its status, workflow automatically manages that content. For example, a component marked with "Ready for review" can be compiled automatically into an information product such as a brochure, after which the brochure is automatically routed for review and approval.

Reduced costs

Metadata can reduce costs in a unified content strategy. For example, existing content identified with metadata can be easily retrieved and reused. The work required to create it again is eliminated. Metadata can also be used to automatically identify source components that have changed. Triggering a translation process for the component saves time otherwise spent identifying the content to be translated. Additionally, if a reusable component is already translated, the metadata can facilitate the automatic population everywhere the source component is reused to ensure that the component is not translated again.

Types of metadata

We've seen an example of entering metadata into Microsoft Word. You can imagine how this could enable customers to search for specific files. But to actually implement metadata in a consistent (and therefore useful) manner, you have to think about why you're entering the it and how it will be used. You need to understand that there are different types of metadata for different purposes.

Unified content requires two types of metadata: descriptive and component. Customers tend to retrieve information based on descriptive metadata, whereas authors tend to retrieve information based on component metadata.

Descriptive or publication metadata is used to help customers find information—books in libraries, PDF files on a company fileserver, or content on the Web.

Component metadata is more granular. Although it can be used to find published information, its primary purpose is to give those creating content (or anyone involved in the content creation process, such as reviewers, editors, and subject matter experts [SMEs]) the ability to find information so it can be reused in different content assembly or for different purposes. We break down the component metadata into two subcategories: metadata for reuse and retrieval, and metadata for tracking.

Descriptive or publication metadata

Today, if you go into a number of libraries, you'll find that the information (books, magazines, and other nonprinted material such as videos and multimedia assets) are organized in a fairly consistent manner from one library to the next. It wasn't always this way.

For centuries, individual libraries were organized by whatever scheme the chief librarian was comfortable with. That's not to say they were disorganized, but the librarian was free to categorize the information in the library in a manner that suited him. It might not be logical or obvious to someone familiar with another library's categorization system, but it would be internally consistent within that library or within a related group of libraries.

In the late 1800s, Melvil Dewey was put in charge of the library at Amherst College in Amherst, Massachusetts. Dewey was a born reformer and organizer, and within a few years he had devised his own system of categorization, now known as the Dewey Decimal Classification system. Many of us used his system when we searched through card catalogs in libraries (see Figure 15.7). He organized all the information in the library into ten top categories, with repeated subcategories to more clearly define and segregate more detailed information.

This system spread throughout the world and remains one of the most common library categorization systems.

But why does it work?

Figure 15.7   Card catalog.

The file cards contained information about the books that people were looking for, such as title, author, publication date, subject, and a brief description (abstract) of what was contained within the books. In today's world, the items on the card would be referred to as metadata.

We use the metadata (embodied in the Dewey decimal system) to find the book. Although the days of the physical card catalog are largely behind us—with the physical cards being replaced by computer systems—it's very difficult to find a particular book in a large library without resorting to the catalog. Walking back and forth up an aisle of books is time consuming and inefficient. Even worse, without metadata it's nearly impossible to find content online (for example, on the Internet, a company intranet, or within a content management system). Online you don't have the option of walking the aisles; you must use some form of search tool, and the best search tools are driven by metadata.

The increasing use of portals has encouraged organizations to make the portal the central location for access to organizational content. However, as each new piece of content is added, customers' ability to find content decreases. Corporate information needs to be just as accessible as library content, which means organizing content in a logical structure, categorizing it, and using the categories to add metadata to the information. Descriptive metadata is like the old card catalog, presenting information to customers in context and enabling them to quickly find relevant information.

Creating descriptive metadata

Often it's the job of a corporate librarian or information architect to manually identify and tag content appropriately. Corporate content can be any content the corporation creates, receives, or wants to make available to its employees, customers, or suppliers. This body of content is much broader than the content we refer to in this book; it encompasses email, reports, correspondence, strategic analysis, and much more. The volume of this content grows at a tremendous pace, making it difficult for organizations to maintain it manually.

If you have a lot of content to categorize, check to see whether a vertical taxonomy already exists for your industry, and check with vendors to see whether they can support your information set. Creating descriptive metadata is a large, sometimes costly, and intensive ongoing task. If you don't have to do this task on your own, don't try to. If you do decide to tackle the job, consider including corporate librarians or information architects on the team.

Vertical taxonomy

Some industries have created industry-specific taxonomies, sometimes known as *vertical taxonomies*. Vertical taxonomies have been developed to help save organizations from the task of having to create everything themselves (thereby creating inconsistent taxonomies from company to company), and to facilitate the sharing of content. For example, online bookstores use a taxonomy that helps them categorize books so readers can more easily find their desired genre: non-fiction, reference, travel reference, European travel, and so on. Vertical taxonomies have been created for such areas as IT, health care, telecommunications, HR, financial, legal, eLearning, sales and marketing, and geography, and more are being created daily.

In the absence of a vertical taxonomy, industries are creating standards for the format, structure, and syntax of metadata to enable different organizations and even different departments within an organization to share metadata. For more information on metadata standards see "Metadata standards," later in this chapter.

Understanding your customer

To begin the process of creating descriptive metadata you need to understand your customers. You need to know who they are, what they're trying to accomplish and how they're looking for information.

- Who are your customers and what are they trying to accomplish?

   Are they prospective purchasers? Are they comparing your product to your competitors' products? Are they looking for reviews? Have they already purchased your product and begun looking for accessories?

   You're likely to find that you have more than one set of customers (or audience) for both your product and your content. You can use that to your advantage, and learn from it.

   Because each audience is slightly different they will be interested in different things. Some will be focused primarily on price, others are more interested in particular features. Still others might want your product immediately, so they're focused on current availability.

   Prospective purchasers might share some interests and concerns with existing customers (availability of accessories). On the other hand, while prospective customers might be interested in the size or weight of your product, existing customers (who already have your product) probably won't be.

- How are they looking for the information?

  If people are searching the Web, they'll use some form of search engine and type a word into the search field that they think will help them find what they're looking for.

  For printed content, people use the index like a search engine, but rather than typing in a search word, they look for the word in the index, and then turn to the page they think is most likely to contain the relevant information.

  You want to ensure that the search terms people enter online or look for in an index lead them to the information they need. It's difficult to anticipate what search terms people will use, but if you've thought out who's searching for your material and what they're trying to do, you have a much better chance than if you guess.

  Think back to your analysis of who your customers are and what they're looking for. Ensure that your content has been tagged with the terms that the various sets of customers are most likely to use as search terms.

Categorize your content

The next thing you have to do is to group or categorize your content. Why?

Imagine you want to find a photo on your computer. If you know the name of the photo, you can search for it pretty easily. Just type the name (or part of the name) in the search box. But if you have a lot of files on your drive, it's going to take some time. If you have a bunch of files that share a part of that name, you're not only going to get a long list of possible files, but some of them might be documents, others spreadsheets, and others pictures or movies.

You can speed things up by ensuring that you limit the search to only photo files such as JPEGs. Tell the search tool on your computer to look only for files with the .jpg file extension, or only "files that are photographs." Now instead of looking at all the files on your computer, it only has to look at photo files.

Congratulations—you've performed what taxonomy geeks call a "faceted search." Facets are what normal people call categories or groupings.

If you examine your material, you'll find that you have common groups of information. Start by identifying these.

Grouping or categorizing related content

As you start to examine your content, you'll probably find content that covers a broad range of information. For example, a quick perusal of the glycemic index (GI) content shows the following topics, among many others (see Figure 15.8).

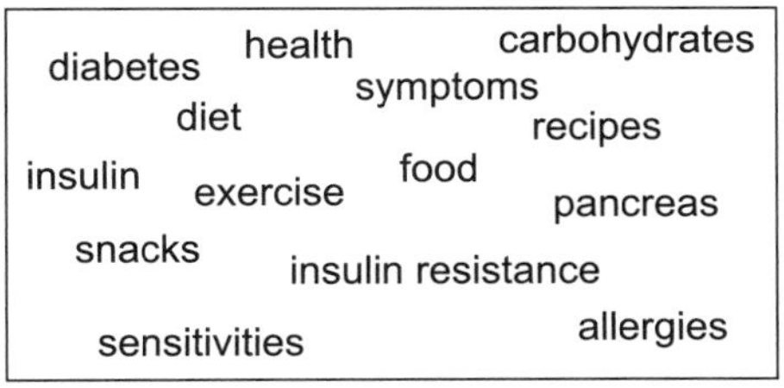

diabetes   health   carbohydrates
    diet   symptoms
                    recipes
insulin   exercise   food
                    pancreas
    snacks
        insulin resistance
    sensitivities   allergies

Figure 15.8   Topic cloud.

These could be grouped in many ways, as shown in Table 15.1.

Table 15.1 Topic categorizations

Health	Food	Physical
Exercise	Diet	Pancreas
Food	Recipes	Insulin
Snacks	Allergies	Insulin resistance
	Sensitivities	Symptoms
	Carbohydrates	Exercise
		Allergies
		Sensitivities

Note that you can have topics that appear in more than one group.

Finding existing categories

Often the best categories are ones that already exist. Look at how websites are organized, and look at existing libraries of information. Talk to information architects, writers, and trainers. If you can, talk to your customers. If you can't, speak to people who work with your customers and find out what people are looking for. Don't forget to look at material provided by your competitors, for example, look at their website to see how they organize it. The goal isn't to copy their organization, but to observe and understand how someone else looks at and categorizes similar information.

Talk to the people in charge of your website (or websites). Websites are a bit like an iceberg: when you visit them, you're only seeing the tip of the information that's really there. Behind that website is a vast trove of information, which can be accessed by web analytics.

Web analytics gather information about the visitors: what search tool they used to find the site, what keywords they entered to get there, what pages and products they were most interested in, and what products or information no one appeared interested in.

Each piece of information you can gather helps you make good decisions about how to categorize your information to make it easier for your customers to find it.

Too much information?

You might find, after researching existing categories, that the problem is that there are too many categories, too many ways of organizing and storing information, rather than too few. There are ways of comparing them, the most common being known as a *crosswalk*. A crosswalk can be used to compare information at the top or at the more detailed level of component metadata. For more details, see "Crosswalk," later in this chapter.

Metadata standards

One of the most valuable aspects of a unified content strategy is the ability to reuse content. As long as you're using one system, sharing content among customers of the system is relatively easy.

However, many organizations have multiple systems because they have existing legacy systems, or because one system is unable to meet all the organization's needs. For example, your organization may have a web content management system, a learning content management system, and a document management system. Sharing content across multiple systems can be problematic. The effective use of metadata requires common conventions for defining the semantics (meaning) of metadata. But typically each system carries its own metadata with its own semantics and its own structure, and there are no matches or very few matches across the systems. In addition, if content is stored in multiple locations that use multiple metadata structures, the task of descriptive metadata is even more difficult. Information retrieval becomes very complex because customers need to learn multiple methods for retrieving content. To address this problem, standards for the structure and semantics of metadata and for sharing metadata are being created.

Dublin Core

The Dublin Core Metadata Initiative is an organization promoting the widespread adoption of interoperable metadata standards. The Dublin Core Metadata Element Set defines 15 elements of semantic metadata (Contributor, Coverage, Creator, Date, Description, Format, Identifier, Language, Publisher, Relation, Rights, Source, Subject, Title, and Type).

Dublin Core has been designed to be easy to understand, and relatively easy to implement. Using the Dublin Core standard, you can define, store, and retrieve metadata that can be used across a number of knowledge domains, including corporate content. Dublin Core is also extensible to allow for site-specific or application-specific metadata, which means that you can customize it. Dublin Core is now Resource Description Framework (RDF) compliant (see the following).

Continued...

Metadata standards continued

RDF

RDF was developed by the World Wide Web Consortium (W3C). Unlike Dublin Core, RDF is a framework for describing and interchanging metadata; it doesn't actually define metadata. Because RDF uses XML, RDF imposes a specific structure that explicitly defines semantics, ensuring consistent encoding, exchange, and machine-readable processing of standardized metadata.

RDF provides a model for describing resources (content). Resources have properties (attributes or characteristics). A resource is an object that can be uniquely defined by a Uniform Resource Identifier (URI). RDF allows descriptions of Web resources (any object with a URL as its address) to be made available in machine-readable form.

RDF helps solve the problem industries have faced in exchanging metadata and its associated content among different systems. It doesn't define the metadata; rather, it enables organizations to define the metadata they need for their applications, yet still share that metadata with other RDF-compliant metadata applications.

Like Dublin Core, eXtensible Metadata Platform (XMP)—described below—has adopted RDF as the underlying structure for its standard.

XMP

XMP is a metadata framework (way of labeling content) created by Adobe that provides a method for combining metadata from "documents" and all their associated components. The metadata for each component is preserved within the container content assembly.

XMP can also be used to facilitate workflow. The label of different types of content (for example, photograph versus text) can help in appropriately directing content through workflow or to databases. Developers of workflow tools, particularly those designed to support the publishing process, are seriously looking at XMP as a potential metadata standard in their products.

Adobe has made XMP public and extensible and has distributed it to developers of content creation applications, content management systems, database publishing systems, web-integrated production systems, and document repositories.

Component metadata

Component metadata has a different focus than descriptive metadata. Whereas descriptive metadata is designed to help customers find completed content, component metadata helps content creators find information before it's published. In particular, it allows content creators to find information at the component level so it can be used in multiple outputs.

There are two main types of component metadata:

- Reuse and retrieval metadata
- Tracking or status metadata

Reuse and retrieval metadata

This first type of component metadata is designed to help authors find content so they can use it in multiple areas. Before even beginning to write, authors can search the content management system (narrowing the search results by picking the applicable metadata) to find reusable content. For example, if an overview already exists for Product 1, you can use metadata like "content type = overview, product = Product 1" to help you find the correct content to reuse.

Alternatively, the content management system can automatically search for appropriate reusable content (based on models and metadata) and deliver it (automatic reuse) to authors. In both cases, metadata is very important to correctly identify the components of content.

As with categorizations, where different departments often have competing views on how the information should be organized, those departments may also have different sets of what might be considered component-level metadata. Sometimes it's formal metadata; most often it's just what people call things.

Only in the rarest of cases will these multiple worldviews match. Marketing may refer to something as a Title, while the service people refer to the same information as a Subject. As we first noted in the explanation of what metadata is, metadata has to be consistently applied to be useful.

When you find these inconsistencies, you can apply a crosswalk to compare them and help sort out the differences.

Crosswalk

In many large organizations, the problem may not be a lack of metadata, but rather too much competing metadata. Different departments often use different terms for the same thing. Marketing and sales may share data in a customer relationship management (CRM) system. Service may store their own information (with their own internal relationships) in a knowledge management (KM) system, and the product content department may have a content management system (CMS) of their own.

Continued...

Crosswalk continued

A crosswalk can help you compare these competing information sets. It's not without its challenges, but completing one can give you a great start in organizing your own information so it meets a wide variety of needs and can tap into the shared knowledge in the company.

A simple example of the differences in the three systems is in how a document is named. The CRM system refers to the name of a document such as a brochure with the metadata tag Title. The KM system calls it Subject, and the CMS uses a combination of Information product and Title. The CMS introduces further complexity: it uses Title in multiple ways, because a title can exist at many levels in an XML document—for example, document title, section title, and subsection title are all considered titles, but are clarified by their location in the document hierarchy. Figure 15.9 illustrates a sample crosswalk.

CRM	KM	CMS
Title	Subject	Information Product
		Title

Figure 15.9   Crosswalk.

The first purpose of the crosswalk is to identify shared and diverging usage of information between different information systems. Once this has been done, you can use it as a basis of rationalizing the information in them, either by renaming the different elements, or by linking them together—using a system to equate the Title in the CRM system and the Subject in the KM with the Information product and Title in the CMS. If you do plan to set up a crosswalk to link information, be sure to clearly identify the rules that were used to make the connections and track the decisions that were made.

You can also consider using crosswalks when your metadata terms change. For example, a product may have had a specific name for a year, but is renamed in a new product offering. You don't want to have to try to retrieve both the old product name (particularly when new people start and don't even know the old product name) and the new product name. Instead, you can use a crosswalk to map the old product name to the new product name.

To determine what metadata you need to enable reuse, you need to first determine the business result you're trying to achieve and build your metadata backward to achieve that result. Think about the following.

Where is content going to be reused?

Across product? Across information product? If you answered "yes" to either of these, then you need to create metadata to identify each reuse, for example:

Product, such as:

- Product 1
- Product 2
- Product 3

Information product, such as:

- Marketing brochure
- Web
- Training course
- Marketing copy

Note that metadata such as information product can be derived from the template type.

What type of content is it?

You also need to know the component content type for which the content is valid. Your metadata might include Content type, for example:

- Concept
- Task

Note that metadata such as content type can be derived from your component model or semantic tags.

What else do you need to know about the content to ensure that the correct piece of content is reused?

You may need to know the region or location where the product is being sold or used so that you can identify content such as safety regulations, language, and configuration. In this case, your metadata might include geography metadata such as:

- Country level
  - United States
  - Canada

- Region level
  - South America
  - Europe
- Language
  - English
  - Spanish
  - French
  - Italian

You may also need to know the audience so that appropriate content is provided for each audience:

- Audience
  - Doctor
  - Pharmacist
  - Caregiver
  - Patient

Some component metadata is the same as descriptive metadata. Both customers and authors might want to find information by the title, by the author's name, or by a specific keyword. Both component and descriptive metadata can contain these metadata components; the crucial difference is that in component-level metadata the metadata is applied to the individual reusable components, not to the completed product.

- Title/Subject
  This type of metadata can be entered by the author, or the system can use the title that appears in the content to create this metadata.

- Author
  The system usually generates this type of metadata automatically, based on the author information.

- Keywords
  This metadata can be entered by the author; however, it's preferable to provide the author with a list of keywords from which to choose, which ensures that keywords will be used consistently.

  Not all component metadata is the same as descriptive metadata. Because the component metadata is usually used within a controlled authoring/editing environment, some metadata isn't applicable to the general public. For example, the system has to be able to determine if a particular author can see the available reusable components. If an author does have permission to see them, access is probably limited to viewing the components, with no permission to change them. The level of access that people have is determined by a security policy, and that policy is managed by the application of metadata.

- Security level (who can view the content)
  This type of metadata is usually applied by the author from a selected list of options.

Metadata for tracking (status)

Metadata for tracking is particularly useful when you're implementing workflow as part of your unified content strategy. By assigning status metadata to each component, you can determine which components are active. You can also control what can be done to a component and who can do it. Generally, status changes based on the metadata are controlled through workflow automation, not by customers. Sometimes, though, an author will identify a status change such as "Ready for review" because the system can't automate this type of information. Status metadata can include such tracking items as Draft (under development by the author), Ready for review, and so on.

Again, as with your other metadata, you identify tracking metadata by determining the business result you're trying to achieve, and then build your metadata backward to achieve that result. Design your metadata for tracking after you've designed your workflow (refer to Chapter 14, "Designing Workflow"). This enables you to identify what metadata needs to be applied to the content at each stage of workflow to enable the workflow system to manage it.

For example, the metadata for the review and approval workflow shown in Figure 15.10 could look like the following:

- Content status
  Indicates the status of the content. Before it can be reviewed the content must have the appropriate metadata attached to identify that it is ready for review. For example, the metadata could include:
  - Draft
  - Ready for review
  - In review
  - Final
  - In approval
  - Approved

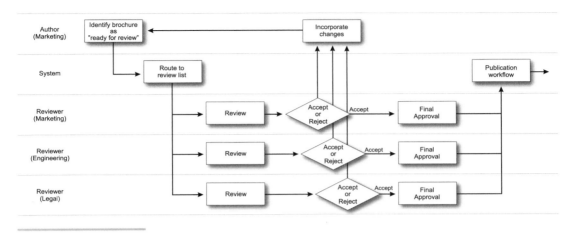

Figure 15.10   Review and approval workflow.

When the content is ready for review, authors apply the "Ready for review" metadata. When the content includes the feedback from review and is ready for final approval, authors apply the "Final" metadata. When the final approval reviewers approve the content, they apply the "Approved" metadata.

The system needs to identify the status of the content at any point in time. When the content has been passed to review, its status is automatically changed to "In review," and later, when it's passed on to final approval, the status is changed to "In approval."

• Review status

Indicates the status of the review content. A reviewer can either accept the content without changes or reject the content by asking for changes and returning it to the author. For example, the review status metadata could include

   • Accept
   • Reject

If the metadata is "Accept," the system moves the content to the final approval stage, but if the metadata is "Reject," the content is routed back to the author for changes.

Tracking metadata

After you've designed your metadata to support your workflow, you need to identify other metadata that can help you track your content. For example:

- Who created the content (author)?
- When was it created/modified (date)?
- Who modified the content (editor)?
- Who reviewed/approved the content (reviewer/approver)?
- How long did it take to create/modify/review (time)?
- Where has it been reused (information product, product)?
- Has it been translated (content status)?

Most content management systems automatically create some of this metadata (for example, author, date), whereas other metadata may already be defined in retrieval metadata and reuse metadata. We recommend that you go through this exercise to make sure that you've identified all the possible metadata you require for tracking and reports.

Metadata relationships

Component and descriptive metadata are closely related. In some cases, even the names are the same, but it's applied to different content.

For example, a particular author may have written all the content for a brochure and therefore the author's name was associated with all the components that make up the brochure. As the brochure works its way through the creation, revision, approval, publishing, and distribution process, it's easy to promote that author's name from the individual components to the categorization or product level. If there's more than one author, the system can gather them all and roll them up into a list of authors.

Other types of metadata are similar but applied at different levels. Separate creation, revision, and approval dates would be managed and tracked for both the individual components and the final publication. Each of the metadata elements has the same name (Date = Approved, for example), but they're maintained separately.

Living the GI Way: Metadata

Customers of LGIW can get information in many ways: through books, training, brochures, and the Web. Each has strengths and weaknesses; we wanted to be able to take advantage of the best features of each without having to rewrite content. The problem was that it was impossible to keep track of what we'd written, for which medium, at what level, and for whom, so we kept rewriting content.

By thinking about our customers' needs and the different information products we needed to generate, we were able to streamline our processes. For example, Figure 15.11 identifies the type of information we needed to be able to find so we could reuse it in a number of information products.

Category	Information Product	Type of Customer	Customer Engagement Level
Metadata	Book	Doctor	Mild interest
	Website	Health care professional	General knowledge
	Training	Pharmacist	Signifcant needs
	Brochure	Caregiver	Sunstantial needs
	...	...	Research level information

Figure 15.11   Metadata matrix.

More importantly, we developed a consistent tagging scheme that enabled us to find that information.

In addition, wherever we can, we roll up that component-level metadata into the information products so the system can identify what the information product is about. We've exposed those tags to our own search engine on our website so it can quickly find the information our customers are looking for.

Summary

Metadata is critical to the success of your unified content strategy. It's more than just data about data; it's the encoded knowledge of your organization. Metadata can be used to describe the behavior, processes, rules, and structure of data as well as add descriptive information.

Descriptive metadata categorizes your documents and is usually used by content users to retrieve content.

Component metadata identifies your content at the element level and is used by authors to retrieve content components. There are three kinds of component metadata. Metadata for reuse is used to identify the components of content that can be reused in multiple areas. Metadata for retrieval is used to retrieve content. It may consist of metadata for reuse as well as additional retrieval metadata. Metadata for tracking (status) is used to identify the status of your content in a workflow system.

To define your metadata, start by identifying the business result you want to achieve with your metadata and work backwards to identify what metadata will achieve that result.

Chapter 16

It's all about the content

Your unified content strategy is only as good as your content. Successful content is:

- Well-written

- Appropriate for the customer and the context

- Customer-centric

- Clear, concise, and consistent

This chapter focuses on the aspects of content that are unique to a unified content strategy—structured collaborative content. We discuss why it's a good idea to separate content from format and we describe the structured writing principles that allow authors to focus primarily on content. This chapter also introduces the concepts of collaborative authoring.

Writing structured content

Structure is the hierarchical order in which content occurs in an information product (for example, web page, brochure, or article) or component. Components have recognizable structures that are repeated each time the information type is created, for example, a value proposition is always structured in the same way. Structure frees you to think about the content, not how content should be organized and written because that's already done for you—in templates and guidelines that authors have used for years.

Structure is everywhere in content. The more consistent the structure, the easier it is for users to read and use, and the easier it is for authors to write. Structured content can be automatically adapted to different needs and devices.

The importance of structuring content

By creating and using well-structured content, you create more opportunities for reuse across product lines, audiences, and information products. In a structured-authoring environment, when authors follow the same rules or guidelines for each element of content, the potential for reuse is greatly enhanced.

Many problems arise when content is not structured. Not only is unstructured authoring difficult for readers to follow, it's also difficult for authors to create.

For details about the benefits of structured content, refer to Chapter 2, "Intelligent content."

What is structured writing?

Structured writing is the way elements in a component are written.

- Structured writing is based on cognitive psychology.
  Structured writing is based on how people read, process, and understand information. Within a structured writing environment, authors follow standards developed for different component types, ensuring content is always written consistently.

- Structured writing follows guidelines.
  Information standards—after they are defined—provide consistency. The standard tells authors such things as a step must always contain the condition under which the step is performed, the action, and the result of the action, in that order. The structure can apply to individual steps, to the whole procedure, or to individual elements within a step.

- Structured writing applies at numerous levels, depending on your content models, for example:
  - Sentence
  - Paragraph
  - Section

  In a structured writing environment, standards apply at the level where you want consistency and reuse. The more granular your information, the more structure you will need, as well as more adherence to structure.

Principles of structured writing

Structured writing is governed by principles that describe how people process information.

- Chunking

  At best, people can hold five to nine chunks of information in their short-term memory. Each chunk is an independent unit of information that can either stand on its own or contribute to a larger unit. Mobile devices display fewer chunks of information while desktops can display many more.

- Labeling

  Chunks of information are labeled (titled) to identify the type of information they contain. To be effective, labels are substantive, indicative of the information they contain. Clear labels also make it much easier for users to scan for the correct information. Every chunk of information should have a substantive label.

- Relevance

  Only information that relates to one main point is contained in a chunk, eliminating "nice to know" information.

- Consistency

  For similar subject matter, use similar words, labels, formats, organizations, and sequences. Consistency, like relevancy, is critical for both reuse and usability. From a usability perspective, when information is presented consistently, customers form expectations about what it contains, which reduces their learning curve as well as their cognitive load.

- Reuse

  The reuse principle dictates how a chunk of information can be reused in similar information products, so that wherever it is repeated, it's the same. The reuse principle also ensures that when a chunk is updated, it is updated in all places it appears, ensuring ongoing consistency.

Structured authoring guidelines

Structured authoring is the process of authoring according to standards that dictate how content should be written. When implementing a unified content strategy, it's critical that authors structure and author their content consistently.

The goals of structured authoring are to:

- Help authors create consistent content that can be reused transparently.
- Enhance the usability of content.
- Make all content appear unified whether it's reused or not.

From the viewpoint of modeling, structure is the *hierarchical order* in which the information occurs in the information product. From the viewpoint of authoring, structure is the way *content* within each hierarchical element is written.

Let's use the example of the recipes again (refer to Chapter 2, "Intelligent content"). The recipe guidelines might read something like this: The model for a recipe will specify which elements make up a recipe, which of those elements are mandatory and optional, and the order in which they appear. However, the model does not specify how each of those elements must be written. Even though the model will specify that recipes contain mandatory steps, authors may still write their steps differently. Some authors may include a result as part of their step, some may not. Some authors may describe an ingredient as "tomatoes, diced" while others might use "diced tomatoes." This is where structured authoring comes in. In addition to the architecture (reflected in the models), authors need content development and style guidelines that will help them write content so it's consistent, no matter where it's used and who wrote it.

Structured authoring follows standards. When the structure of the content is defined (for example, the structure of a recipe), whoever writes a recipe must follow that structure. The standard tells authors such things as a step must always contain the condition under which the step is performed, followed by the action, followed by the result of the action. If all authors follow that standard, recipes will be clear and consistent. Ideally, that step can be reused wherever it's needed and its reuse will not be jarring.

Structured authoring guidelines apply to every single element in a component model, whether content is planned for reuse or not. Structured authoring guidelines ensure consistency and readability as well as reusability.

Returning to our recipe example, Figure 16.1 identifies the authoring guidelines for our recipe.

Semantic	
Recipe	
Title	Mandatory. Capitalize only the first word in the title.
Description	Optional. Create a short, one- or two-sentence introduction to the recipe to entice the reader to read on.
Ingredients	
Ingredient	[quantity] [measure] [ingredient] Include the quantity, measure (for example, Tbsp), and ingredient.
Directions	
Step	Mandatory. A step must always contain the condition under which the step is performed, (for example, in a medium-sized bowl), followed by the action (mix the ingredients for the rub).
Suggestion	Optional. Provide a suggestion for serving or preparing the recipe.

Figure 16.1   Recipe structured authoring guidelines.

Applying the model

Depending on your need for control and precision in your unified content strategy, and also depending on the tools you're using, you can provide explicit models that guide authors through the process of creating structured content using authoring templates, forms, and XML structures. Or you can provide written guidelines that authors follow manually (instead of being guided by a tool.)

Writing to a model is critical in adopting structured writing because the model contains the rules that govern not only what elements belong in which information product, but also how each element in a component is structured (based on the type of information it contains). When implementing structured writing, models serve three purposes:

1. To provide guidelines for authors—Authors use content models to determine what content goes in which information product, as well as how to structure each element. For example, by referring to the content model, they can determine that an information product requires a value proposition, they can determine the structure of a value proposition, and they can get hints/rules about how to write a value proposition. Refer to Chapter 2, "Intelligent content," for this model.

2. To provide guidelines for information technologists—Information technologists (refer to Chapter 18, "Changing roles") use models to build the templates or XML structures that authors must follow. Instead of referring to written guidelines, the tool guides authors through what to include and how to structure it. Some tools make it possible to include authoring guidance that provides the guidelines in the element. Even in a structured writing environment supported by tools, authors still need to understand the model to follow what the tool is asking them to do.

3. To provide guidelines for reviewers—Model reviewers check models to ensure that they support customer and information requirements. Editors use models to review authors' drafts. They compare the draft against the content model to ensure that it contains all the necessary elements.

Models showing different channels

Figure 16.2 introduces a new model for a product description. This model shows the elements for a product description and how they are reused to accommodate different channels and information products.

| Product Description | | | | | | |
| | | | Where Used | | | |
Semantic	Product Sheet	Brochure	Press Release	Website	eCatalog	Mobile
Product Name	X	X		X	X	X
Product Description	X	X		X	X	
Product Desc. Short	X	X	X	X	X	X
Product Desc. Medium	X			X	X	
Product Desc. Long	X			X		
Graphic	X	X		X	X	
Features						X
Feature Item						X
Benefits						
Benefit Item						
Tagline						X

Figure 16.2   Product description showing channel and information product.

In writing for this model, authors would know that a product description must contain a product name, a product description (divided into short, medium, and long components), and a graphic, in that order. Each element within the product description must be structured this way to accommodate its different uses. If this model is supported by an automated authoring tool, it would guide the authors through the product description, prohibiting entries that are not included in the model. If the model is not supported by an authoring tool, authors would refer to the model to understand how to put each element together.

Writing guidelines tell the author how to write to the model. It's a good idea to include an example of each element, showing authors such things as how the long product description should be structured and written, based on the type of information it conveys.

For further information on models, refer to Chapter 12, "Content modeling: Adaptive content design."

Using the building block approach

Another way of separating content from format is to use the building block approach. The building block approach allows you to identify core information that is applicable for all information products/users, and then build on it to customize information for different uses and users, as follows:

- Identify the core information (the information that is applicable for all uses).

- Identify what has to be added to the core to meet other needs, such as training, or different audiences.

- Tag additional elements according to where they belong.

For example, you might start with a product description that contains the elements in the model shown in Figure 16.2. The short description would become your core information and you would then add the medium and long descriptions to it to create a more comprehensive piece of information.

In the building block approach, each element is identified by the information product in which it belongs (for example, product sheet, eCatalog, or mobile), and supported by stylesheets that format it for the appropriate channel. In this way, authors create content elements, augmenting the core sequentially. The format is applied after the content is published—*not* as it is written.

Same content, different uses?

So, what about using a product description in a number of different places and publishing it to a number of different channels? Can the same content *really* be written so it's appropriate for all its potential uses? Can a product description that is used in a brochure *really* be reused for mobile? Shouldn't the brochure have a different tone?

We believe that content can be reused effectively, simply by following writing guidelines that are applicable to all the potential uses for the content. In addition, the building block approach allows content to be augmented as required, so the core is written in a style that is applicable for all uses and the augmented parts are written to successively build on the core.

The Product Desc Short is your core and appears in every information product. The Product Desc Medium is used in the product sheet, website, and eCatalog. The Product Desc Long is used only in the product sheet and the website.

The writing guidelines for each element are documented in the model (along with the structure guidelines) and are based on the type of information each component contains, as well as its potential uses and reuses. The difference is in how much information is provided and how it's presented.

Writing guidelines for different uses

We've been developing content for both online and print media for more than 20 years, and experience has taught us that well-written online documentation makes good paper documentation and vice versa. The same is true of mobile. Mobile is short and succinct, as the first element of any component should be. Consequently, we've developed guidelines to ensure that content really can be used in a number of different ways. Many of these guidelines are simply guidelines for clear communication and make for better content, regardless of reuse. What is true for the Web is also true for mobile (see Table 16.1).

Table 16.1   Writing guidelines that apply to the Web and mobile.

	Web	Mobile
Write succinctly	✓	✓
Write so users can scan	✓	✓
Layer information	✓	✓
Write useful titles	✓	✓

However, if you look at these guidelines closely, you'll find that they are just as valid for paper (see Table 16.2).

Table 16.2   Web and mobile writing guidelines applied to paper.

	Paper	Reasoning
Write succinctly	✓	Clear, concise content can greatly improve the quality of paper materials.
Write so users can scan	✓	Long passages of text that extend down a page or over pages are hard to read. Chunking that information can make it much easier for a reader to comprehend.
Layer information	✓	This is a bit harder in paper. You don't want to have a lot of "go-tos" in the text that take the reader back and forth. However, layering of content is appropriate for things like overviews, summaries, and checklists versus placing all the detail in the body.
Write useful titles	✓	Useful titles make it easier for users to find what they want.

All guidelines help writers achieve consistency and reuse, especially when standards accompany each guideline.

So what's different for mobile?

So if all these guidelines are the same regardless of whether it is print, Web, or mobile, how do we make this work? We know there's no way that content designed for print will work on mobile. That's because content written for print or the Web is often one monolithic chunk of content.

Go back to the model for the product description (in Figure 16.2) and look at how the description itself is structured. Look at the section on the building block approach. Take the concepts of the building block approach to heart and write your content to match these guidelines.

Write to models that clearly identify short and critical information. If you don't have fine granular models, then write a topic sentence for every paragraph so the first sentence could be extracted automatically for mobile content. Ensure that the topic sentence clearly states the central idea that you're expressing.

Example: Same content, different uses

The Reo Auto Company is preparing for the annual auto show and the launch of its new vehicles. This year they are launching their first hybrid sports utility vehicle (SUV)—the Tsai. They require a variety of information products: a press release to announce their new lineup, brochures to hand out at the show and dealer show-rooms, updates to the website, a show catalog, and a mobile app. The content strategist and marketing group determine that the information products are to be provided through four channels: paper (show catalog, press release, brochure), the Web (website, press release), email (press release), and mobile. Mobile will be an app, not a mobile website. Each information product requires different content and design:

- A show catalog for the entire lineup (photo, short description, and key features, three cars to a page)

- A brochure for the Tsai only (photo, long description with all the features, and benefits)

- A press release for the Tsai only (no photo, short description, features and benefits)

- A website for entire lineup (home page for each car with photos, list of full features combined with a pricing calculator)

- A mobile app (page for each car with photo, list of features, and interactive experience for exploring the interior of the car)

Working with the model, the website team and marketing group proceed to develop the content, as shown in Table 16.3. (The metadata column indicates in which information product the content will appear.)

Table 16.3 Content development for Tsai product description.

Element	Content	Metadata
Product Name	Tsai	All
Product Description		
Product Desc Short	The new Tsai is a totally new experience in SUVs. The revolutionary Tsai combines a gas engine with an electric motor resulting in a fuel-efficient and environmentally conscious SUV. Yet, none of the features like roominess and ruggedness are lost. The best of all worlds, the Tsai.	All
Product Desc Medium	The Tsai features an all-wheel drive with an in-line four-cylinder engine. The powertrain includes a five-speed automatic transmission and has a towing capacity of 1,000 pounds. Integrated light-weight roof rails and fold-down rear seats with 70/30 split make carrying loads a breeze.	Brochure
Product Desc Long	The revolutionary light-weight body is manufactured with dent-resistant polymer. Front and side air bags add to safety and security. The car friendly height makes it easy to get in and out of and to load all your essentials on top.	Brochure
Graphic	TBD	Show catalog Brochure Website Mobile app
Features		All
Feature Title	Features	Brochure Press release
Feature Item	2L engine	All
Feature Item	Anti-lock brake system	All
Feature Item	Power brakes	All
Feature Item	Stabilizer bars	All
Feature Item	Low-emission Vehicle Standards	All

Element	Content	Metadata
Benefits		
Benefit Item	The only SUV that is truly environmentally friendly from its construction to its operation.	Brochure Press release Website
Tagline	Practicality of a car, power of an SUV.	Brochure Press release Website Mobile app

The finished product

Once the content is written, it's published to each information product and the format is applied based on the content's use. Figures 16.4 and 16.5 show how the same product description is reused effectively in each medium.

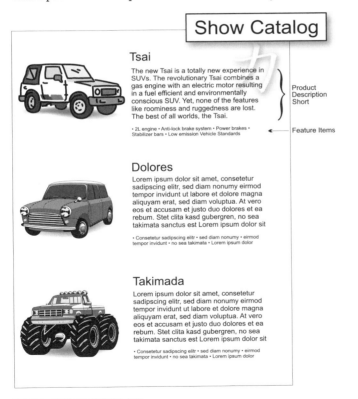

Figure 16.3   Reuse across channels, Show Catalog.

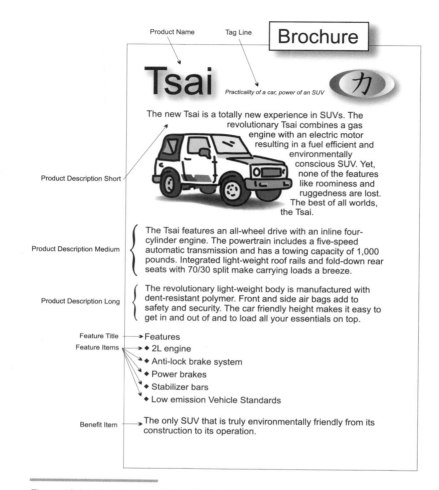

Figure 16.4   Reuse across channels, Brochure.

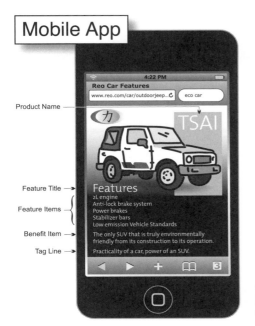

Mobile App

Product Name

Feature Title
Feature Items
Benefit Item
Tag Line

Figure 16.5   Reuse across channels, Mobile App.

Press Release

Product Description Short

Feature Title
Feature Items

Benefit Item

Tag Line

REO

REO announces Tsai   Jane Smith 2:04 p.m.
October 7, 2011   416-613-1852

The new Tsai is a totally new experience in SUVs. The revolutionary Tsai combines a gas engine with an electric motor resulting in a fuel efficient and environmentally conscious SUV. Yet, none of the features like roominess and ruggedness are lost. The best of all worlds, the Tsai.

Features
♦ 2L engine
♦ Anti-lock brake system
♦ Power brakes
♦ Stabilizer bars
♦ Low emission Vehicle Standards

The only SUV that is truly environmentally friendly from its construction to its operation.

Practicality of a car, power of an SUV.

Figure 16.6   Reuse across channels, Press Release.

Figure 16.7   Reuse across channels, Web.

Collaborative authoring: Breaking down the silos

A key concept of a unified content strategy is the sharing of content and collaboration on its development. Collaboration ensures that the content components, such as product descriptions, are consistent and can be reused wherever they're required: in a printed brochure, on the Web, on a mobile device. To ensure that content elements will meet all needs, everyone involved in creating content must work together to figure out exactly what their needs are and make decisions about how such elements are to be reused, structured, and written.

As we discuss in Chapter 1, "Content: The lifeblood of an organization," content is often created by authors working in isolation from other authors. Silos are erected between departments and even within departments, which leads to content being created, recreated, and recreated again, which causes extra work and introduces inconsistencies. Individual authors working in isolation is not possible in a unified content environment. When content is compiled into its various information products, it must appear to be completely unified; there is no room for different "colors or textures." The finished product must be seamless. The goal of collaborative authoring is to break down the silo walls so authors can create content consistently.

Collaboration, however, is harder than you might imagine. Collaboration, regardless of the tools in place to support it, is a human endeavor and must be supported by strong teams willing to undertake collaborative efforts. Collaboration requires everyone working together towards a common goal—unified content. To realize this goal, organizations will have to change the way content is authored, starting from the modeling process and continuing through each new project.

What is collaboration?

Collaboration is not a new concept. Think of the many books authored by more than one writer or the albums produced by more than one musician. The common element in successful collaborations is a goal that all players are aware of and support. Everyone involved in the collaboration knows what the goals are, knows his or her role, knows others' roles, and knows how to address issues.

Players should also have a stake in the outcome, whether it's content that's easier to access and use, a more productive authoring environment, or even a share of company profits. With all those requirements, figuring out a way to make collaboration work in an organization, especially a large one, can be problematic. But, in a unified content strategy, it's necessary.

More and more, effective information requires many people—often with varying skills and backgrounds and from different departments or even different professions—to work together on the same project, or more accurately, to work together on different aspects of the same project. Authors cannot work in isolation from subject matter experts and customers; marketing cannot work in isolation from product documentation and support; product developers and engineers cannot work in isolation from authors. This is certainly true in a unified content environment. Yet, collaboration in relation to writing is often misunderstood. Collaboration involves more than different authors creating content for different aspects of a project.

Exploring collaboration further

Doing a search for collaborative authoring or collaborative writing on the Internet turns up thousands of hits, most with one thing in common—the human element implicit in collaboration. For example:

- On the website for the University of North Carolina at Pembroke, a law professor posted guidelines for collaborative writing, with the number one guideline being:

  "Take time at the start of your project to build cohesion. Begin your project by developing a shared understanding of your assignment and discussing basic procedural and logical issues. Build group cohesion and establish good interpersonal relations among members."[1]

- In a thesis on computer-supported collaborative writing, the author defines collaborative writing as follows:

  "In a true co-authoring process, the peers collaborate on every task as opposed to the situation in co-publishing [and] co-responding…In co-publishing the individuals produce a collaborative text based on individual texts. Interaction in a co-responding environment takes place only during the revision process… In peer collaboration, the group assignment is a truely [sic] joint task, all members contribute to the interaction most of the time and each of the peers has equal control over the text as well as within the interaction."[2]

- In the OII Guide to Workflow Management and Collaborative Authoring, collaborative authoring is defined as follows:

  Collaborative authoring can be defined as "the use of workflow techniques to manage the creation of integrated data sets by more than one author." However, collaborative authoring is normally seen to include more than simply the application of workflow. It also requires facilities for defining how data created by different, parallel processes is to be combined or linked.[3]

  For an effective collaborative authoring environment to be set up, the team must define how information is to be written, linked, and unified. The tools then support what the team decides.

- In another paper on collaborative authoring of web content, the authors state:

  "Information content publishing may also be performed collaboratively, where multiple geographically dispersed authors contribute to the publishing of

---

1   www.uncp.edu/home/vanderhoof/syllabus/colab-rt.html

2   infolab.kub.nl/pub/theses/w3thesis/Groupwork/collaborative_writing.html

3   www.diffuse.org/oii/en/workflow.html

semantically related pieces of information…The authors bring together expert knowledge needed to provide parts of the content. Collaboration enables the authors to work together on the authoring tasks by sharing the knowledge needed in the process of producing content."[4]

What does collaborative authoring require?

From an organizational perspective, collaborative authoring requires that all authors have an understanding of how content is used in multiple situations and the ability to work together to create it. This normally requires organizational change, specifically in the way content is authored. Authors must be involved in development teams (so they can plan for reuse from the beginning), they must have solid content models (that they have helped to create and been trained to follow), they must have usable authoring tools that assist them in following models and sharing information, they must have a stake in the outcome, and most of all, they need an understanding of what they are trying to accomplish and the support and resources to do it.

Collaborative authoring also requires technology's assistance with some things, such as access to shared information, workflow routing, version management, and check-in and check-out, as well as tools to assist authors in writing to models. While tools are important, they play a supporting role; the focus of this section is on the organizational strategies for collaboration. Further information on tools and technologies as they relate to collaboration can be found in Chapter 20, "The role of content management."

Strategies for organizational change

Many companies are not structured to support collaboration. Their structure is hierarchical and, as a result, many of their projects come together horizontally and in isolation. When a company introduces a new product or service, many of the people involved in the project don't even know who the other people are or what aspect of the project they're working on.

Once you've developed content models—especially if you've developed them by looking beyond the content that your group creates—you'll be more aware of the content that other groups create. Yet the content models themselves are a collaborative effort, and they will need collaborative revisiting at the start of new projects to ensure they still accommodate the information needs of the new project,

---

4 Kovse, J., Härder, T., Ritter, N., Steiert, H., Mahnke, W. "Supporting Collaborative Authoring of Web Content by Customizable Resource Repositories." Department of Computer Science, University of Kaiserslautern, Kaiserslautern, Germany.

for example, is the granularity still sufficient to deliver content dynamically over the Web? For collaboration to occur, change must occur at many levels:

- In the way groups are organized and managed
- In the way groups work together
- In the way individual authors work
- In the way models are implemented and used

In the way groups are organized and managed

For authoring to be collaborative, project members must know and understand each others' roles, even if they perform different functions. The content model will indicate what information products are required. Based on your knowledge of who does what in your organization, you can organize your team around the information products being developed. For example, if you are creating documentation for medical devices, the authoring team will consist of everyone involved in creating any type of documentation (brochures, doctors' manuals, patients' guides, or press releases) for the medical device—medical writers, marketing writers, and public relations specialists.

A unified content strategy requires that all groups collaborate on their efforts so they can complement one another. As groups become more familiar with one another, they can also work together to make sure models continue to meet their needs.

When you're documenting a new product or service, hold a project kickoff meeting at the project's inception (you can do this virtually if you're geographically dispersed). Discuss the information requirements, ensure that the current content models support them, and establish how you will share information that is reusable. Make sure the writing standards for elements are explicit and understood by everyone in the group.

When you're working on updates to existing content, revisit the content model to make sure everyone on the team understands what information is being reused and what the writing standards are for the elements being revised. Don't assume that your group is the only group involved in an update; check the elements requiring revision against the content model to see who else is involved. As a group, you can make sure the model is still effective as elements are updated; you can also keep it current with what you've learned from users, so you continue to deliver what readers really need, not just what the models say they needed five iterations ago.

Organizing based on content requirements

Collaboration also implies a change in the way work is organized. In many organizations, individual groups handle a number of projects, separate from one another. A marketing group, for example, will often work on a number of different projects for a variety of other groups in the organization. Those projects are, for the most part, independent of one another in how they're staffed, funded, and managed. It's difficult for groups to collaborate with an independent, project-oriented organizational structure in place.

In a unified content environment, organizations need to be resource-based, focusing on content requirements across the organization, not just for one project. When planning the information products required for a project, departments should think about what they will add to and use from the definitive source. As they develop their content, they should plan for its other uses as well. Consider allocating budgets for content development across an organization, not to individual departments. This allows you to move to a resource-based content development model instead of a project-based one.

Resource-based project planning also reduces time and costs for content creation. When content is tagged and stored for easy retrieval, authors can retrieve it and either incorporate it into their information product as is or modify it for their purposes (based on their content model). The model will tell the marketing group that technical publications also needs the product description and that it must be written and structured in a certain way so that it's usable for both purposes. To reach this common understanding of the product description, technical publications and marketing must collaborate.

In the way groups work together

Even in a collaborative environment, authors don't have to work together in groups the whole time. They can do plenty of work on their own. But, crucial decisions must be made together and reaching consensus is key to successful collaboration. One author may find that the current level of granularity is insufficient, but before changing it, everyone who is affected by the change must agree. Collaborative teams, when they work, do not proceed by democratic vote. Instead, they struggle to reach consensus, even though it takes longer than voting. Consensus means that everyone agrees to a change, not just the 7 out of 10 who vote for it. With consensus, everyone buys into the change and will support it in their writing.

Furthermore, collaboration is significantly different from cooperation. When we cooperate, we work together, but we each produce and "own" our own project. We retain our separate styles and in the finished product, we can usually tell which portions are "ours," and we can certainly tell which complete information products we created. This kind of independence doesn't work in a unified content environment, when information products are compiled from a number of different elements, often written by a number of different authors.

Relinquishing ownership

In a unified content environment, the concept of ownership becomes irrelevant. For instance, in an "independent but cooperative" environment, my colleague writes a procedure, which I edit. I write another procedure, which my colleague edits. But, ultimately, my colleague is in charge of his, and I'm in charge of mine. We negotiate changes and we (often delicately) suggest improvements. But we "live with" what the other person produces. We do not really merge our thoughts so that it becomes transparent who wrote what. However, if a particular author's style is discernible, the content may not be reusable in different information products. Independence often leaves documentation uneven, which is unacceptable in a unified content environment.

Instead of the usual, cooperative approach to writing that many groups use, a unified content strategy requires true collaboration, which means working together so thoroughly that you no longer own any part, any section, any sentence, or any content assembly. Components are truly unified, based on the content model, and authors can't tell who did what. This is difficult for many authors to get used to; they claim it takes away their creativity. We frequently dispute this belief, emphasizing that the *real* creativity comes in analyzing customers' needs and figuring out the best way to meet those needs, often dynamically. The creativity also lies in building strong models, based on possible uses and potential users for content. In this way, authors truly become content strategists, with more and more emphasis on the analysis and design that drive the content. Collaboration is critical in creating and sharing the information design and the standards that everyone follows.

In the way individual authors work

Collaboration requires that authors not only work with other authors in their own department, but also with authors from different departments. In a collaborative environment, authors work together to ensure that content is not written more than once by more than one author, and more importantly, that similar content is not written about differently. The content models must be clear about what the information requirements are; the organizational structure must be clear about which department authors which elements.

Developing new skills

What does this mean in the workplace? It means that authors may need new skills to help them analyze content and design. They'll also need skills for modeling, structured writing, and conflict management to help them in the transition from independent to collaborative work. Strategies for helping authors switch to a collaborative authoring environment include:

- Training authors in analysis, content modeling, and design; emphasize analysis of information and users' needs so authors learn to model based on needs.

- Involving authors from across the organization to develop models and review them on an ongoing basis.

- Training authors in how to follow and use models.

- Training authors in structured writing.

Also, often overlooked in favor of the more "technical" skills of analysis, design, and writing is the ability to handle conflict. A certain amount of conflict is needed to motivate change and encourage creativity. However, unmanaged conflict can quickly turn to chaos. Conflict will certainly be present as groups try to reach consensus, and it's important for team members to understand conflict responses and how to deal with them. Furthermore, in collaborative efforts across departments and even within departments, there are likely to be turf wars. Departments or individual authors may feel they are being compromised and when this happens, conflict is imminent. Jean Richardson and Lisa Burk's paper *Conflict Management in Software Development Environments* provides a good description of conflict management techniques, as well as a thorough bibliography.[5]

In the way models are implemented and used

Models are the key to a successful unified content strategy. While not everyone in your organization can get involved in the modeling process, you should have representatives from every area that creates content. Their input is critical in defining information requirements and potential reuse. Once models are developed to accommodate needs across the organization, anyone involved in authoring content must learn how to follow them. We recommend the following:

- Run workshops introducing the concept of models and how to use them for authors *and* for reviewers of content *and* for managers of content creation groups. Stress how important models are for unified content and stress how important it is that different groups contribute to and follow the models.

---

5 Burk, Lisa and Jean Richardson with Lisa Latin. "Conflict Management in Software Development Environments." Proc. PNSQC 2000 (online): 298-357, 2000.

- Test new authoring tools and authoring scenarios for usability with all the groups that will be using them. Provide real authoring scenarios to each group, including such things as their ability to:
  - Follow the model (whether it's supported by a tool or referenced in a writing guide or spreadsheet)
  - Identify and retrieve reusable information
  - Populate a document with reusable information
  - Create components
  - Publish components
  - Store components

Strategies for technological change

Although tools are not the way to implement collaborative authoring (change must occur at the organizational level), their role is a critical supporting one. They don't replace the teamwork, understanding, or cohesion that collaborative authoring requires. In fact, tools can make collaboration easier, but they do not guarantee success. In working with a tool that is not conducive to the creative process, authors often feel like they're submitting rather than creating.

The tools required for collaboration involve more than giving everyone access to the same directories on the same file server, regardless of how user-friendly the file server may be! Some elements critical for effective collaboration are:

- Access to shared information
- Check-in and check-out
- Access and version control
- Transparent authoring to support models
- Managed workflow
- Event notification

Summary

Structure is everywhere in content. The more consistent the structure, the easier it is for users to read/use and the easier it is for authors to write. Structured content can be automatically adapted to different needs and devices. Structured writing is the way elements in a component are written.

To structure information effectively, you need to separate content from format, which means:

- Defining writing standards that focus on meaning rather than format

- Thinking about what you want the information to *do* rather than what you want the information to look like

- Creating a writing environment that enables authors to structure their content consistently by either supporting them with tools or providing comprehensive models to follow

- Following writing guidelines to ensure that content is written effectively for *all* channels and all uses

Collaborative authoring is key to breaking down silo walls. Collaboration means everyone working together to achieve the common goal of unified content that is truly seamless. Collaboration sounds easier than it is, though. To ensure successful collaboration it is necessary to:

- Know everyone involved in creating content and what their roles are; look to models to provide advice about information requirements; consider including "responsible party" for each information type in your model so you know *what* information is required as well as *who* is responsible for creating it. Hold kickoff meetings at the beginning of projects.

- Think about how your organization is structured. Does your structure allow for collaboration across departments? How do departments know what other departments are working on?

- Provide authors with a stake in the outcome and an understanding of how collaborative authoring will benefit them.

- Consider moving to a resource-focused approach to developing content; develop budgets based on content requirements across the organization instead of department-specific budgets.

- Encourage authors to relinquish ownership of their content; content with a discernible style is not necessarily reusable.

Chapter 17

Change management and governance

Change is the one constant in business, because business has to change in order to stay competitive. Perhaps because small changes have become part of the daily business culture, they're perceived as less problematic than larger changes.

Surprisingly though, small changes can add up and become significant over time. Unless those small changes are tracked and managed, over the medium-to-long term they can wreak havoc on an initially well-designed and implemented system. We need to govern them.

What is change management?

Change management is the process of communicating and managing change throughout the organization. Change has to be managed to ensure that all employees are aware of and comfortable with the changes. Lack of change management can result in resistance to the project involving the changes—and potential failure.

What is governance?

Put simply, governance is the process of managing change.

Based on a Greek word meaning "to steer," governance is exactly that: steering or directing the content, the people who create it, and the systems that support it through both the day-to-day and long-term content lifecycles.

In order to be effective, governance must consider both the people and the systems involved. If proper governance of both of these facets is maintained, then the content governance will be much simpler.

You need to develop governance guidelines for every aspect of your unified content strategy:

- Content models
- Content
- Reuse
- Workflow
- Metadata

We suggest setting up a steering committee or governance board to set the initial conditions and then manage and maintain those conditions over time. The basic needs of such a group are similar whether they're managing content or the "under the hood" stuff—the taxonomy and metadata.

Change management

Never underestimate the impact change will have on your organization. If you have change management personnel in-house, get them involved in your project as soon as you make the decision to adopt a unified content strategy. If you don't have change management personnel, consider hiring consultants who specialize in change management. This section provides suggestions to help you effectively manage the change associated with a unified content strategy.

Identify the pain, issues, and consequences

People are unwilling to change unless there is a very good reason for that change and they can see the benefits. Identifying the benefits means first identifying the pain, issues, and consequences. What are the real issues facing your organization? What is the impact of not addressing these issues? Once you've identified your reasons for change, communicate your findings to everyone involved.

Reach out and listen

Reach out to people within the organization and listen to what they have to say about the issues and the solutions. Be sure to thank them for their input. When you've summarized their input, go back to them and verify that you understood them correctly. Then as you move into design, testing, and implementation, involve them and ask them to help you in determining if your design correctly addresses their concerns and needs. If you involve people early on, really listen to what they have to say, then show them that you're addressing their requirements, they'll be among your strongest supporters.

Communicate

Communication is critical to successful change. You need to communicate the reasons for change, your plan, and the project's status. Projects that are developed under wraps are viewed with suspicion. Lack of communication results in anxiety and starts rumors. The longer that information is withheld, the more anxious people will become and the harder it will be to convince them of the need to adopt the change. Communicate as early in the project as possible and continue to communicate throughout.

Develop a communication plan to help keep everyone involved aware of what's going on. But don't make the all-too-common mistake of confusing a communication plan with communication. A communication plan must be effectively implemented and must involve full two-way communication to be truly useful.

What to communicate?

- Why change?
  Frequently communication plans tell people only what's happening and what they have to do; they don't tell people *why* it has to be done. When people don't understand the *why* they have a tendency to ignore or resist the change.

  Use the results of your analysis, summarize your findings, and present your findings in a clear manner. Don't play down the current issues or the dangers that face the organization; lay them on the table so people see the reasoning behind the change. Take care not to frighten people with the issues and dangers, but be honest in your presentation; they'll appreciate the honesty and clarity. Emphasize that the current concerns are no one's fault and that the change is possible with their help.

- The plan

  Explain your plan, including an approximate timeline for implementation. This gives people an understanding of the scope and timeline for the project. Informal lunchtime sessions provide a nonthreatening atmosphere and allow people to ask questions. Informal does not mean a whiteboard session with food; it must be a truly informal session—a lunch with a discussion afterward is usually more effective.

- Ongoing status

  Keep people up to date as the project progresses even if only specific groups are involved in the beginning. A newsletter is a good vehicle to communicate ongoing progress and answer commonly asked questions.

  If your company culture is a positive one, a wiki or blog can be used rather than a more formal newsletter. This can give you instant feedback from the employees about what's working, what's not, and how the process could be improved.

- Successes

  Ensure that you communicate the successes you've achieved. This will enable people to understand that it's possible to achieve a unified content strategy.

- Problems

  No project is without its problems. As you start to implement the unified content strategy in additional areas, point out the problems you encountered, how they were addressed, and how they'll be avoided as you move forward. Admitting problems brings them into the open and ensures that people understand that problems are inevitable and solvable.

- How it will affect them

  Let them know how the changes will affect them. Don't tell them that there will be no changes to their daily routine or their methods of work. You know there will be and they know it too. Be up front and honest about the changes.

  We talked about why the company needs to make the changes. Ask them about their own workload, their own pressures and problems. Show how making the changes to the existing process will not only help the company, but also improve their working conditions and processes.

  In some companies, the system will require significantly different skills and mindset. Ensure that you know how the changes will affect each role in the company and that you will be able to explain the changes to the people in those roles.

Elicit the help of change agents

Communication will help people understand what's going on and why, but it won't necessarily convince them to participate. The best way to convince people about the value of a change is to have one of their own communicate the excitement and possibilities. To do this you need "change agents." A change agent is someone who's not necessarily part of the assigned implementation team but who will be a user of the new system and methodologies.

The best way to create change agents is to bring together a group of representative users who have shown an early understanding of the problems or who are open to change. Help them clearly understand the pain, issues, and dangers, and have them voice their own. Take them through a short content audit exercise to help them see the possibilities. Discuss their specific opportunities and the ways in which this change will apply to them. Discuss how they can share their learnings with others on their team. Make sure you address all their questions and concerns. When they have an understanding of why this change should happen and are excited about the change, they'll begin to communicate this to others on their team, easing the transition to the unified content strategy. Make sure that you help the change agents prepare a consistent message to take back to their team. A consistent message reduces possible misinterpretations.

Get a champion

The broader the scope of your unified content strategy the more likely you are to have disagreement. A champion (someone high up enough in the organization to effect change) needs to endorse the cause and ensure that different content areas understand the need for change and buy into it. If a group resists the change despite having their concerns and questions addressed, the champion may have to insist on them adopting the change or make a change in personnel to facilitate adoption.

Overcoming resistance

Many of the challenges of a unified content strategy are common to any new process or system, while others are unique to a unified content strategy. The following are some of the more common challenges associated with a unified content strategy as well as suggestions for how to overcome them.

Not invented here

People find it hard to believe that content somebody else created could possibly meet their needs. After all it was written for a different purpose and channel, and the author couldn't possibly know their customer/audience/requirements.

In some ways, this is true. If content is written for a different purpose, audience, or channel without considering how the content can be reused, it won't work. However, content can be reused if it's:

- Written according to models and structured writing guidelines

- Written in the form of building blocks so content can be selectively used as required

- Written using good writing principles

- Written without format in mind

In some cases the content can be reused identically; in other cases, it must be modified, resulting in derivative reuse. But, regardless of the type, reuse is possible.

So how do you convince people of that? The best solution is "seeing is believing." Bring together different groups who create similar content and work through a mini-content audit exercise with them. It's a good idea if you have an understanding of where reuse is possible and select appropriate materials in advance so the analysis can be rapid. Having different groups identify the potential areas of reuse is an eye-opener. Many people are unaware just how much content is reused or could be reused. Once they see the volume of potential reuse, they're usually convinced that reuse is possible.

The channel issue may be more of a hurdle. Prepare for this one in advance. Create an example using some material that was written differently for different channels, but that could be written the same for all channels. Show the group the original materials. Show how the content could be written for multiple channels. Show them the content in each channel (for example, on paper, on the Web) using your current design templates.

We do it differently

It's not unusual for different departments and different business units to have their own values and ways of doing things. Many organizations even encourage different parts of the organization to compete with one another. They may not talk to one another or cooperate.

In this case, the content coordinator needs to find a balance between similarity and diversity. The overall business needs must be identified and communicated to the different areas. They're all in business together and the focus should be on their business competitors instead of on competition with other departments.

However, even when departments compete with one another, find out what their commonalities are and share them. Let each department or business unit focus on what is unique and optimize those unique qualities.

You might also consider adopting variations on the solution to meet the needs of different areas. For example, one area may use a full authoring tool, another area may use templates and forms, and yet another may use modified traditional authoring tools (refer to Chapter 20, "The role of content management"). This makes it easier for each area to author in a way that supports its processes.

It's okay for processes to be different in different areas. As long as the result of these processes is the same—effective, reusable content—different areas can continue to follow different processes. It's not necessary to create one unified process for the whole organization.

Loss of creativity

Authors often feel that they'll lose their creativity if they're forced to write structured content and write to models. First you need to identify what they consider creativity and what value is being added to the content through that creativity. Frequently, creativity is the work authors put into the layout rather into than the content. It's true that in a unified content environment, authors no longer have creative control over format and layout. However, authors who enjoy layout and design may want to participate in the design of templates and stylesheets in addition to creating content.

For authors who enjoy the content creation process, point out that they can be more creative since they no longer have to worry about format and layout. Their creative efforts can be put into designing the most effective information products possible and ensuring that content is readable and usable.

Others welcome the structured content and models as these free them up to do what they do best—creating content—what some consider to be their "real" job.

For teams such as marketing, where unique design and layout are integral to the effectiveness of information products, consider providing authors with the ability to modify the stylesheets. Structure *must* remain the same so content can be reused, but give authors the flexibility to change the look and feel generated by their stylesheets and develop the materials to meet their customers' needs. Alternatively, consider giving the authors the ability to pick from a selection of visual representations for components so they can specify to a certain extent the "look and feel" of the content by channel.

There are benefits, but this is too much work

Developing a unified content strategy is a lot of work. However, the work comes at the beginning, not throughout the content lifecycle. Once your strategy is implemented, the average author will have a reduced workload. When speaking with authors, don't overemphasize the amount of work it takes to implement the strategy. Instead, emphasize what they'll save by working this way, and how much time will be freed up when they don't have to create everything from scratch.

For management, who will be concerned about the amount of work a unified strategy requires, emphasize that all new methods and systems require up-front work, but the investment is returned later in benefits and reduced costs.

If fewer people can do more, I may lose my job

Companies and departments never have enough time, money, or resources to do all the work they need to do. Less work in one area means more time and resources are available to do work in another. Rarely are jobs lost. More frequently, organizations reorganize the workload and pursue projects and initiatives that they didn't have the time, money, or resources to do before. You can do *more* with the same resources.

Why some projects fail

Failure is always a possibility when organizations change the way they do business. These are some of the reasons projects fail or falter and some ways you can address these issues.

- Resistance to change

  Failing to address people's concerns during implementation can result in the project's failure. This is addressed in detail above in "Overcoming resistance."

- Failure to address both technical and nontechnical issues

  Focusing on nontechnical issues alone may obscure the issues of technology. Yet focusing on only the technological issues may result in failing to realize the impact a unified content strategy will have on the organization, its culture, and its political processes. Ensure that you address all the issues, both technical and nontechnical.

- Failure to recognize that analysis and design take time

  Implementing a unified content strategy and realizing the benefits will not happen overnight. It's important to recognize that time must be spent up front to produce an efficient, flexible, and robust unified information architecture. Departments or business units that recognize the opportunities for a unified content strategy and spend the time to develop an effective one should be rewarded for their efforts.

- Lack of a champion

  Starting a unified content strategy at the grassroots of an organization then gradually extending it to address the enterprise may only succeed in meeting the immediate needs. You need a champion to endorse your project and to make sure that different areas understand the need for unified content and buy into it.

- Biting off more than you can chew

  Organizations that try to do it all at once may fail due to the complexities of the content, the technology, or the organizational issues. It's more effective to develop the strategy in phases. Start with a prototype, implementing in one area, then move into other areas. Implementing in phases provides small-scale successes that allow developers and managers to build the necessary skills and confidence. And it provides you with the opportunity to work out the bugs in a small, controlled environment.

- Economic issues

  Different departments or business units may operate as different cost centers. Reusing content could be a disincentive. You may need to develop a new way of identifying the cost of creating and maintaining reusable content that is fairly distributed across the organization.

- Cataloguing reusable components

  It is hard to catalog (for example, add appropriate metadata) and retrieve reusable content across multiple business units or departments. Authors often find it hard to locate suitable reusable components outside their own area.

  Employing systematic reuse can reduce this issue. Information architects who have a thorough understanding of the entire domain of content can also help through the effective categorization of content (metadata).

- Organizations lack core competencies

  The organization may lack the core competencies necessary to design, create, and integrate reusable components. Implementing a unified content strategy means you should be thinking about content in a new way, and many in your organization may lack the skills to recognize the opportunities that unified content offers.

  Key personnel should receive appropriate training. Where necessary, consider using consulting resources at the beginning of the project to help you get started. Develop the strategy in stages to ensure that appropriate skills are gained and lessons learned are implemented with the next phase of the project.

- Lack of communication

  Lack of communication breeds rumor and resistance. It's important to communicate what is happening, why it is happening, and what is going to happen to ensure that everyone is aware of the project. Change is not as great a shock when information is communicated over time.

But remember that communication is not one-way. If you restrict communication to one-way only—the company telling people how things will change without listening to their concerns or their suggestions—the project will have a significantly higher chance of failure.

- Failure to involve others

  Often when teams are assigned, they go off and do their job on their own. Their results depend on how clearly they've identified the full scope of the project and its issues. To be successful, they must involve all the parties affected by the issues and the change.

  Perform a thorough analysis to ensure that you understand the scope of the issues and goals, invite people to participate in the design and testing process, communicate how you've implemented their suggestions, and employ the people who have assisted in the process and are convinced of the value of the unified content strategy to act as change agents (see "Change management").

- Relying on only one type of reuse

  The most common form of reuse is manual reuse, which results in the lowest incidence of reuse because it puts the responsibility on the authors to decide to reuse content, then find the content they want to reuse. Alternatively, automatic reuse ensures that content is reused and reduces the onus on authors to know that reusable content exists, find it, and reuse it appropriately. However, authors may perceive automatic reuse as overly restrictive. Using a combination of reuse types provides the greatest results and the most flexibility.

- Project-by-project reuse

  While it's a good idea to start small and work in phases, it's not a good idea to develop a unified content strategy on a project-by-project basis. This can lead to a lack of awareness about how content needs to be structured and modeled for optimum reuse, resulting in a lot of rework later on. You can implement project-by-project or area-to-area, but design for the entire scope of the unified content strategy.

- Selecting the wrong first project

  Selecting the right first project to begin your unified content implementation is very important. Picking the wrong one can lead to failure. Don't pick a mission-critical project with a very short deadline, because developing an effective unified content strategy takes time. You need the time to do it properly. You also need the opportunity to make mistakes and learn from them. The pressure to perform quickly may sabotage the development team's desire to do it right.

  Pick a project that will show return on investment, but not one that's a make-or-break proposition. You should also pick a project where content already exists but requires a major revision to meet current needs. The changes required for a unified content strategy will be less onerous if the content has to change anyway. Using existing content will also enable the analysts and architects to have a real rather than abstract example to work with.

- Reuse everything you can

  Reusing content for the sake of reusing content or to show high levels of reuse may not be effective. You could compromise the quality and effectiveness of your materials. Reuse content only where appropriate and effective, and always ensure that the reuse won't compromise the quality of your materials or make the reusable content difficult to create, find, and manage.

- No facility for change

  Some organizations may implement their unified content strategy, then either fail to support ongoing change or discourage change. They do this to ensure the greatest use of the system and most effective implementation of the strategy, but situations change and models, processes, and even technology need to be revised. Ensure that there's open communication between the authors and the business owners to enable your organization to adopt change when required and to respond to unique needs where appropriate.

- Failure to provide ongoing resources

  Once a business case is in place, organizations fund additional resources to take the project from concept through implementation. But what they sometimes fail to do is budget and provide for ongoing resources. Management and oversight doesn't end at implementation; it continues on an ongoing basis. There are a lot of shifts in people's behaviors and best practice in a unified content strategy and without ongoing oversight people can backslide into their old ways, sometimes resulting in long-term failure. Over time new behaviors become habit, but it often takes years.

Content governance

Changes to content must be managed at the content level (writing), the structural level (models), and the reuse level.

Content guidelines

Content guidelines help direct the author in creating structured content. Structured writing guidelines should be managed just like editorial guidelines.

An editor should own the structured writing guidelines and ensure that they continue to reflect ongoing corporate authoring guidance. It's preferable to include

Case study: Lack of ongoing oversight, a lesson in failure

We approached a client to write a case study for this book. They indicated that while they would have loved to provide the case study, they had to decline because the project was no longer successful. We were extremely surprised, because they'd had a significant success story.

Success of the project

- Implemented a unified content strategy
- Implemented a content management system
- Realized millions of dollars of savings in translation costs
- Responded to new requirements twice as fast as in previous years
- Developed a relationship of content sharing on a global basis
- Measured significant productivity gains

Failure of the project

So what happened?

They had funding and resources for the design work and pilot implementation in the first year, then two more years of dedicated resources to support the global rollout. Once the rollout was complete, regions were on their own. The global content team continued to work on the premise of reuse and content sharing, but when the regions were pressured by tough economic times and resources were lost, they began to lose sight of the requirements.

Two years after full rollout, the technology was no longer being used as a content management system; instead it was used as a "glorified word processor." Reuse continued in the corporate content, but nowhere else.

Lessons learned

This is the first time in over 20 years of consulting we've seen this happen. This was a very ambitious project; it spanned the globe, which made it more difficult than a departmental or single-region enterprise. But it was the failure to allocate resources that resulted in the breakdown. If there's no coordinated oversight, the project may fail. This is not an unusual requirement. When a company rolls out corporate branding standards, someone is responsible for the program overall and works to ensure the standards are followed.

Companies don't like to add headcount, but the financial savings of a unified content strategy far outweigh the cost of additional resources, particularly when translation is involved. Change is hard, but change is constant in today's world, and it's the only way that companies can survive. The increasing costs in this project will eventually trigger a new project, but they'll have to start all over again.

the authoring guidance in the structured authoring tool or guidelines. Then if the guidelines change, they're automatically updated. Consider allowing authors the option of turning the guidelines off when they're comfortable that they know the requirements but have the guidelines automatically turn back on again when a change occurs so that authors are immediately notified of changes.

Content models

Content models should be governed by the content strategist or the governance board. Consistent models are critical to content reuse and for supporting adaptive content. Changing the models arbitrarily will result in reduced or even full loss of automation. Work with the content creation teams to ensure that models remain consistent and are implemented consistently.

However, review necessary changes to the models on a regular basis to ensure that they continue to meet organizational needs, and develop new ones as required.

Reuse governance

A reuse strategy identifies what types of content will be reused and at what level of granularity, how they'll be reused, and how to support authors in easily and effectively reusing content. Once you've defined your strategy, you need to establish rules to govern reuse.

Reuse governance identifies the processes and business rules associated with reuse. For example, what happens when an author creates content that's approved? This content then becomes the source. Another author chooses to reuse the source content. They're in the process of modifying it when a third author decides to reuse the source, and begins making changes to it. What do you do? Will there be two derivatives (variations)? What if a change is made to the source while the secondary authors are working on their content?

On the surface, it may sound like a lot of work to figure out these rules, but think about the state of your servers, file system, and content right now—they're probably a mess! That's one of the reasons you're moving to a unified content strategy: to control your content. And if you work in a regulated industry, then controlling not just your documents, but also your content components, will be critical to regulatory compliance.

We know of customers who cost-justified the move to a unified content strategy using a risk-avoidance business case. Within one year of implementation, they were able to show how they managed to prevent a risk situation through governance of regulator-approved content (for example, prevention of a derivative version).

If your governance is designed into your unified content strategy from the beginning, it's just one more change that authors adjust to rather than an imposition at a later date.

Business rules

You use business rules to govern your reuse. Business rules can be implemented in your content management system (CMS) and controlled by workflow or controlled by your staff (manually); however, it's important that you develop the business rules before deciding how they'll be implemented. Once you know what your business rules are, you can then determine how to implement them.

You need to ask yourself, "What happens when…?" For example, Table 17.1 illustrates a few business rules associated with reuse.

Table 17.1   Sample business rules for governance.

What happens when:	Decision:
A source component is changed by someone other than the owner?	The changed component becomes a derivative.
A source component that has been identically reused changes?	Authors who reused the component are notified of the change to determine if they want to make the change to their usage of the component.
	If they choose not to use the changed component, their version of the component becomes a derivative.
A derivative component is created and approved?	An approved derivative goes through an approval process to determine if it should become the "new source" or an alternate source.
	Derivatives approved for a specific use cannot be used as a source for reuse.
	The system generates a report for review of derivative versions to determine which should become the source.
New content is created?	It is not part of the source until approved.
	Authors can reuse unapproved content which is in progress, but their information product cannot be published until all components are approved.

Workflow governance

Workflow guides the content through its lifecycle, from design and creation all the way to publishing. A complete workflow will even include feedback loops from the customer to improve the quality of the next version of the content. So it's no surprise that you can't manage your workflow on an ad hoc basis. Like any part of the content creation process, it must be well managed.

This management involves a level of commitment similar to that needed for the taxonomy and metadata. It will require a small group of people who ensure that the workflow supports the business rules, who guide changes if the workflow doesn't, and who change the workflow if the business requirements change.

The same governance board can manage the workflow as well. They tend to understand the content requirements, the business requirements, and the interrelationships between the different departments.

As with the changes to taxonomy and metadata, most of the changes to the workflow come in the early days of the system setup and testing. Once the system is up and running, there are usually very few changes to the workflow, so any additional work for the governance board members is very light.

Taxonomy and metadata governance

Taxonomy and metadata are the "under the hood" things that make your system work the way you want it to: smoothly and cleanly, without any fuss.

No matter how well a system is initially defined and implemented, small changes made over time can add up to trouble—that is, unless they're properly managed. It's not as though we want to forbid change. Your taxonomy and metadata must change. You'll need to keep your structures, taxonomy, metadata, and relationships up to date. Product names change, products are retired, and new ones appear. Your business grows, either through natural growth or mergers. The market changes, and with those changes, the terms used in your taxonomy change.

And although those changes must be implemented by your information technology (IT) department, you don't want them making the decisions on what to change and when. Likewise, you don't want IT to make each and every change that anyone wants. If every change that any author or editor ever considered were implemented, the system would quickly break down. For all intents and purposes it would be as though no system had ever been designed and implemented. Suggestions for change must be examined, and that's where a governance board comes in.

What do you need to manage?

A taxonomy identifies content, defines metadata, and manages the relationships between those pieces content and the metadata. It specifically manages the organization of information—how the system can help people find the information they need.

For example, a new series of glycemic index (GI) products might be planned for. It's targeted at a particular demographic, for example, 30- to 40-year-olds, people who are just starting to be concerned about their health. They have a busy social and work life, and have spent years with a mobile phone in their hands.

But now they're starting to notice that they can't eat like they used to without being concerned about a bit of weight gain. They make jokes about it, but are willing to start making some changes to their lifestyle. However, one of the things that they're not going to do is carry a book or list with them to check the GI values of their food. They do have a smartphone with them at all times though. Therefore the main product is a mobile app that allows them to compare the GI influence of foods, but it's not just a list of foods and their GI numbers. It uses social media and gamificaton theory to make it more interesting for them to use. And background material will be created, including notes and tips geared to their previous requests for information. These notes and tips are pushed to them via social media and texts, not email or web page browsing.

In order to support those new products, the governance board will have to look at the existing metadata. Will it support the creation and management (and ePublishing) of the tips and notes? Has this target market been identified in the metadata, and can you tag information as being specific to that market? If so, do you need to go further? Should you set up a special tag that identifies content specifically created for this series of products?

There are many questions that need to be asked (and answered) to support the new product. The changes and additions must not only support the new product, they must not impede existing products. You might initially think that because this new series of products is aimed at a particular age market, all you need to do is identify the material with an existing tag—one that defines the same target market. This might cause a problem in the future, however, if the volume of the notes and tips swamps the CMS with small pieces of information applicable only to the new series and not to other products aimed at the same age group. A better decision might be to tag the new information with the series identifier, and allow the CMS to segment the information for initial search and retrieval.

We want to ensure that adding new information doesn't make it harder to get access to what already exists.

Governance board

A governance board has a dual role. It must set up long-term strategic goals that reflect the business aims of the organization. On a day-to-day basis, the board must also manage and maintain the systems (content, taxonomy, and workflow) in such a way that it allows change but ensures that the approved changes strengthen and improve the organization's goals. In some companies, the same people are involved in both roles; in others, it's split between two different groups (with some overlap). No matter how it's organized, there are some basic rules for setting up a governance board.

Who's on the board?

Getting the size of the board right can be tricky. We're often asked how big the board should be, and we usually answer "As big as necessary, but no bigger." Because that's accurate but not helpful, we usually have other suggestions.

First, we recommend that you keep it under ten people if possible. We've found that committees made up of more than ten rapidly become unwieldy. One wag once defined a committee of twelve as an animal with twelve stomachs and six brains. That's not an animal you want to feed.

The goal is to have a representative from each group involved in creating, managing, and publishing the content. In addition, you'll need to have some management or executive representation as well as representatives from IT or systems who'll be able to tell you if a change someone wants is technically possible. Also don't forget to bring in someone who can represent your customers. Depending on your organization, this could be marketing, sales, or training. It could also be someone who speaks to the customers on a regular basis, such as service or support.

How often does it meet?

How often the board meets changes over time. Initially, the board will probably meet quite often. In the first year, it will probably meet six to eight times, and in subsequent years, it will probably meet on a quarterly basis.

The high number of meetings in the first year serves a number of purposes. During that first year you're likely to want to make a significant number of small but important changes. These are the types of things that you want to address quickly rather than drag out. This doesn't mean that you can hold off on implementation decisions with the excuse, "We need to take this to the governance board, and it's not scheduled to meet for two weeks." The board is designed to make decisions, not delay them. If there's an urgent decision to be taken, without which the implementation can't take place, it's imperative that that decision be taken, even if it requires a series of phone calls and quick consultations.

However, after that first flurry of implementation-level decisions—most of which tend to take place in the pilot, often in the first two or three months of the implementation—you can count on meeting every five to six weeks or so.

These regular meetings will help the governance board members become familiar with the processes of the board, with the types of decisions they will have to take, and with the board's internal processes.

In the second year, fewer changes will be required, and most of them can probably be scheduled. For example, everyone will know that a new product will be released at the end of the summer. Marketing and sales will know its name and its prospective audience. Training will be working on new material to support the product. Writers, illustrators, and other content creators will be working on new materials as well. In order to support the new product, new product names will have to be created, links made between new and old products, and new audiences may have to be determined. None of these changes should be a surprise, so they can be planned for. If the product is a new information product, rather than a product that needs documentation, the same scheduled set of changes can apply. The publication date is set and all the changes required to support the publication can be determined backward from that date.

Not all industries operate on such a planned basis, of course. Some industries are in what can only be described as a state of churn. Mobile phone carriers, for example, must react much more quickly and often have to make changes within a few business days.

Most industries aren't under the same type of pressure and have a few weeks to make most changes.

What happens at the meetings?

We strongly recommend that participants have all the information they need to make a decision on a change at least a week in advance of the governance board meeting. During the week prior to the meeting, they're expected to do some homework. They need to learn about the suggested changes, understand how these changes will affect their department, and be ready to make recommendations to the rest of the board (accept/reject) when they meet.

Summary

It's important to ensure that your content strategy is governed. You can't expect it to work in the long term unless it's properly managed and guided.

That governance starts even before the strategy is implemented. The change management sessions are crucial: during these sessions, you'll talk to and work with employees to ensure that they understand the need for change, and learn about their concerns and needs. If everyone is on board with the changes, the chances of success improve greatly.

Once the strategy is implemented, there are two main focuses of governance: the content, and everything that supports it.

Changes to content must be managed at the content level (writing), at the structural level (models), and at the reuse level.

The supporting structure for the content must be governed as well. The taxonomy and metadata that allow authors to find content for reuse can't be random. These must be maintained over the long term to remain useful. Changes must both enhance existing content and support new content and products.

It's not possible to govern on an ad hoc basis. A structure must be put in place to ensure that changes are understood and that they have broad acceptance before they are implemented.

When we discussed workflow, we talked about the similarities of designing and creating content and designing and building a house. The analogy can be extended to the governance board: the board is like a combination architectural design review panel and building inspector. Together they ensure that the house is built as designed but they also have the expertise to make intelligent changes if circumstances change and another room is needed in the house. The architects and inspectors can make changes and ensure that the changes are safe, that the foundations can support the extra weight, and that the plumbing, heating, and electrical systems can be expanded to deal with the extra load.

Likewise, the governance board ensures that the basic systems are in place to support the creation, management, and publication of content. They also review requested changes to the content strategy or the system used to support the content to ensure that requested changes are effective and that the processes used to create the content are not adversely affected by the changes.

Part 5

Supporting your unified content strategy

No strategy can be implemented without a full and complete complement of people to carry it out. In Chapter 18, "Changing roles," we explore what *collaborative authoring* means for the people who produce the content. We also examine what types of roles—existing roles and new roles you might not know you need—should be integrated into the organization to effectively support the unified content strategy.

And along with the right roles to support your strategy, you also need the right technology. XML is the underlying technology that makes modern content management systems (CMSs) possible. The best part about XML? It's like driving a car—just like you don't have to know how an internal combustion engine works in your car, you don't have to know how XML works to be able to use it. But we do encourage you to read about it in Chapter 19, "The role of XML," because it will give you a solid foundation for understanding how the use of XML affects your unified content strategy.

In Chapter 20, "The role of content management," we discuss how you integrate content management into your environment, the types of authoring tools you can use, the workflow systems you can set up, and the delivery mechanisms you can choose. Each aspect of content management affects your organization and requires careful planning and implementation to ensure that the full potential of content management can be realized.

Chapter 18

Changing roles

Implementing a unified content strategy together with the designated tools requires new roles, a modification to existing roles, and new skill sets. Part of managing change will be getting new roles in place and adjusting others to meet the new requirements.

Senior content strategist (new role)

Working in a unified content environment means working in a collaborative environment. With a collaborative environment, someone needs to understand all the content and the overall content requirements to ensure that content comes together in a logical manner. This task falls to a senior content strategist to work with all the stakeholders involved in the design and development of content to ensure that the unified content strategy is effectively addressed.

This is a management role. In particular, the senior content strategist needs to communicate the concepts and advantages of reuse on an ongoing basis to facilitate agreement among project teams.

The senior content strategist must also be able to oversee many projects and determine the unified content strategy required to address both the needs of all the stakeholders and the needs of the content as a whole.

In addition, the senior content strategist must work with all the content creation teams to ensure that models and guidelines are followed and that everyone is in agreement on how to most effectively support the unified content strategy.

Skills and knowledge required include:

- A broad-based understanding of business needs.
- The ability to determine an effective unified content strategy.
- An in-depth understanding of customer needs and the ways in which the unified content strategy can support those needs.
- An in-depth understanding of the unified content lifecycle and the authors' requirements for success.
- The ability to manage diverse requirements.
- Negotiating techniques.
- Strong people management skills.

This is primarily a management role that requires extensive coordination of people, processes, and change, and a desire to implement and manage best practices.

This role could be combined with the role of content strategist.

Content strategist (modified role)

Content strategy plays a key role in analyzing, designing the content strategy, and working with stakeholders.

The content strategist is responsible for building the information product models, component models, metadata, reuse strategies, and workflow. He or she works closely with information architects and user experience designers to ensure that the content can support the desired customer experience.

The content strategist needs the following skills:

- Analysis
  - Analytical problem-solving
  - Customer needs analysis
  - Content analysis
  - Content organizational analysis
- Design
  - Information product and component models
  - Metadata (content management system)
  - Information retrieval
  - Reuse strategy
- Standards
  - Usability
  - Information

A lot of this work will be done as part of the project, but it is an ongoing task, required to meet new and changed needs.

Content owners (modified role)

In a unified content strategy, content can be used in many different information products. Common content, and product- and channel-specific content, must be owned. The owners of common content need to ensure that the content is maintained and is appropriate across multiple products.

Owners of product-specific content need to ensure that the content is created and maintained throughout the life of the product and they also need to ensure that it integrates effectively with the common content.

In a traditional authoring environment, authors own the content they create because they are also responsible for creating a specific information product. However, in a unified content strategy, content can be used in many different information products. The concept of the content owner needs to change to accommodate this.

In a unified content strategy, the person who authors the content still owns it, but may not own all the content that comes together to create an information product. There may be many authors, all of whom may not be responsible for creating an entire information product. Rather, they may be responsible for creating content about a certain subject that goes into many different information products.

In addition, there needs to be an owner of the unified content, someone who can oversee the creation of all the content related to a particular product, service, product family, or any other associated content set. The unified content owner facilitates the collaborative authoring process and ensures consistency and quality of the materials.

The role of the unified content owner could be assumed by an existing author, business owner/analyst, or project manager, reporting to the senior project manager. The skills required of the unified content owner include:

- Information analysis
- Information design
- Ability to determine an effective unified content strategy
- Ability to manage diverse requirements
- Negotiating techniques
- Strong people management

External authors (modified role)

Working with external authors is more difficult than working with internal authors, as you cannot always control how they provide content. To support structured content and a clean conversion of their content to structured content, create structured templates for authors to use.

Internal authors (modified role)

Creating materials in a unified content strategy separates the creation of the input (content) from the output (channel or information type). This means that internal authors, as proficient communicators, will now rely less on the tools used to display the final information.

Internal authors no longer have to worry about applying styles or becoming involved in the formatting of the information; formatting is automatically handled by the authoring and delivery systems. Instead, authors can concentrate exclusively on the content they create and combine.

Internal authors identify the building blocks of information and how the blocks will fit together. They also identify opportunities for content reuse and write applicable content components for reuse. Their skill set must expand to include:

- Working in a collaborative environment
- Creating structured content and writing to models
- Writing reusable content

Business owners/analysts (modified role)

Business owners/analysts are very important to an effective unified content strategy. They determine the requirements of the business and frequently, the customers' needs as well. Their role is to ensure that products, services, and content are designed to effectively meet the customers' needs. However, they must also ensure that any strategies and solutions meet the needs of the employees, the individuals tasked with creating the products, services, and content.

Too often organizations bring in a technological solution to business problems. It is critical that business owners/analysts participate in the effective design of your unified content strategy. Their role is to ensure that content meets the needs of the customer, and the unified content strategy meets the needs of the authors.

To support a unified content strategy, business analysts/owners should expand their skill set to include:

- A broad-based understanding of business needs

- The ability to determine an effective unified content strategy

- In-depth understanding of customer needs and the ways in which the unified content strategy can support those needs

- In-depth understanding of the unified content lifecycle and the authors' requirements for success

Editors (modified role)

Standards and consistency are important in creating seamless unified materials. In a unified content environment, it's particularly important that editors look not only at the words, but also at how the information is used to ensure it is written effectively for reuse.

To support a unified content strategy, editors must understand:

- The unified content strategy

- The information product models and component models

- Editorial techniques

- Writing for multiple channels, information products, multiple audiences

- Structured writing techniques

Information architect (modified role)

The role of information architecture expands from web information architecture to:

- Web

- Mobile

- eBooks

- Apps

Each platform has a different set of navigation systems and organizational structures. The information architect needs to determine platform specific:

- Organization
- Labeling
- Navigation
- Taxonomy and metadata (customer facing)

The information architect should work closely with the content strategist to ensure the unified content strategy effectively supports the architecture and vice versa.

Information technologists (modified role)

In a traditional authoring system, many authors are responsible for creating the output for their content. In a unified content strategy, this is handled automatically by the system. An information technologist is required to handle the technology of the system. This may be a role that resides in the information technology area or within the content area.

An information technologist is skilled at implementing content models in the various tools, including programming and supporting stylesheets to meet specifications provided by the information architect.

Information technologists should be well-versed in a wide variety of tools and technologies, including XML. Specifically, they should understand the tools and technologies you choose for your system.

Their skill set includes designing and developing:

- DTDs or other supporting content frameworks
- Authoring and publishing stylesheets (XML-based)
- Authoring templates
- Workflow creation
- CMS configuration

Art (modified role)

Art is likely to be a team with the following roles:

- Graphic design (Web, mobile, eBooks)
- Interactive design (Flash, JavaScript, Ajax)
- Media (illustration, photography, video)

Multiple renditions of all assets are required to support all platforms.

Metadata must become richer to ensure that assets can be found regardless of where they have been used in the information set.

Publishing roles

The primary change in publishing-specific roles is the move from strictly print publications (books) to print, eBooks, and apps.

Acquisitions editor (modified role)

Acquisitions editors are typically responsible for identifying market requirements and seeking out authors to meet those requirements. Acquisitions editors will be responsible for acquiring content for information product suites, including:

- Books only
- eBooks only
- Books/eBooks with associated apps
- Courses only
- Courses with associated books/eBooks

Development editors (modified role)

Development editors work with the authors to ensure that the quality of the content meets the desired publishing requirements and deadlines. They also coordinate activities between the author and graphic designers and production. Their role is relatively unchanged but they will work online more with the author and add eBooks and apps to the materials they manage. The role of development editor will also include:

- Checking revisions from authors
- Completing art and photo requests
- Reviewing copyedits
- Reviewing art and photos
- Entering copyright information
- Contracting with an indexer (at XML stage)
- Checking pages and page proofs
- Checking the integrity of the eBook

Assistant editors (modified role)

The assistant editor's role changes quite a bit, with more and more work moving online and many manual activities eliminated.

The assistant editor is no longer responsible for:

- Printing copyeditor files for the author (assumes that all edits have been done online)
- Incorporating author revisions (assumes that revisions are done online so there are no revisions to incorporate)

Assistant editors will be responsible for:

- Converting external authors' manuscripts to XML
- Adding art, photos, and video, or creating placeholders in XML
- Checking that art, photos, and video have been imported correctly
- Reviewing art, photos, and video with the development editor to ensure that they are acceptable
- Incorporating the index in XML if the indexer does not do it directly
- Adding credit lines for art, and so on, where appropriate
- Identifying that content is ready for production (changes workflow metadata to "ready for production")
- Checking pages
- Checking indexes, and front and back matter
- Checking printer's proofs
- Testing eBooks

Copy editor (modified role)

The role of the copy editor is the same, but copy editors will perform their tasks using a collaborative online review tool.

Production-print (modified role)

This role expands to the design of print books, eBooks, and apps. You may have production teams that specialize in one or the other, but not necessarily all.

Production creates page layout templates that are designed to import XML content. Standard templates are required for the standard information products. Production imports the XML, just as they would the Word document and adjusts the template to accommodate the size of the content.

Changes to the content can be made by others in the XML and then they can publish to styled print themselves. Alternatively, production could reimport the XML and adjust the template for any content changes (e.g., more content).

This process reduces the burden on production to manually incorporate changes and optimizes the role of page design experts.

Production is no longer responsible for:

- Incorporating the author revisions into final layout; this is now done in the XML.

- Uploading files for the printer. This can be triggered automatically once all the appropriate approvals are complete by identifying that the content is ready for printing via the workflow.

Summary

Implementing a unified content strategy together with the designated tools requires new roles, modification of existing roles, and new skill sets. Part of managing change will be getting new roles in place and adjusting others to meet the new requirements.

There are a number of new and modified roles:

- Senior content strategist (new role)
- Content strategist (modified role)
- Content owners (modified role)
- External authors (modified role)
- Internal authors (modified role)
- Business owners/analysts (modified role)
- Editors (modified role)
- Information architect (modified role)
- Information technologists (modified role)
- Publishing roles
  - Acquisitions editor (modified role)
  - Development editor (modified role)
  - Assistant editor (modified role)
  - Copy editor (modified role)

Chapter 19

The role of XML

XML is the underlying technology that makes modern content management systems (CMSs) possible. It allows us to break content into reusable elements, and helps us find them so we can arrange them into new information products. It allows different types of computer systems to talk to each other—to send information back and forth—allowing us to share information between departments and companies.

The best part about XML is that you don't really need to know too much about it to use it. It's like driving a car. You don't have to understand how an internal combustion engine works to start and drive the car; likewise you don't have to understand the internals of XML in order to use it well.

On the other hand, knowledge is a good thing, so we encourage you to read through this chapter. In it you'll learn a bit about the history of XML, where it came from, and what it can do. We'll compare XML with HTML and then introduce a little bit about Darwin Information Typing Architecture (DITA) and other XML tagging schemes.

Perhaps most importantly we'll start off with a question we hear a lot from writers and other content creators.

Should you fear XML?

It does sound complicated and geeky. At one point it was; most writers had to be able to edit text like they were creating code. But that was a long time ago.

Remember, there was a time when mainstream word processing packages like WordStar™ and WordPerfect™ required writers to memorize complicated key-stroke commands and "dot codes" for formatting content. WYSIWYG editors took over as soon as the computer platforms became powerful enough to run them, and the dreaded "dot codes" were hidden under a nice, clean, easy-to-use interface. Those who pined for the days of ugly screens could opt for the "codes on" mode, but most authors quickly dispensed with them.

The same has happened with XML editors. Early editors were famous for display-ing the text in "tags on" mode. In this mode, you see all of the underlying structure and coding needed to create the final document. Like the earlier "codes on" mode in word processors, the screens were cluttered and the programs fairly hard to use.

XML authoring tools have moved on, and like their word processing ancestors, sport easy-to-use interfaces. The interface can look just like a modern word pro-cessing program (like Microsoft Word, or they actually can be Microsoft Word) or can be totally customized to meet the specific needs of the writers.

For example, in Figure 19.1 we see a sample document in an XML authoring tool that is Microsoft Word with XML structure "under the covers." It looks like Word because it is Word, but it has a lot more functionality than traditional Word with-out the overt complexities of XML.

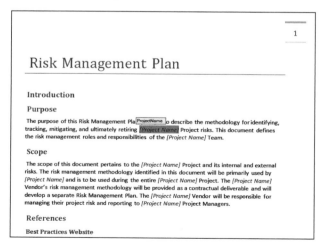

Figure 19.1   Sample structured document in Quark XML Author™.

The origins

In the beginning (all the way back to the 1970s), there were disparate software applications that really did not play well together at all. Charles Goldfarb, a researcher at IBM, observed that many systems at IBM could not share information with one another, that they each used their own "language" (incompatible file formats) to format the text. SGML (Standard Generalized Markup Language) was born out of a project to build a system for creating, managing, and publishing legal documents. A markup language is a set of annotations (tags) on text that describe how the text is to be structured, laid out, or formatted. HTML, which is used to define the appearance of content on web pages, is probably the most widely known markup language. Any application that formats text has an underlying markup language. For example, RTF (Rich Text Format) was for many years the underlying markup language for Microsoft Word.

SGML was based on the following three principles:

- Computers need to share files in a common format (they need to "speak" the same language).

- The markup of a document has to be extensible.

- There needs to be a way to identify the structure of documents so that different documents of the same type will share the same structure or rules.

  As the World Wide Web came into being and developed, the community recognized that although HTML was useful for formatting information displayed on the Web, it had its limitations (insufficient tag set, could only describe format and not the content itself). It also realized that SGML was essentially overkill. So a working group under the World Wide Web Consortium (W3C) began work on XML.

The goals of the W3C in developing XML include the following:

- Web-based delivery

- Open standard

- Based on SGML

- Formal and concise

- Easy to author and create

- Easy to develop applications for

- Extensible

The first point is extremely important. To be suitable for the Web, the working group needed to create a streamlined version of SGML—SGML Lite—that would provide a lightweight markup standard, with all of the needed features and without the bulkiness that would overwhelm the Web.

XML was that streamlined version of SGML.

XML has been a great success. Use has spread beyond content markup to all sorts of other business and software applications.

Why XML in content creation?

From a content and publishing perspective, XML has become an extremely important technology for both big and small publishers. For complex content management with information reuse, XML is the technology of choice.

XML provides the ability to do a whole lot more than what can be done with traditional tools. The characteristics of XML that best support publishing are:

- Structured content
- Separation of content and format
- XSL (eXtensible Stylesheet Language) stylesheets

XML and structured content

Authors typically have a high-level understanding of the concept of structured content. For example, they understand that books have front matter, body chapters, and back matter. They also recognize repeatable structures at a lower level. Chapters have titles, overviews, sections containing the "meat" of the chapter, and a summary.

However, when you examine similar information products, you find that structures are not consistent from product to product. Even among documents of the same type, structures will vary from author to author, from department to department, from division to division. Even information written by a single author will vary over time. This is a problem for a number of reasons.

For customers, the impact of changes in structure can range from distracting to confusing. As creatures of habit, they get used to seeing things in the same places. When things move, it takes them time to get used to the changes. Changes in structure may be seen as inconsistencies, and may lead customers to distrust the material.

Inconsistency also has a major impact on reuse. Effective reuse is built on predictability. The initial analysis of the content and customers' needs for that content will define the structure of your information products.

What is XML?

XML is a set of rules for defining markup languages. We're all familiar with markup languages, with HTML being the most common example available. We've all looked at HTML code and in many cases we create content directly in HTML.

The XML standard is based on the SGML standard, which was designed with many of the same goals as XML. XML has been streamlined—reduced in complexity and capability— from SGML to make it practical for the Internet. However, XML retains enough of the characteristics to make it very effective for all sorts of publishing and specifically content management for publishing.

The advantage that XML has over HTML is that it allows you to define a tag set that meets the specific needs of your content. It's a set of rules for creating markup languages (like HTML). Unlike HTML, where the tags are defined, XML allows you to create the tags to suit the needs of your content and your authors.

But what *is* XML?

XML can best be described by walking through a sample of XML markup.

XML files are made up primarily of elements and attributes. Elements have start tags, end tags, and content. Attributes have names and values.

```
<Procedure Audience="All">
<Title>Logging On to AccSoft </Title>
<Text>You must log on to the system before you can complete any tasks.
</Text>
<Intro>To log on to AccSoft:</Intro>
<ProcedureSteps>
<Step>Double-click the AccSoft application</Step>
<Step>Type your USERID into the <Fieldname>Name</Fieldname> field</ Step>
<Step>Type your password into the <Fieldname>Password</Fieldname> field.</Step>
<Step>Click the OK button to log on to AccSoft.</Step>
</ProcedureSteps>
</Procedure>
```

In the sample, <Title> is a start tag. Tags are enclosed by angle brackets. </Title> is an end tag: end tags always begin with a slash (/) after the opening angle bracket. The Title element is the start tag (<Title>), the end tag(</ Title>), and everything in between. Audience is an attribute name; All is the value. The combination of name and value make up the attribute.

In the example, some elements, like Title, Text, and Intro, just contain data. Others, like ProcedureSteps, contain other elements. Some Step elements contain both data and elements (Fieldname).

What do XML tags do?

XML tags:

- Describe your document's content (meaningful tag and attribute names).

- Describe the structure of your document (document/node tree).

- Indicate hierarchy of data through embedded elements.

- Do not include formatting or "style" characteristics.

Comparing XML and HTML

There are a number of differences between HTML and XML. HTML is a set of tags that you can use to present content in a browser. Its primary application is presentation. It was not designed to capture structure. On the other hand, XML allows you to create your own markup languages with a focus on capturing the structure of content. The XML standard does not provide any specific capability for presentation.

From w3schools (http://www.w3schools.com/xml/xml_whatis.asp):

- XML was designed to describe data and to focus on what data is.

- HTML was designed to display data and to focus on how data looks.

A procedure in HTML

Consider what the sample procedure above might look like if it were marked up with HTML.

```
<h2>Logging On to AccSoft </h2>
<p>You must log on to the system before you can complete any tasks.</p>
<h3>To log on to AccSoft:</h3>
<ol>
<li>Double-click the AccSoft application</li>
<li>Type your USERID into the <i>Name field</i></li>
<li>Type your password into the <i>Password</i> field.</li>
<li>Click the OK button to log on to AccSoft.</li>
</ol>
```

The h2 tag indicates that you have a second-level heading, but you must interpret the content to determine that the content is a procedure.

Advantages of XML?

The advantages of XML are that it:

- Promotes consistency through structured documents. Documents follow the same structures, with similar documents having the same content pieces.

- Separates structure from format, allowing authors to focus on writing.

- Enables single-sourcing (component reuse). Structured information is easy to break into individual components for reuse or repurposing.

- Enables multiple outputs (formats and content). Publishing information is isolated from the content and is easily changed/replaced/added to.

- Enables dynamic documents. Documents can be built from components, enabling you to select components dynamically.

- Increases output flexibility. Structured information is easy to manipulate to reconfigure or republish.

An example

Consider a procedure. The content model for a procedure could be expressed as:

- A procedure contains a title

- Followed by a description of the procedure

- Followed by a heading to introduce actual steps

- Followed by one or more steps

- Followed by links to related procedures

The content model is a specific relationship of elements of content.

DTDs and schemas

In XML, structure can be defined in a schema or DTD (Document Type Definition) that specifically defines all the elements (tags) that can be used in a document as well as the relationship of those elements to other elements. You can specify the hierarchy of elements ("a chapter contains…"), the order of elements, even the number of elements.

DTDs and schemas:

- Are formal documents, written in a particular syntax that specifies an XML vocabulary (set of tags)

- Describe which elements and entities may appear in associated documents, including:
  - Elements
  - Attributes
  - Child elements
  - Number of children
  - Sequences of elements
  - Mixed content
  - Empty elements
  - Text declarations
- Document content models in a formal manner

Advantages of schemas over DTDs

DTDs and schemas are similar in that they both define the required structure of a document. However, schemas are, in effect, an updated version of DTDs. As XML use on the Web increased, developers realized that DTDs were limited in what they could do, and that a more able mechanism for defining structure was needed. Schemas provide that increase in capability.

Schemas include all the capabilities of DTDs, plus:

- They are written as well-formed XML documents (DTDs are created using a different language).
- Data can be validated based on built-in and user-defined data types.
- Programmers can more easily create complex and reusable content models.
- Schemas support local and global variables in the XML document.

The two key differences (for authoring and publication) between schemas and DTDs are that schemas are written using a specific XML markup language, while DTDs require you to learn a separate, unique language. Most importantly, schemas offer what developers like to call "rich data typing capabilities for elements and attributes." That translates to enabling much greater control over the structure of content and the content itself. For example, in a DTD, you can create a "year" element as part of a date. You can also specify that the "year" element contains only content and not other elements. But that is all you can specify within the element. A DTD can only specify the correct arrangements of elements to other elements. In a schema, not only can you define a "year" element, you can also specify that it must be four characters long and that all characters must be numeric (1, 2, 3,…). It allows control over the data itself.

A schema can be invaluable for authoring and publication. Many authors take as much time figuring out the structure they need to write to as they do actually crafting the information. Do I need an overview? Should my procedure have an introduction? With a schema, you can mandate the structure that is required. This consistency is also very valuable for customers. Consistency leads to predictability. Customers learn where information is to be found and can navigate to it automatically, finding what they need quickly and efficiently.

For structural consistency, having a defined structure in a schema is important. However, you need to be able to confirm that your content matches the content model defined in the schema. This functionality is provided by specialized tools called parsers that can read a schema and enforce the structural rules defined in it. The parser "reads" the document and reports an error when the structure and content do not match the schema.

Most XML authoring tools have built-in parsers to parse the content as you enter it, and to ensure that the elements and content match the requirements of the schema. Some authoring tools will allow you to enter elements only in their defined places and will not allow you to enter elements that break the rules of the schema. By providing authors with an editor and a schema, you can ensure that all your information products are structurally consistent.

Separation of content and format

Word processing and desktop publishing tools revolutionized the way content was created. Authors quickly gained the opportunity to take control of formatting their documents. The long lead times and production cycles of formal layout for printing were eliminated as authors began producing their own camera-ready, hot-off-the-laser-printer copy.

However, these new formatting capabilities come with issues. For some, having responsibility is a burden, for others, a distraction. Many authors become more concerned with how content looks, than with what the content says.

XML by itself is not acceptable for display to the average customer. It must be formatted for presentation.

There are a number of technologies available for formatting. XML presentation is created using XSL stylesheet. Unlike traditional stylesheets, which provide only formatting commands, XSL is a powerful mechanism for both transforming and formatting XML documents.

Using a stylesheet gives you the ability to describe all your formatting needs, including fonts, colors, sizes, margins, bullets, list numbers, and so on, in a WYSIWYG editor.

XSL

Of course, your job is probably not to deliver XML files, but rather printed books, eBooks, PDFs, or HTML pages. For content management and publishing, a large measure of the advantages of XML comes from XSL. You use XSL to transform (or convert or publish) to the output formats you want to deliver.

XSL:

- Is XML markup language itself (there is an XSL vocabulary)
- Can format content for online display or for paper-based delivery
- Can add constant text or graphics (like the icon in a note)
- Can filter content
- Can sort or reorder content
- Is really divided into three parts:
  1. XSLT—a transformation language
  2. XSL-FO (XSL Formatting Objects—a language used to format XML)
  3. XPath

But rather than simply formatting the information in a document, XSL gives you the ability to transform it into something else. That is, you can manipulate the information to reorder, repeat, filter out information, or even add information based on details in the file. This is where XSL transformation, also known as XSLT, fits in. XSLT allows you to transform an XML document into another markup language. The most common use of XSLT is to transform information to HTML for display on the Web. But XSLT can also be used to convert information from XML into markup for mobile.

The flexibility of XSL and its pieces is extremely valuable for information publication and presentation. Unlike traditional tools, which associate one stylesheet with one document, you can create any number of stylesheets for a single XML document or information product. If you want to post the document on the Web or mobile, create an XSL stylesheet to HTML. For print, create an XSL stylesheet to XSL-FO or better yet, to an XML-aware composition tool.

Despite the unstoppable growth of the Internet and display technologies, paper will continue to be a required output for information. XSL-FO has been designed for that purpose. If you want paper, create an XSL-FO stylesheet. XSL-FO provides stylesheet capabilities for converting XML to paper-based formats like PDF. It provides for all of the required formatting, including page layouts, headers, footers, recto/verso (odd/even) pages, portrait and landscape pages, and so on. Many organizations are skipping XSL-FO completely and going from XML to a composition package such as Adobe InDesign and QuarkXPress.

When the information is ready to publish, you can process the file against all stylesheets simultaneously and get all required outputs at the same time.

What about DITA?

You've probably heard a lot about DITA, and might be aware that it's related to XML in some way. So what is it, and why might you be interested in it?

With all that, why do we need DITA?

First of all, starting an XML implementation from scratch can be expensive. The process of creating content models, DTDs or schemas, and stylesheets can be quite time-consuming. DITA is an existing markup standard, and being able to start out with an existing, well thought out standard can take you a giant step along the development timeline, saving you both time and money.

DITA was developed primarily by IBM in response to the changing needs of their business. Those needs are the same needs that we all face:

- Figuring out how to get products to market faster
- Finding ways to reduce unnecessary expenses
- Delivering content in an increasing number of output formats
- Finding ways to react faster to changing demands (more flexibility)
- Increasing the effectiveness of content

Changes in corporate goals, changes in technology, and changes in customer expectations and needs all have to be met. DITA is the mechanism IBM chose to meet those needs.

Recognizing that DITA would benefit writing departments everywhere, IBM has passed the standard to the Organization for the Advancement of Structured Information Standards (OASIS), a not-for-profit, international consortium, that drives the development, convergence, and adoption of eBusiness standards.

Design goals

Before discussing the details of DITA, it's useful to understand some of the goals that led to the development of the standard.

Move away from a single format to multiple formats and outputs

One of the largest impacts of technology on information development is the addition of so many new formats for delivering information. No one just delivers to one format any more. There is an increasing need for information to be delivered in multiple formats. While some improvements have been made, many of the technologies in use today are not efficient tools for creating multiple outputs from a single source of content. The standards that have been available to date, like DocBook, have been book-based.

Move away from SGML to XML

IBM had been using SGML for some time but recognized that XML, with its stated focus on Internet applicability, was a better option. Web-based and mobile formats and delivery have become crucial tools for delivering effective information to customers.

Move towards the trend to minimalism

The goal of information development and delivery should be "the right information, at the right time, in the right format, to the right person." For IBM, that meant reducing information "glut," lessening the volume of irrelevant information presented to customers, and focusing on providing only the information that customers *need*. This approach reduces the time it takes to both create and maintain information, facilitates quicker information delivery, and reduces the effort required to keep information up-to-date.

Provide more flexibility in structures and move away from "monolithic" DTDs

The trend in the past was to create a DTD focused on the needs of individual departments and specific information products they produce. This approach, however, can have a negative impact on wide-scale reuse, as content created by one department may be difficult to reuse in other departments. DITA is intended to provide a mechanism that establishes a clear base of common structures, making it easier to create specific structures needed by different departments.

Support maximum reuse

Reuse is today's best practice for information developers. DITA was developed specifically to promote content reuse and reduce redundant information.

Benefits of DITA

Considering the benefits that come with SGML and XML, you might wonder why you should consider DITA instead of just developing your own XML markup scheme. That might be the right way to go; there are still many, many applications that cry out for XML solutions other than DITA. And there are many other XML solutions that compete with DITA, like DocBook and S1000D. So what are the arguments in favor of DITA?

First, starting from scratch is expensive. DITA is an open standard that includes a set of predefined structures for capturing topic-based content and gives you a set of tags and structures to use as-is or as a starting point for creating your own specialized structures.

DITA is output independent. That is, as a basic principle of its use, topics are written in DITA to be output into other formats as necessary. When authoring in Microsoft Word or standard FrameMaker, for example, you are authoring in an interface that has been designed and optimized for creating paper output.

DITA was designed to support reuse. From the beginning, DITA's developers recognized reuse as a best principle of content creation. By focusing on the information, rather than the output, you can write information once and use it in other formats and contexts as needed. This does take planning to get the structures right, effort to teach people to write in a new way, and discipline to actually write that way. But you can save money, save time, and improve quality if you do it right.

Topics, the building blocks of DITA

The DITA standard defines the topic as the basic building block of content. Users author content using specific topic structures. There are four different topic structures—that is, four different kinds of topics—delivered with DITA (see Table 19.1).

Table 19.1   DITA topics

Topic	Example
Concept/Generic[1]	
Task	
Reference	

1 Note that at the top level the structure for a generic topic and a concept topic are the same, hence one illustration.

The base definition for all topics comes from the generic topic. It is defined with a relatively simple structure, including elements for title, short description, prolog (for metadata), the topic body, and related links. The topic body is defined with mostly generic HTML tags for structure, with the notable exception of a section substructure, which allows you to break up a long topic into sections.

One of the strengths of DITA—and where the Darwin angle fits in—is that the other three topic types (concept, task, and reference) all borrow their base structures from the generic topic structure. In other words, they inherit the same basic structure as a generic topic. However, because the DITA creators recognized that generic structure will not always provide the necessary authoring or output control, the three specialized types have additional structure that is specific to the kind of information they represent. For example, the task topic has a defined substructure for capturing procedures, with steps, actions, and results, among other specialized elements. The reference topic includes structure for documenting a screen or an interface.

It is that topic structure that gives DITA much of its effectiveness. Users capture content in individual topics that can be included into different outputs to create different information products.

Topics and DITA Maps

Creating topics is effective, but not what we typically deliver. DITA is based on a topic architecture that sees output products built from topics aggregated by a DITA map. This means that DITA maps provide an index of the topics that are associated with an individual book or help system, for example.

Broken down, a map is really just a series of topic references; the references point to the topics to be included in the output when you process the map (see Figure 19.2). You can set the order and the hierarchy of the topic references. The map does not contain content, it just points to it. This simplifies reuse, as you can point to the same topic from as many maps as you want. You can change a topic's hierarchy level in different books. In one map, a topic can be at a "chapter" level, while in another book, it can function as a "section" or "subsection." You can also point to the same topic in the same document as many times as you want or need. The map basically operates as a table of contents for a virtual document.

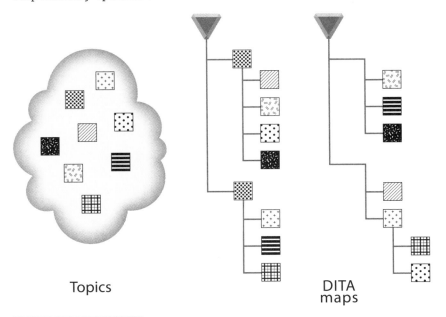

Topics

DITA maps

Figure 19.2   How topics can be assembled into DITA maps.

It's not perfect for all purposes

IBM's business has long been focused on delivering software and services. Accordingly, much of their documentation needs is centered on managing software and the documentation for that software.

When you look at the DITA standard, you'll see many internal references that make this apparent. Examples used in the specification often reflect DITA's roots. That doesn't mean that you can only use it to structure software documentation; far from it. It just reflects its origins.

Recent updates to the standard have widened the scope considerably. DITA 1.2 includes new elements to support the specific needs of training departments. This is a welcome development. DITA is now being used in the publishing industry as well.

Alternatives to DITA

DITA is not the first XML initiative to become popular or widely used. Companies implementing XML solutions have always had alternatives, including building custom DTDs from scratch. Industry-standard DTDs, like DocBook, and NLM, have also existed for people to use. Each has strengths and weaknesses, as does any initiative or approach.

DocBook

If you approached XML editor or CMS vendors five years ago, they would at some point during the conversation ask you if you had considered DocBook. For publishing, it was really the first industry-standard DTD for the publications focus.

It was originally developed as an SGML markup language for converting, sharing, and ultimately authoring technical manuals for UNIX computer systems. Eventually, its development was taken over by a technical committee of OASIS.

The standard has undergone multiple revisions since its initial version, with wide contributions from many customers. As a result, it's a very robust model, which accommodates pretty much any model of documentation guide imaginable. However, with over 300 individual elements, it's very complex and can be difficult to use. To help alleviate the problem, the DocBook developers have designed the model and DTD to facilitate the use of a customization layer. This layer is built on top of Doc-Book to simplify the models actually used by authors.

DocBook is a stable, tested, mature software documentation model. It's been used and refined over a long period of time and over varied applications. As a result, it has built-in models to cover most, if not all, typical software documentation applications. DocBook is not just for technical documentation, though; many organizations such as publishers and companies that write a lot of articles and reports use DocBook.

However, DocBook has lost some of its appeal in the last few years for several reasons. DocBook:

- Was designed for the creation of books, not materials on the Web
- Does not support reuse well
- Is overly complex

DocBook is still in use and is not likely to go away for a long time to come. DocBook is appropriate for content that is largely print-based. DocBook is frequently used for narrative documents and in areas like government.

DocBook is seeing a resurgence in the increased use of XQuery. XQuery is a recommendation of the W3C and is supported by all the major database engines (IBM, Oracle, Microsoft, and so on). XQuery is to XML what SQL is to database tables. That is, it's a language for extracting data from XML repositories, just as SQL is a query language for extracting data from relational databases. In fact, XQuery is semantically similar to SQL, but is designed specifically for finding and extracting elements and attributes from XML documents. Many companies are converting their existing content to DocBook because XQuery can:

- Query/search any XML-based content, regardless of schema.
- Automatically extract and reassemble content in any desired configuration.
- Repurpose content without pre-chunking.

XML formats for publishing

A variety of different XML formats can be used for XML publishing including:

- Text Encoding Initiative (TEI)
- National Library of Medicine (NLM)
- DocBook
- DITA for Publishers

TEI

TEI (Text Encoding Initiative) is an extremely rich and complex tag set, consisting of nearly 500 elements. In practice, most practitioners use far fewer tags. A typical document is likely to use fewer than 50.

TEI is managed by the Text Encoding Initiative Consortium that develops and maintains a standard for the representation of texts in digital form. The complexity of the TEI tag set is caused by TEI's goal of providing "a framework for encoding (in theory) any genre of text from any period in any language."

http://www.tei-c.org/index.xml

NLM

National Library of Medicine (NLM) is a DTD developed by the US National Library of Medicine to structure information for publication in scientific and medical journals and other publications.

NLM is fast becoming the de facto XML standard for scientific journals and publications, especially those in the medical field.

The US National Library of Medicine is the world's largest medical library. In order to structure and organize information, including information published in medical journals, the library chose XML as the tagging methodology. In order to capture the data required, they developed their own DTDs. These DTDs are known as the NLM DTDs.

http://www.nlm.nih.gov/news/electronic_archiving.html

DITA for publishers

The DITA for Publishers project is an open-source community project to enable the quick and productive use of DITA by publishers. DITA for publishers provides:

- DITA specializations for common publishing document components (article, chapter, subsection, sidebar, part)
- Plug-ins for HTML, PDF, EPUB, and Kindle
- Ability to convert styled Word documents to DITA
- Ability to produce InCopy and InDesign documents from DITA content

http://dita4publishers.sourceforge.net

Summary

There is no need to fear working with XML; today's XML authoring tools are Microsoft Word-like or are even Microsoft Word itself, which makes it simple to create XML-based content.

XML is not the only technology solution for reuse, but it's the most powerful by far. XML provides the best functionality of SGML and the ease-of-use of HTML, the best of both worlds.

XML provides powerful support for a unified content strategy through:

- Structured content
- Separation of content and format
- Built-in metadata
- Database orientation
- XSL stylesheets
- Personalization

Chapter 20

The role of content management

This chapter discusses the different ways to manage your content through authoring tools, many types of content management systems (CMSs), workflow, and delivery tools.

Authoring tools

Before content can be managed, manipulated, or reused, it must be created. Authoring tools enable authors to create that content. To support a unified content strategy, authoring tools must allow content to be written so it can be structured and reused according to the content lifecycle you identified earlier.

An overview of authoring tools

Authoring tools are among the oldest and most mature tools available for the desktop. The dominant authoring tool on the market is Microsoft Word, which has become almost ubiquitous. However, there are still many other tools, all with different capabilities, strengths, and weaknesses. There are also an increasing number of XML authoring tools on the market. Additionally, many of the traditional tools are adding or have added XML capabilities. For the purposes of this discussion, authoring tools are broken into two types:

- Traditional word processing and page layout tools

- Structured editors

Traditional word processing and page layout tools

If you plan to stay with traditional tools, you should understand what they are, as well as what they're capable of doing. There are really four types of traditional tools: word processing tools, page layout tools, hybrids that combine the functionality (to some degree) of both word processor and page layout tools, and web authoring tools.

- Word processing tools were originally designed as memo and letter authoring tools; they are focused on authoring. They have been designed to make it easy to enter text and apply formatting.

- Page layout tools typically have had weak text entry capabilities; instead, they rely on importing text from word processors. Their focus has been on formatting content for page layout. Page layout tools are the tools of creative services and they have tremendous typographical control for exacting output standards.

- Hybrids are a cross between word processors and page layout tools, typically designed to manage long documents. Their text editing capabilities are better than page layout tools, but not always as complete as word processors. Their formatting capabilities are better than word processors, but not as good as the page layout tools.

- Web authoring tools are designed to enable authors to create web content. They are usually based on custom-designed templates that match the organization's requirements and provide rudimentary formatting capabilities. Because authors are not creating large documents, web authoring tools don't always have features like search and replace or tables.

Structured editors

If XML is part of your authoring environment, you have the option of using structured editors as your authoring tool. Structured editors enforce the structure of content, typically based on a model such as a DTD (Document Type Definition). There are XML-aware tools (traditional tools with integrated XML), native XML editors (editors that allow authors to create and produce content directly in XML), and other editors that enforce structure in different ways.

There are four types of structured editors:

- Full function editors

  A full function editor is based on XML as its data format and it provides the equivalent functionality of something like Microsoft Word, but for XML. It includes spell checkers, table tools, book building tools, and all the usual functions that authors expect to see, but it enforces the structure of content as that content is entered and uses XML. Usually, full function editors provide a WYSIWYG view of the text that is familiar to most authors: a view that shows the structure of the content (displays tags and hierarchy), and a full XML view that displays the XML.

- Simple XML editors

  A simple XML editor is a capable editor, but includes only the functionality for the basic entry of text and XML markup. It does not include any of the book-building tools of traditional or full function tools. It might be more suited to programmers than authors.

- XML-aware tools

  XML-aware tools attempt to combine the ease of use of a traditional word processor or desktop publishing tool with the power of XML. They embed XML functions directly in the familiar authoring tool so the interface looks much like the one that authors are used to, but provides XML as the output.

- Forms-based authoring systems

  Forms-based authoring tools are usually provided as optional functionality on XML-based CMSs. They are used to create web-based HTML forms that provide text entry capabilities. They are most effective for simple structures. Form-based authoring can also provide benefits to geographically dispersed content creation teams or individuals with special remote access needs.

Capabilities and requirements for structured content

When deciding what you want an authoring tool to do, it's vital that you consider the needs of authors, not just the interests of the tool evaluators. Too often, solutions are chosen based on an incomplete interpretation of what authors need, not their true needs. That means you have to talk to the authors and determine their real authoring needs (refer to Chapter 9, "Analyzing the content lifecycle"). You also have to look at your unified content lifecycle vision to determine what kind of authoring functionality you will need to support the vision (refer to Chapter 11, "Envisioning your unified content strategy and lifecycle").

When you evaluate authors' needs, you may find that you need different tools for different groups throughout the enterprise. You will probably have casual authors who submit content occasionally, authors who submit content on a continuous basis, and authors who compile and configure content into multiple information products. Even authors who submit content frequently have different needs; some contribute small pieces of information with simple structures and others create large, complex information products.

Familiarity

Given that people do not always accept change easily, there can be an advantage to sticking with the tools they know. The main advantage of traditional word processing tools is that they are familiar to most employees. Tools like Microsoft Word are very common on the corporate desktop and authors have become accustomed to their look and their functionality.

Structured authoring tools, on the other hand, have been around for many years, but have not gained the same popularity. The tools with embedded support have a familiar interface, but the technology and the technological concepts behind the interface are new. For other XML tools, both the interface and the concepts will be new to authors.

If you are dealing with casual, nontechnical authors, there is a distinct advantage to staying with a familiar tool. With the release of Microsoft Office 2007, the entire Office suite was XML-enabled by Microsoft. This means that your authors can continue to work in their familiar Office products and have the content converted to your XML structure. However, note that authors do need to use styles and adhere to specified structures.

Technical complexity

Traditional authoring tools are easy for even casual authors to use. That is not the case with most structured editors. In selecting a structured editor, a key factor to consider is how much of the underlying technology is exposed to authors. Do you have them edit the codes directly, or do you hide the code from them?

Of course, if you do choose XML, you have additional options. Since XML is markup that is application-independent, you can select different authoring tools for different groups of authors in your organization. Authors with very simple authoring tasks can use an editor with simple editing functionality. Authors who have more complex authoring tasks will need a more complex tool. Structured editors range from simple file editing tools (that is, tools that are used for editing a file but have no capacity for book building) to full function tools that include all the usual capabilities of standard authoring tools.

Structural and stylistic control

The biggest disadvantage to traditional word processing and page layout tools is that they offer too much flexibility. They do not prevent authors from creating new styles or applying formatting to suit their own views of how information should look on the page. The result is inconsistent formatting and style names. There is also no built-in functionality to ensure that authors include all the components required for the information product they are writing. In other words, there is nothing to enforce structure. Style names imply structure only. Users can easily ignore the styles and format directly.

Documents created with traditional word processing and page layout tools might all look alike on the surface, but they may not look alike "under the covers" with authors manually creating the look-and-feel rather than using consistent style tags. This process is inefficient for authors and has a major effect on conversion to other formats; content that is not consistently formatted (tagged) cannot be automatically converted to another format. It requires manual cleanup. An alternative is to enforce formatting and structure through policy and procedure (editorial or review), but such reviews are never 100 percent effective. The result is inconsistency. Inconsistency means unpredictability, which is a killer for reuse and multichannel output.

Structured editors do not have the same problems with format. As the name suggests, the focus of *structured* editors is on the structure of the document. Most structured editors provide the ability to attach a stylesheet to documents, which serves primarily to provide a certain comfort level for authors. The obvious advantage of structured editors is that they use XML, with great advantages for reuse (see Chapter 19, "The role of XML"). More importantly, structured editors are capable of reading and enforcing a DTD or schema. At their simplest, structured editors allow authors to validate the structure of a document by identifying any structural errors in the document, including when components are not allowed or when they are missing.

Some editors do not allow authors to insert invalid elements of structure. For example, they would not allow authors to insert a table in a title. The most capable tools provide authors with drop-down lists or menus of elements that are valid in the document. As authors move the cursor around the document from element to element, the drop-down menu changes to show the valid elements. This capability prevents authors from entering tags where they are not allowed. This type of structured editor does not allow authors to make structural mistakes.

Separation of format and content

Traditional tools make it easy for authors to make documents look good and, in doing so, they have turned authors into desktop publishers. But from the perspective of reuse, this is not a good thing for many reasons.

Word processors and desktop publishing tools helped to make documents very attractive and, potentially, more usable. Authors enter the characters that form the content, then select them and apply the formatting. For reuse, you need to remove this formatting to make the content device independent, then apply formatting that is appropriate to each intended use. Stripping and reapplying formatting always requires correction by hand or complicated scripting.

XML does not have this problem. The presentation information (styles) is maintained in separate files that can then be associated with the document when it is published or used.

Integration with a CMS

While authors can create content, save the content, and then check the file(s) into a CMS, it's preferable to have the authoring tools integrated directly into the CMS. This means that when authors select File > Open, the authoring tool automatically goes to the CMS to select content and when authors do a File > Save, the content is automatically saved to the CMS and any version control information is gathered. In addition, if your organization has decided to use automatic reuse, it is important that the content be automatically populated to the document open in the authoring tool.

To pick authoring tools, whether for department use or for enterprise use, you must start by developing a list of criteria to match prospective solutions against. The authoring tool you choose for your department, division, or company should be picked based on its ability to meet specific criteria. These criteria should definitely include functionality, but must also take into account broader concerns like price, environment, and the capabilities of your authors.

Content management systems

Content management is an integral component of a successful unified content strategy and selecting the right CMS can be a lengthy investigational process.

One of the hardest decisions is selecting the type of CMS to use. To help you make this choice, this chapter outlines the many types of CMSs and their advantages and disadvantages.

Understanding content management

Content is created in an authoring tool and then saved into the CMS. Content may be saved as individual components, after which the metadata is added (see "Metadata" later in this chapter). Within the CMS, content is managed and then delivered to the appropriate channel.

Segmentation/bursting

To assist authors in writing contextually, content can be authored in documents or components, but content may be reused at a much more granular level (for example, step or paragraph). Before being stored in the CMS, content is broken apart into its individual components and then stored. The process of breaking content into its element parts is called segmentation or bursting.

You define the level of segmentation in a segmentation map or bursting map. For example, you may decide that content should be saved as individual components only at the third-level head, but not within the content of the section that is contained under the third-level head. Alternatively you may decide that content needs to be broken down at each element. Organizations often have different segmentation maps for different types of content.

Metadata

Metadata may be applied to the content in the authoring tool or it may be applied to the content as it is checked into the CMS. Wherever possible, you want metadata automatically applied to the components of content.

The management system

The management portion of the CMS manages the content through such features as access control, check in/check out, and version control.

Access control

Access control secures content and identifies who can read, create, modify, and delete content.

Access is based on roles. For example, you may determine that authors can create, modify, and delete their own content, editors can only modify content, designers can modify templates but not content, and others can only view (read) content.

Certain components may be accessible only to a certain group (for example, marketing can access all content, but engineering can only access their own materials). Check to ensure that you can set access control at any level of granularity. If the information product is secured at a specific level, then all the content in the information product should be secured at the same level of security as well.

If content is reused and secured at one level in one document, the access control should automatically be the same level wherever it is reused. You may decide to have individual component access control levels as well as container and information product model access control levels. For example, the company logo has no security restrictions associated with it. But for an audit report, the company logo is restricted to senior management viewing only (restricted viewing at the information product level). In an information product where the viewing of the logo is not restricted (for example, a brochure), anyone can view that component. The logo element takes on the restriction of the information product where it is reused.

Version control

Version control ensures that each time content is checked in, another version (copy) is created and is assigned a new version number. This ensures that content will never be accidentally overwritten and that every change can be tracked. It also enables you to use multiple versions of the same content in different situations (for example, more recent versions of products where the previous version is still being supported). Reviewers like to look at previous versions of content to see what has changed and to ensure that changes have been correctly incorporated.

It's important to be able to version each component, not just at the information product level. It's also important to be able to version an entire approved information product as it is delivered (for example, an instance of the website as it was posted on a particular date, the final version of a report, the latest version of the brochure). In this way you can easily identify the information product with all its individual components as it existed on a specific day for tracking, legal, or retrieval purposes, or go back to that version rapidly. Sometimes this version is called a released version, the delivered instance, or in the case of a website, an edition.

Updates

Reused content can be updated in a number of ways. Authors who reuse the content can select which type of update they want the reusable content to have. There are three types of updates available:

- Automatically update

  Automatically updates the reused component when the original (source) component is changed. This means that authors who reuse the content are not notified; instead, the content is automatically updated. Automatic update can save a lot of time for authors since they do not have to check and verify that they want to reuse the content. However, an automatic update could cause problems. The update may not be relevant or correct in the reuse situation. Automatic update could then result in incorrect information.

- Optionally update

  The CMS notifies authors of the changes so they can decide if they want to update the component or not. This helps authors ensure that the update is relevant to them, but requires them to review the update and decide to accept or reject it.

- No update

  If the original component is updated, the reused component will not be updated and authors will not be notified if the original component changes. The reused component now exists as a separate component (similar to copy and paste). This option should be discouraged unless there is a good reason for the choice (for example, branching of information) since content will diverge and become inconsistent over time.

Authors reusing the content are responsible for determining what type of update they want on the reused components. The system default is usually "optionally update."

Check in/check out

When authors want to work on content, they check it out (sign it out) and check it back in again when they are finished with it. This ensures that only one person is working on the same content at any one time and that multiple people cannot concurrently change (or save) the content and create a conflict (which version is correct?) or even destroy the version that was saved by the first person. It's possible to check out previous and current versions of content; when changes occur to both versions, the content branches. This should be discouraged unless it's absolutely necessary (for example, a product that starts off as one product then splits into two products) because it could cause confusion or inaccuracies if the wrong version of the content is used.

Search and retrieval

Good search and retrieval functionality is important in ensuring that authors can easily find and retrieve content for reuse and delivery. It should be possible to search and retrieve content based on individual components, containers, and whole information products. Full-text retrieval searches on the text of the content. Metadata can be used to narrow the focus of the search.

Archive

Previous versions of content that are finalized and approved but no longer current should be archived (stored). Content is archived based on a set of rules that specify the period of time in which the content is considered to be valid or accurate. The CMS can automatically delete expired content or can prompt a manager to review the content and determine if it should be archived.

Translation

Managing content in multiple languages becomes important if you translate your content. It's not enough just to store the multiple language versions of your content; you must ensure that the CMS can create a relationship between your source language (original language) and the localized content. A relationship between the source language and the localized content ensures that when the source language changes, the localized content is identified (using metadata) as requiring new translation. Without a relationship between the source language and the translated content, managing the identification of change is very time-consuming and error-prone.

Many organizations use memory translation tools to assist in the translation process. It's advantageous for the CMS to integrate directly with a translation memory tool to further facilitate the translation process (for example, the translators can retrieve content directly from the CMS rather than having to extract the content, send it to the localization firm, and then reintegrate the translated content).

The types of content management systems

One of the hardest decisions to make about content management is which type of CMS makes the most sense to purchase. There are many different types of CMSs that focus on many different content lifecycles. Web content management is the most familiar type of CMS but there are a number of other types of content management. Each type of CMS has its advantages and disadvantages. In this section we describe the types of content management.

Web content management systems

The term *content management system* has become synonymous with web content management systems. There have been document management systems for over a decade, but it was the advent of the Web and the issues of managing large websites that popularized content management and content management systems.

Web content management systems (WCMSs) assist an organization in automating various aspects of web content creation, content management, and delivery. Delivery to the web is its primary format, but many WCMSs also deliver to mobile.

Advantages

The interface and functionality of a WCMS are designed to support website creation and management content lifecycle, and to provide strong support for collaborative authoring, testing, and controlled delivery of content to a website.

Typically, WCMSs include their own authoring tool, either an HTML editor or web-based forms. Some provide an automatic conversion of content from traditional authoring tools into HTML that can be processed by the WCMS.

Authoring and management is managed in stages with authors working in their own content work area to create content, view and review the content, and test functionality. When content has been approved, it's moved into a staging area where it's assembled according to your design and integrated with content from other work areas. When content in the staging area is approved, an edition (version) of the content is created. This edition can then be posted to the site to replace existing content. The editions can be archived so that if there is a problem (for example, error introduced to the site) content can be rapidly rolled back (returned) to a previous edition.

Support of the web content lifecycle is very valuable to organizations as it ensures that content is thoroughly reviewed and tested before it is delivered to the site. It also ensures that only content that meets certain criteria is posted to the site, which prevents problems of incorrect content or content that does not function (for example, error 404). A WCMS can also hold content until a specific date when it becomes effective and can automatically remove content from the website when the content has expired (no longer current/relevant).

Personalization is also a strong component of many WCMSs supporting dynamic creation of content. Personalization enables the WCMS to provide personalized content to users.

Delivery to the Web and often to mobile devices is directly integrated in the WCMS, unlike a paper-oriented CMS where an additional publishing tool is often required.

Disadvantages

A WCMS is designed to create, manage, and deliver web-based content and potentially mobile content only. In an enterprise environment where paper and the complexities of paper (for example, sophisticated page layout and support of table of contents [TOC] and index) are required, a WCMS fails to meet these needs.

In addition to the lack of support of other types of content, the level of granularity of reuse may be insufficient for your requirements. Granularity of a web page is supported and often granularity of components within a web page is supported, particularly if the WCMS also provides personalization functionality. However, functionality like conditional reuse and granular content that can be exchanged among different types of content is rarely supported.

If the WCMS relies on an HTML editor or forms for input, the complexities of other types of content will not be supported.

The majority of WCMSs are not XML-based systems. They can sometimes import XML and possibly export XML, but they tend not to manage XML in its native format. Instead a WCMS manages XML as just another file type.

If you plan to create an enterprise unified content strategy with a wide variety of information products support and a variety of channels, a WCMS is probably not the best solution for you. Treat the Web as a channel and manage your content elsewhere.

Transactional content management systems

A number of CMSs have been specifically designed to manage eCommerce transactions (B2B or B2C). Transactional CMSs (TCMSs) are focused on managing the exchange of money over the Web and product eCatalogs. They typically integrate with legacy systems for inventory, pricing, and shipping. In addition, they provide shopping cart functionality that enables customers to select products for purchase and track the cost of their potential purchases.

Most TCMSs manage transactional information and provide full WCMS capability.

Advantages

TCMSs' greatest strengths are their strong support of eCommerce interactions and their ability to interface with legacy systems for the transfer of product information.

Disadvantages

Like a WCMS, a TCMS is web-based only and does not support the requirements of enterprise content.

A TCMS can be one of your channels but should not be your primary content management system.

Document management systems

Document management systems (DMSs) have been around much longer than WCMSs. Document management systems have traditionally managed enterprise documents (for example, correspondence, reports, publications). A DMS can interface with multiple types of authoring tools to manage multiple types of content. However, unless the content is converted internally to a common format, it cannot be reused among different types of content.

A DMS can deliver content in the original source format (for example, Word in, Word out), frequently convert to other formats (for example, Word in, HTML out), and produce PDF versions of content.

A common function of many DMSs is the imaging of content. Many organizations require the ability to image paper-based content that comes in from an external source (for example, customer correspondence, patient records), and then manage that image as they would their other content.

DMSs have gained widespread acceptance in organizations where security of content and strong control of content are required (for example, organizations that produce products regulated by government or agencies). To support this usage, many DMSs have very robust audit trails (clear history of what has occurred for every piece of content, who made the change and why, and the series of authorizations the content has gone through). They may also include electronic signatures to securely verify authorization of content.

Some DMSs may have CRM (customer relationship management) and web content management components.

Advantages

DMSs have been around much longer than any other type of CMS so the interface is stable. In addition, the vendors that sell them tend to be financially stable.

DMSs are very strong on traditional content management (check in/check out, version control, access control, workflow, archiving, and audit trails).

Some provide the ability to deliver publications and web content.

Disadvantages

Because DMS tools have come from the document management world, they do not always provide effective component content management. While most can output HTML, not all support the web content lifecycle.

Because DMSs have come from the document management world, they typically do not provide good support for a unified content strategy.

Component content management systems

A component content management system (CCMS) manages content at a granular (component) level, rather than at the page or document level. Each component represents a single topic, concept, or asset (such as an image or table). Components are assembled into multiple content assemblies (content types) and can be viewed as components or as traditional pages or documents. Each component has its own lifecycle (owner, version, approval, use) and can be tracked individually, or as part of an assembly. A CCMS is typically used for multichannel, customer-facing content (marketing, usage, learning, support). A CCMS can be a separate system or a functionality of another content management type (such as an enterprise content management system).

A CCMS can come in five "flavors": dedicated, web, publishing, learning content management, or enterprise.

Dedicated

Dedicated systems developed out of the technical documentation industry's requirement for multichannel publishing—first to print and help; then to print, help, and web; and now also to mobile devices. Component management was built into these systems to address not only the specific requirements of multiple channels, but more importantly, differences in product, platform, audience, and content type. Many of these systems have existed for more than a decade, working first with SGML, and now with XML.

Note that these systems typically publish to HTML or produce websites, but they do not have the capability to manage such functionality as deployment, dynamic personalization, or more generalized website management.

Dedicated CCMSs have component content management down to a fine art, managing multiple levels of granularity, complex reuse, reuse governance, and integration with multiple systems for content/data integration and publication.

Web component content management

Component-oriented web content management systems (WCCMs) are full-fledged web content management tools that have a component orientation rather than a page orientation. They usually have the capability of publishing to multiple channels—including print—but rarely can manage complex print projects. Most WCCM system vendors regard their products as WCMSs.

Publishing

Publishing-oriented component content management systems (PCCMSs) are designed to meet the needs of the publishing industry. Content is managed as native XML and content as components.

PCCMSs are designed with the publishing workflow in mind. They support internal and external authors, the copyediting lifecycle, and publication to both composition tools for print layout and eBooks. They can interface with traditional word processing tools and structured editors.

They can typically publish to HTML, though they are not designed to manage websites. Most also publish to mobile.

Consider a PCCMS when your primary focus is print books and eBooks.

Learning content management systems

Learning component content management systems (LCCMSs) are designed assist in the creation, management, and delivery of learning materials. They support the complete process of content authoring, content management, reuse, workflow, and delivery. They are XML-based and support the creation of print-based materials like ILT (instructor-led training), PowerPoint slides, eLearning, and mobile. They have a simple-to-use interface that makes it easy for instructional designers to create structured content.

For more information, refer to the section below on learning content management systems.

Enterprise

There are often situations where component content management needs to span the enterprise. Technology that can meet enterprise requirements could be an ECM system that can handle component content management, or it could be a component content management system that can support enterprise content. The numbers of vendors that can do this is still small, but it is possible to find a few that do. To be successful at component content management, an enterprise system must:

- Manage XML, not as just another file type, but recognize and use the structure of XML to manage the content.

- Manage content components.

- Support content reuse at a fairly granular level (i.e., smaller than a component), track reuse, manage derivatives, and move components through workflow.

- Support multichannel publishing.

  Consider an enterprise system with a component content management focus when your content needs to bridge departments (silos) in the enterprise.

Learning content management systems

Learning content management systems (LCMSs) are content management systems that support the web-based learning materials content lifecycle and the components of learning content (for example, text, graphics, simulations, multimedia).

An LCMS supports text-based content, but it also supports multimedia components (sound, video, animation). Many of these tools are actually web-based learning authoring tools combined with a content management system that handles traditional CMS functionality, reuse, and delivery. In addition to standard web-based authoring, the LCMS may include tools for the creation of simulations and animations.

Traditional learning content management systems are dedicated to eLearning and do not publish well to any other channel.

Some LCMSs contain learning management system (LMS) functionality such as registration, course tracking, and evaluation, but most integrate with a separate LMS.

Advantages

LCMSs were specifically designed to manage the learning content management lifecycle. No other CMS can currently handle this lifecycle effectively. LCMS vendors have been working hard to implement SCORM to ensure that their customers can create reusable eLearning materials.

An LCMS can deliver the functionality of an eLearning authoring tool with the added functionality of a content management system.

Disadvantages

Like WCM systems, LCM systems have been specifically designed to manage web-based eLearning content. A few provide paper output but it is very rudimentary.

The LCMS is a closed environment. The vendors assume that authors will author only in the tool and not need to accept content from other systems, nor share content with another type of content management system. Therefore, this means that it is very difficult to share reusable content with other content areas in the organization.

Enterprise content management systems

Many WCM and some DMS vendors have started to use the phrase *enterprise content management* (ECM) to describe their products. As organizations have looked around and said web content management is good, but we need to manage other types of content as well, vendors have begun to respond with ECM systems.

The meaning of enterprise content management varies from vendor to vendor, with vendors approaching ECM in different ways. Some now provide XML-based systems that can interface with XML-based publishing tools to provide paper output, while others have continued to focus on web-based delivery but now include eCommerce functionality or customer relationship management functionality. Some have simply incorporated PDF delivery. Some DMS vendors now support more robust web delivery and call themselves enterprise content management systems.

Advantages

ECM vendors support a broader-based content management lifecycle.

Disadvantages

There is currently no consistency in what is called an enterprise content management system. The increased functionality may or may not meet your enterprise content management needs.

Other

There are other types of content management systems, but they usually do not address the requirements of a unified content strategy.

Customer relationship management (CRM) systems collect and integrate customer information. They manage information such as customer contact information, products and configurations of products they have purchased, the kinds of questions they have asked, and buyer profiles. When integrated across an enterprise, CRM systems can allow the company to consistently present one face to the customer and work toward improving customer retention. These systems tend to manage data, but they often need to share data and content among other systems in the organization.

Database versus CMS

Content management systems use a database for storing content. Frequently, organizations consider whether a database alone is sufficient for their requirements.

You could use a database for storing your content and many organizations do, but a database provides only a portion of the functionality of a content management system. A database begins life as a blank slate where there is no structure, no functionality, no interface until you create it. Think of the CMS as a user interface to the database. A CMS provides a tremendous amount of functionality out of the box such as:

- Predefined content repository model
- Support for content relationships
- Built-in reports (such as where used, history, relationships)
- Simplified creation of metadata
- Pre-configured system triggers (for example, notification of change)
- Version control
- Access control (security)
- Integration with authoring tool(s)
- Workflow

To recreate and maintain this functionality could be more costly then purchasing an off-the-shelf product.

Can one CMS do it all?

Can one content management system meet all your enterprise content requirements? Unfortunately the answer to this question is "maybe." As you can see by the description of the many types of content management systems available, they each have their advantages and disadvantages. And, each type of CMS supports different content lifecycles.

We recommend that you select a component content management system. If one of the different types of CCMSs can meet the majority of your needs, then select that type of system. Treat your web content as a channel only. Do not manage source content in your WCMS. You still need a WCMS to manage all the functionality but consider storing your source content in a CCMS and pushing it to a WCMS.

The key to a single solution is the ability to share content among the CMS, the authoring tools, and the delivery tools. If your organization has chosen to use XML, this can greatly facilitate the sharing of information. If you haven't chosen to use XML, but your CMS can import content from a variety of authoring tools, combine the content appropriately (for example, convert into a common format), and then provide appropriate reusable content back to the authoring tools, you might be able to use a single solution.

If your organization decides to go with "best of breed" tools, like a web content management tool that is really good at creating web content but poor at creating paper content, you still have to share information among content management systems. After all, the key to a successful unified content strategy lies in the ability to share content. Effective sharing of content requires the systems to interpret content as it moves from system to system. Interpreting content is dependent on:

- Common information models (structures)

- Common ways of tagging content (style/structure tags)

- Common metadata

Workflow systems

Workflow systems are critical in a unified content strategy because they help to ensure that content flows smoothly through the content lifecycle. Workflow systems make sure that everybody contributes their required content, that content is reviewed and approved at the necessary stages, and that it is delivered to its various outputs. Rather than relying on manual processes, workflow systems automate them, handling the interrelationships among processes and tracking the status of the project at any given time. Workflow systems allow work to be assigned, routed, approved, acted upon, and managed using system-controlled rules that you set up when you design your workflow. (For more information about designing effective workflow, refer to Chapter 14, "Designing workflow".)

Workflow systems may be included as part of the CMS you select or they may be stand-alone systems. If your CMS has workflow included, it's particularly important to ensure that it meets your needs. Sometimes embedded workflow systems are specific to only one application of content or they may be more rudimentary than stand-alone systems.

Creation

The creation component enables workflow authors (for example, content strategists, business analysts) to create and test workflow processes. Creation typically consists of:

- Process flow creation

  Workflow authors create graphical representations of the workflow, selecting from predefined interactions (for example, print) or creating new interactions if required.

- Process testing

  Workflow authors can simulate a process using test data. Testing workflow under a variety of circumstances before implementing it can be extremely beneficial.

- Ability to learn

  Some workflow tools learn from user interactions, creating new workflows based on their analysis of user processes. The automatically created workflows can then be reviewed for validity and usefulness by your organization. This capability is not the norm in most workflow systems and it's not a must-have; it's nice to have. By identifying repetitive processes, the workflow system can help to point out areas where workflow could be automated.

Processing

The processing component of a workflow system activates and manages workflow, handling such things as routing work based on rules you set up when you design workflow.

Routing

Routing moves work through the workflow system. For example, once content is identified as ready for review, it is automatically routed to the reviewers or reviewers are notified that the content is ready for review so they can link to it. Work can be routed in a number of ways:

- Sequential

  Sequential routing moves work through the workflow in a linear fashion. As a step is completed, work is automatically routed to the next step in the process. For example, content that is identified as ready for review is automatically routed to reviewers. Sequential routing is the simplest form of workflow.

- Rules-based

  Rules-based routing enables the system to determine how to route content based on logic. For example, if this is content for Product X, it should be routed to the Product X reviewers, but if it is for Product Y, then it should be routed to Product Y reviewers. Rules-based workflow enables the system to make intelligent decisions about how to handle work based on certain conditions. Rules also assist in handling exceptions. For more information, see "Rules" later in this chapter.

- Parallel

  Parallel routing routes work simultaneously, so one part of the work isn't delayed while another part is completed. For example, content for a new brochure can be assigned at the same time as the graphics; the graphics don't have to wait for the content to be finished. However, you may want to include a "wait" step at the end of the parallel processes before the work continues through the flow. For example, if graphics are completed before the content, you could include a wait step to hold the graphics until the content is complete so they can be integrated for review.

- Ad hoc

  Ad hoc workflows do not follow a set of rules. Instead, they involve human decisions. Ad hoc workflow is the least used, but can be useful to assist in one-time or unplanned situations. For example, if you have to issue an addendum immediately to announce a change in staff, or to correct a problem users are having with a product, ad hoc workflow lets you route content only to where it's needed immediately, bypassing others. Ad hoc workflow is also useful when it's not possible or necessary to apply a rule to a decision.

Rules

Rules define what happens under what circumstances. They determine how content and tasks are routed through workflow. For example, when content has been identified as "ready for review" (that is, the author has selected "ready for review" metadata), that content is either routed automatically to the reviewers, or reviewers are notified that content is ready for them to review. The rule may look something like:

```
if metadata= "ready for review" then step 3
```

Exceptions to the rule

Rules should also include exceptions to the normal situation. An exception to the rule tells the system how to process a task when it does not meet all the requirements to continue through the workflow. For example, what happens if three reviewers have been assigned to review some content, two reviewers have completed the review, and the third is on vacation?

The exception tells the system to automatically route the content to an alternate reviewer. What happens if that reviewer is off sick and no one else is identified as a reviewer in the workflow processes? If the rule states explicitly that content must have three reviews completed before it can move to the next stage in the workflow process, the content will be delayed until a third reviewer is available. An exception could state that if a third reviewer is unavailable, the content must be routed as though it had three reviews, or it must be routed to a manager to decide if the two reviews suffice.

Administration

The administration portion of the workflow system is where all activity is tracked. Administration matches roles to tasks, assigning who—or which system—does what, it manages security (who can see or do what), deadlines, and reporting when tasks are done.

Players (roles assignment)

In a unified content strategy, different people (players) perform various tasks at different stages in a process, and the workflow system must keep track of who is responsible for what. For example, some players create content while others review it and approve it. In a workflow system, the system itself is also a player (for example, once the content is approved the system may initiate an action to deliver the content to the website automatically).

While players perform many of the steps in the process, it is important to be able to assign a role to an action or a step rather than a person. Many players can then be assigned to a role and a change in a player will not require a change to the workflow. For example, Fred Turnbull was responsible for the final approval for all Product X information. He has been promoted to general manager and is now responsible for final approval of the entire product suite. Rather than changing the workflow to indicate his changed title, he is just removed from the Product X approver role and assigned to the Product X Suite approver role. The tasks stay with the role, not the person.

To move workflow along, it's also beneficial to assign more than one player to a role. That way, if the first person is unable to perform a task, workflow moves the task to the next person whose role is assigned to that task. For example, Nancy Smith is the senior graphic artist who creates graphics for all Product X's web-based information products. If she is on vacation when a request comes through for some new graphics, the workflow system identifies that she is unavailable and routes the request for graphics to Michael Hotley, another graphic designer associated with that role.

Security and electronic signature

Just like content, workflow should have security assigned to it. It should be possible to apply a security level to any part of a workflow to control who can create, modify, delete, and view a workflow. Security can apply to:

- Players
- Groups
- Roles
- Workflow
- Steps
- Tasks
- Objects

Security controls who can start a workflow process, handle an exception, view reports, or change priorities.

Electronic signatures may be a part of security. An electronic signature, like a traditional signature, indicates that work has received some level of sign-off or approval. The ability to use/apply an electronic signature should be strictly controlled. Electronic signatures are particularly important in regulated industries.

Deadlines and escalation

Within a workflow system, each step or activity has a deadline assigned to it. If the deadline is missed, a series of actions should occur (for example, send reminder messages, escalation). Escalation actions can route the issue to a supervisor or manager to ensure that the action is completed and does not hold up the process. For example, imagine that content has been routed to three reviewers, and two of the reviewers have completed their reviews and returned their comments but the third has not. The system sends the reviewer reminder messages that get increasingly more demanding. After the third reminder the reviewer's manager is notified that the review has not been completed and the number of days the review has been delayed. The manager speaks directly to the reviewer and the reviewer completes the review that day.

Deadlines can be defined to occur after a certain period of time elapses (duration), or can prompt the user to enter a deadline. A workflow system can define different deadlines at different levels, including:

- Step

  The step is assigned a duration deadline (for example, three days) or a specific date of completion.

- Task

  The entire task can be assigned a duration or date of completion. This means that the individual steps do not have a specific duration, but the entire task must be completed after a certain period of time has elapsed or by a specific date.

Sometimes you may find that one workflow process needs to take precedence over another process. It's important to be able to change the deadlines to reprioritize the processes.

Reporting

You can create reports to monitor the status of a process as well as individual and group performance (for example, how long does it take to create a new web page?) Reports can also be automatically generated at a specific point in the workflow. For example, a report detailing who worked on a document, how long it took at each stage, and any missed deadlines could be automatically generated and routed to management as soon as a document is approved.

Workflow systems typically provide a variety of reports. Sample reports include:

- Deadline reports identify upcoming deadlines and deadlines that have been missed.

- Work-in-process reports track what steps have been completed, the location of outstanding items, and whether or not a process is on schedule. Work-in-process reports can also determine the volume of work and any backlog in processes.

- Exception reports identify where exceptions have occurred and the frequency of their occurrence. Repeated exceptions may indicate that the workflow needs to be revised to avoid further exceptions.

- Workload balance reports identify how much work a player in the process has waiting to be addressed. The report can assist managers in identifying if one player has too much work while another has insufficient work, so the workload can be rebalanced. If the workload balance is frequently too high or low, it can identify that new rules need to be put in place to avoid these problems in the future.

Delivery

The design and organization of information is a key factor in creating a unified content strategy. But without a capable delivery engine, a unified content strategy is just an exercise in data collection. To turn your data into usable content, you must assemble it, format it, and deliver it to your user community, whenever and however they need it.

Delivery systems have many different capabilities. The content management system may have built-in facilities for delivering content, or you may have to integrate a delivery system with your content management system. Some delivery systems will enable you to deliver to a variety of outputs (for example, web, HTML, PDF), while others may be restricted to a single output.

Some delivery mechanisms reside on the desktop; others are server-based and are available to everyone. Some delivery systems can interface with content management systems, web servers, portal servers, and other systems.

Capabilities

To determine the type of delivery system you need, you must first understand the range of capabilities available in current products. Products may have all or some of the following capabilities:

- Transformation
- Conversion
- Distribution
- Assembly
- Automation

You need to ask the right questions when you are selecting a delivery system that will meet the needs of your authors and the requirements of your unified content strategy.

Transformation

In the past, information was typically delivered to a single channel. It was designed for that channel and republished each time the information changed. That is no longer the case. With the popularity of web-based publishing, information is typically output to multiple channels, including HTML, print, and mobile. The content may be identical, with format optimized for the channel. Or, the content may be tailored for use in the output channel. Whatever the channel, a key function of any delivery system is the transformation of information from its stored format to the required channel. Delivering unified content requires the ability to publish not only to traditional outputs (for example, paper and web), but also to XML, PDF, and mobile.

Output support

An obvious first question is what output formats are supported by the delivery system:

- PostScript?
- PDF?
- HTML?
- XML?
- Microsoft Word?

The next question to ask is whether the tool supports output to multiple formats for a single publishing request? For example, can you create a PDF version and an HTML version with a single request?

XSL support

Most, if not all of the big delivery systems will support some form of XSL, the XML formatting and transformation language. It is actually their support of XSL that gives many engines their apparent power.

In the rush to get market share, companies frequently develop their products in advance of the standard; they develop a product base on what they think the standard will be. Sometimes their interpretation is not correct. Or, vendors will support part of the standard—the part that's easiest to implement—and save the complicated stuff (frequently the most valuable functionality) for later versions.

You should think carefully about any delivery engine that supports only a part of the XSL standard or that supports the vendor's own version of the standard. XSL is growing in popularity by leaps and bounds. Systems that do not fully support XSL now will be forced to play catch-up with functionality, assuming that XML and XSL maintain their current growth in popularity.

You should also think twice about a delivery engine that does not support XSL. There are processing engines that support other style languages, but they are limited in flexibility.

Automation

Gone are the days of big publishing departments, which took files from authors, cleaned them up, and published them to the required output. Today's enterprise model features centralized, automated publishing. Authors submit a file directly or by setting a workflow flag, and the required output is generated automatically.

Summary

Before content can be managed, manipulated, or reused, it must be created. Authoring tools enable authors to create that content. To support a unified content strategy, authoring tools must allow content to be written so that it can be structured and reused according to the content lifecycle you identified earlier.

A content management system controls your content through workflow, access control, and version control. There are a number of different types of content management systems depending on the content to be managed (for example, web, document, component, learning).

Workflow systems make sure that everybody contributes their required content, that content is reviewed and approved at the necessary stages, and that is delivered to its various outputs. Workflow systems automate them, handling the interrelationships among processes and tracking the status of the project at any given time.

To turn your data into usable content, you must assemble it, format it, and deliver it to your user community, whenever and however they need it. Delivery systems have many different capabilities. The content management system may have built-in facilities for delivering content, or you may have to integrate a delivery system with your content management system. Some delivery systems will enable you to deliver to a variety of outputs (for example, web, HTML, PDF) while others may be restricted to a single output.

Authoring

While authors can create content and convert it to the format of choice, it is preferable to use a tool that will minimize the amount of conversion required and will aid authors in the authoring process.

There are two types of authoring tools for your system: traditional word processing or page layout tools and structured editors.

There are four types of traditional authoring tools: word processing tools, page layout tools, hybrids that combine the functionality (to some degree) of both word processor and page layout tools, and web authoring tools.

There are also different kinds of structured authoring tools. There are XML-aware tools (traditional tools with integrated XML), native XML editors (editors that work natively in XML), and other editors that enforce structure in different ways.

Content management

Content management is an integral component of a successful unified content strategy. There are many different types of content management systems:

- Web content management systems (WCMSs) assist an organization in automating various aspects of web content creation, content management, and delivery. Delivery to the web is its primary format, but many WCMSs also deliver to mobile devices.

- Transactional content management systems (TCMSs) assist an organization in managing eCommerce transactions.

- Document management systems (DMSs) assist an organization in managing enterprise documents and content.

- Component content management systems (CCMSs) manage content at the component level and support reuse. There are multiple varieties of CCMSs including dedicated, web component content management, publishing, learning content management, and enterprise.

- Learning content management systems (LCMSs) assist an organization in managing the web-based learning content lifecycle.

- Enterprise content management systems (ECMSs) vary in their functionality. Some support both the web and publications content lifecycles, while others support the web content lifecycle and either transactional content or customer relationship management content.

Workflow

Workflow systems consist of three major parts: creation (enables you to create and test a workflow), processing (activates and manages workflow), and administration (tracks workflow).

The creation component of a workflow system enables you to create graphical representations of the workflow, test the workflow using test data, and may provide the ability to learn from user interaction and automatically create automated workflow.

In the processing component of a workflow system, work is routed using sequential, rules-based, parallel, and ad hoc workflow routings. Rules define what actions should be taken at each step.

The administration component of a workflow system provides the capability to define roles, assign security to different components of a workflow, and set deadlines for each action in a workflow. Reports enable you to monitor the status of a process as well as individual and group performance.

Delivery engine

The delivery engine is an integral component of a successful unified content strategy. You need to understand the basic capabilities of the systems that exist.

Basic capabilities include:

- Transformation
- Conversion
- Distribution
- Assembly
- Automation

Part 6

Resources

Glossary

Access control   Secures content and identifies who can read, create, modify, and delete content.

Adaptive content   Adaptive content is format-free, device-independent, scalable, and filterable content that is transformable for display in different environments and on different devices in an automated or dynamic fashion.

Adobe Digital Editions   Adobe's proprietary eReader and eBook management software. It's an application that runs on Windows, Macintosh systems, and Linux. It's designed to enable the user to download, manage, and read eBooks. It supports PDF, EPUB, and Adobe Flash-based content. Fonts can be made larger or smaller and the text reflows to fit the screen.

Approvers   Approvers provide the final sign-off for content before it is "posted" or published. Approvers can also be reviewers, and while their permissions are similar to the reviewers' permissions, approvers have the final authority to determine if the content is ready to go to the public.

Attribute   See *metadata*.

Audit   See *content audit*.

Authoring tool   A tool that enables authors (content creators) to create content.

Authors   Anyone involved with creating content of any type (for example, text or graphics).

Automated reuse   The process by which the system decides how to reuse content based on information product models, metadata, and business rules. See also *reuse* and *reusable content*.

Basic eBook   A basic eBook includes text, images, and table of contents, but no additional functionality.

Building block approach   Allows you to identify a core of information that is applicable for all information products or customers, and then builds on it to customize information for different uses and customers.

Bursting   The process of breaking content into component parts before storing the content in a content management system.

Categorization metadata   Organizes content into logical categories (groupings) that aid in the retrieval of content. Categorization is used by content users to retrieve content.

Change management   The process of communicating and managing change throughout the organization.

Check in   The act of putting content previously checked out of a content management system back into the content management system. Content is versioned when it is checked back in.

Check out   The act of signing out content from the content management system. When content is checked out, no one else can modify that content because it is locked.

CCMS   See *component content management system.*

CMS   *See content management system.*

Collaborative authoring   Ensures that the content components, such as product descriptions, are consistent and can be reused wherever they're required—in a printed brochure, on the Web, on a mobile device. To ensure content elements will meet all needs, everyone involved in creating content must work together to figure out exactly what their needs are and make decisions about how such elements are to be reused, structured, and written.

Component   A discrete piece of content that is about a specific subject, has an identifiable purpose, and can stand alone. Components can be reused multiple times in multiple information products.

Component-based reuse   The process by which components of content are reused. See also *reuse* and *reusable content.*

Component content management system   Manages content at a granular (component) level of content, rather than at the page or document level. Each component represents a single topic, concept, or asset (such as an image or table). Components are assembled into multiple content assemblies (information products) and can be viewed as components or as traditional pages or documents. Each component has its own lifecycle (owner, version, approval, use) and can be tracked individually or as part of an assembly. See also *content management system.*

Component metadata   Provides the ability to find components of information so they can be reused in different content assemblies or for different purposes.

Component model   Describes the structure of specific types of content, for example, a recipe, a value proposition, or an overview. Component models can be used over and over again with different content. The structure remains the same; only the content changes.

Conditional reuse   The process by which authors provide variants for reusable content in a single component, with the variations identified by conditional tags or metadata. Often called "filtered" content because the content is filtered in or out depending on where and for whom the content is being published. See also *reuse* and *reusable content.*

Content audit   An accounting of the information in your organization. Requires analyzing representative materials and looking for similar or identical information.

Content inventory   A content inventory is a complete list of all the content you plan to manage. For example, a content inventory could apply to the contents of a website, a suite of books, or learning materials.

Content lifecycle   The various phases that content moves through, such as creation, review, management, and delivery.

Content management system   Software or a suite of applications that help an organization to store and manage their organizational content. Includes access control, version control, and workflow.

Content modeling   The process of determining the structure and granularity of your content.

Content models   Define the structure of information products and their constituent content components.

Content reuse   Content reuse is the process of reusing specific pieces of content. Reusable content is written as components or elements. See also *reuse* and *reusable content.*

Content silo trap   A situation created by authors working in isolation from other authors within the organization. Walls are erected among content areas and even within content areas, which leads to content being created, and recreated, and recreated, often with changes or differences in each iteration.

Content structure   The content structure consists of models that represent the desired structure for both your information products and your topics.

Controlled vocabulary   A list of metadata terms in which each concept or subject has a specific term to be used. A controlled vocabulary reconciles all the various possible words that can be used to identify content and differentiates among all the possible meanings that can be attached to content.

Core information   In a building block approach, information that is applicable for all uses. See also *building block approach.*

CRM   See *customer relationship management system.*

Crosswalk   See *metadata crosswalk.*

Customer relationship management system   A system to collect and integrate customer information. Can be integrated with other management systems.

DAISY, DAISY consortium   See *Digital Accessible Information System.*

Darwin Information Typing Architecture Known now by the acronym DITA, this is an open content standard that defines a common structure for content that promotes the consistent creation, sharing, and reuse of content. DITA is an XML-based architecture for creating and delivering content as components, typically as discrete, typed topics.

Derivative reuse   Reuse with change. The derivative component is a "child" of the "parent" (source) component. When the source component changes, the owner of the derivative is notified so the author of the derivative component can review the changes to the source component and determine if any changes need to be made to the derivative. This ensures that content remains as similar as possible. See also *reuse* and *reusable content.*

Descriptive metadata   Used to help customers find information—books in libraries, PDF files on a company fileserver, or content on the Web. Sometimes called publications metadata.

Digital Accessible Information System Known by the acronym DAISY, it's a multimedia publishing system designed to enable the creation of publications for use by those unable to read print. The goal is to provide audio publications that are as easy and efficient for the listener to use as a traditional publication is for a sighted person. DAISY is managed by the DAISY Consortium, which is being incorporated into the International Digital Publishing Forum.

Digital rights management   Digital rights management (DRM) is a term used to describe a form of digital lock that is used to restrict access to content. It's designed to allow the creator (or publisher or copyright holder) of digital content to determine where and how that content can be accessed. It can be used to restrict content to a particular user, device, location, or system. The usual goal is to ensure that only the person who purchased the content has access to it.

DITA   See *Darwin Information Typing Architecture.*

DMS   See *document management system.*

Document management system   A traditional system that manages documents, for example, correspondence, reports, and publications, for an enterprise. It can usually deliver content in the original source format, convert to other formats, and produce PDF versions of content. See also *enterprise content management system.*

Document type definition   A document type definition (DTD) is the form of document definition used to support and effectively describe XML file structures, providing the vocabulary and allowable structure of the elements in an XML document.

DRM   See *digital rights management.*

DTD   See *document type definition.*

Dublin Core   The Dublin Core Metadata Initiative promotes the widespread adoption of interoperable metadata standards. The Dublin Core Metadata Element Set defines 15 elements of semantic metadata (Contributor, Coverage, Creator, Date, Description, Format, Identifier, Language, Publisher, Relation, Rights, Source, Subject, Title, and Type).

Dynamic content   Content that is assembled to meet customers' specific needs, providing them with exactly what they are looking for, when they are looking for it, and in the format they are looking for.

eBook   An electronic book. It may be a digitized form of a printed book or be electronic only. In general, it's an electronic representation of a printed book. eBooks, as opposed to enhanced eBooks or eBook apps, typically consist of text and graphics. They can be displayed on eReaders, tablets, personal computers, and mobile phones.

eBook app   An eBook application is a method of delivering an interactive and media-rich experience to the reader.

ECMS   See *enterprise content management system.*

Ecosystem   An ecosystem describes the "self-contained" nature of a publisher's offerings. iTunes (and iBooks) from Apple, and the Kindle and Kindle Store are probably the best known such ecosystems.

Editors   Editors review and make changes to content; the scope of their changes depends on their role as either substantive or copy editors. Editors can also be reviewers, but unlike reviewers, their permissions allow them to modify the content.

E Ink (e-Ink, e-ink, eInk)   E Ink™ is a proprietary form of electronic paper manufactured by E Ink Corporation, founded in 1997 and based on research started at the MIT Media Lab. This "paper" is used as the screen on most eReaders (such as the Kindle) with grayscale (black and white) screens.

Element   The smallest part of a model that can be semantically defined but not broken out into a separate component.

Element metadata   Identifies content at the element level. Element metadata is used by content authors to identify content for reuse.

Enhanced eBook   An eBook that has been "enhanced" with audio, video, 3D, or certain interactive features like JavaScript.

Enterprise content management system   A hybrid system designed by vendors to manage web content lifecycles as well as document management lifecycles. An enterprise content management system (ECMS) often includes records management functionality.

EPUB   EPUB, short for electronic publication, is an open standard for electronic books from the International Digital Publishing Forum (IDPF). This standard is used by the majority of eReaders.

eReader   eReaders are thin, light (usually single-purpose) devices. They last a long time between charges and they have screens that are very easy to read in bright light (especially sunlight), but because they are not backlit, they are much less readable in dim light. eReaders typically use E Ink software for screen display of eBooks.

Extensible markup language   Extensible markup language (XML) is a markup language for documents containing structured information. A metalanguage, XML contains a set of rules that expand the amount and kinds of information that can be provided about the data held in documents. XML is a subset or restricted form of SGML. A goal of XML is to enable content to be served, received, and processed on the Web in the way that is not possible with HTML. XML has been designed for ease of implementation and for interoperability.

Extensible metadata platform   Extensible metadata platform (XMP) is a metadata framework (a method of labeling content) created by Adobe. XMP provides a method for combining metadata from "documents" and all their associated components. The metadata for each component is preserved within the container content assembly.

Extensible stylesheet language   Extensible stylesheet language (XSL) is a language used to create stylesheets for XML. An XML document must be formatted before it can be read, and the formatting is usually accomplished with stylesheets. Stylesheets consist of formatting rules for how particular XML tags affect the display of the content on multiple devices.

Extensible stylesheet language transformation   Extensible style language transformation (XSLT) is a language for transforming XML to other formats such as InDesign, Word, or HTML.

Fallback mechanism   A mechanism provided in EPUB that allows an eBook to display an alternate if the primary content cannot be displayed. For example, if a video cannot be displayed on a particular device, EPUB can fall back (alternatively display) to a static image.

Flowcharts   A means of depicting a process from beginning to end, using flowcharting symbols to indicate the type of tasks in the process.

Fragment-based reuse   The process by which a piece of a component, such as a paragraph, sentence, or bullet, is reused. See also *reuse* and *reusable content*.

Generated text   Text that is not supplied by authors but is generated or mandated by the structure. Examples are the numbers in a numbered list, numbers in headings, numbers in numbered tables or figures. Standard titles are often created using generated text.

Governance   The process of managing change. Involves steering or directing the content, the people who create it, and the systems that support it through both the day-to-day and long-term content lifecycles.

Granularity   Granularity refers to the smallest reusable element of information. See also *physical granularity*.

HTML   See *hypertext markup language*.

Hypertext Markup Language   Created in the early 90s by Tim Berners-Lee at CERN (the European Laboratory for Particle Physics) as a way for scientists to share information. Hypertext Markup Language (HTML) is the best known application of SGML for the Web.

Identical reuse   Content is reused without change. See also *reuse* and *reusable content*.

IDPF   Acronym for the international digital publishing forum.

In-depth analysis   Part of a content audit; involves further examination of common information found in the top-level analysis to see how or if it can be reused. See also *content audit* and *top-level analysis*.

Information product   An assembly of content components, for example, a press release, an executive profile, a brochure, or an instructional course.

Information product model   A hierarchical ordering of components. The IPM can be used over and over again with slight variations for different content.

Information typing   Information typing is the analyzing you do to identify the type of information a piece of content represents, for example, an introduction, summary, glossary term, or quiz.

Intelligent content   Content that is structurally rich and semantically categorized, and is therefore automatically discoverable, reusable, reconfigurable, and adaptable.

International Digital Publishing Forum   The International Digital Publishing Forum is charged with creating, managing, and maintaining the EPUB set of standards.

IPM   See *Information product model*.

LCMS   See *learning content management system*.

Learning content management system   Designed to assist in the creation, management, and delivery of learning materials. It supports the complete process of content authoring, content management, reuse, workflow and delivery.

Learning management system   A learning management system (LMS) facilitates and manages delivery of content for eLearning materials to students. The focus of an LMS is registration, course tracking, and student evaluation.

Linear flowchart   A means of depicting a process from beginning to end, often using flowcharting symbols to indicate the type of tasks in the process.

LMS   See *learning management system*.

Locked reuse   Reusable content that cannot be changed except by an authorized author.

Mandatory elements   Elements are specified in an information model as either mandatory or optional; mandatory elements are those that must be included for an information product to be considered complete. See also *optional elements*.

Manual reuse   The process by which authors manually find a content component, retrieve it, and reuse it by pointing to the source content. See also *reuse* and *reusable content*.

Markup language   A mechanism to identify structures in a document.

Metadata   Data that describes other data. Metadata is often referred to as an attribute. Metadata is the encoded knowledge of your organization. Metadata are descriptive terms attached to an object (element) that allow for additional information about the element and accurate indexing and querying of the element. XML elements are indexed by metadata that is described in the DTD or in the XML document itself, enabling other applications to interact with it.

Metadata crosswalk   Maps the structure and the semantics of one set of metadata to the structure and semantics of another set of metadata. Usually a table is used to map one set of metadata to the other.

Metric   Measurement of a particular characteristic of a task (for example, duration, effort, quality, cost, value delivered, or customer satisfaction).

Mobipocket   Mobipocket is the eBook format used to create Kindle-based eBooks. Mobipocket was created in 2000 and it quickly spread throughout the personal digital assistant (PDA) market, where it achieved broad acceptance. Mobipocket was purchased by Amazon.com in 2005 and has become the underlying software for the Kindle.

Modular content   See *reusable content*.

Modular stylesheet   A stylesheet that is built in layers; allows layers that are common across multiple stylesheets to be shared.

Module   A collection of content or data that implements one idea or concept.

National Library of Medicine   The National Library of Medicine (NLM) is a DTD developed by the US National Library of Medicine to structure information for publication in scientific and medical journals and other publications. It is fast becoming the de facto XML standard for those journals.

NLM   See *National Library of Medicine*.

OASIS   Organization for the Advancement of Structured Information Standards. This not-for-profit consortium drives the development, convergence, and adoption of open standards for global information.

Optional elements   Not required, but recommended elements. See also *mandatory elements*.

PCCM   See *publishing-oriented component content management system*.

PDF   See *portable document format*.

Persona   A profile of a typical user represented with a description of a "real" individual.

Personalization   Delivery of personalized content (content that specifically meets the customer's needs). Uses dynamic content to automatically assemble appropriate content. Learns from user actions on content and requests for content, and predicts users' content requirements.

Physical granularity   The physical chunk of information stored in the CMS.

Players   Everyone involved in the content lifecycle, for example, customers, authors, reviewers, and publication staff.

Portable document format   A cross-platform file format developed by Adobe Systems, Inc. Portable document format (PDF) documents are created using Adobe Acrobat software and the PostScript language.

Portal   A special web page that organizes access to all online resources about a topic, providing a one-stop shop of sorts.

PostScript   A page description language from Adobe Systems, Inc., PostScript translates the text and graphic images that appear on the computer screen into instructions for the printer. PostScript must be used with a printer that can interpret it.

Process   Part of workflow; the flow of tasks, as performed by the various players, showing the interactions and interdependencies among players. See also *workflow* and *task*.

Publishing   The process of rendering, or outputting, files from the CMS into the required output format (for example, PDF or HTML).

Publishing-oriented component content management system   A publishing-oriented component content management system (PCCMS) is a CMS designed to meet the needs of the publishing industry. Content is managed as native XML and content is managed as components. See also *content management system*.

RDF   See *resource description framework*.

Reflow   The automatic reformatting of text and images in an electronic document to fill the virtual page on an eReader when the orientation of the reader is changed (from vertical to horizontal, for example) or when the font or font size is changed. Like water that flows freely, the content will spread out and flow from page to page, leaving no wasted space.

Resource description framework   The resource description framework (RDF) was developed by the World Wide Web Consortium (W3C). Unlike Dublin Core, RDF is a framework for describing and interchanging metadata; it doesn't actually define metadata. Because it uses XML, RDF imposes a specific structure that explicitly defines semantics, ensuring consistent encoding, exchange, and machine-readable processing of standardized metadata.

Reusable content   Self-contained components of content that can be used more than once in combination with other components.

Reusable learning object   A reusable learning object (RLO) is a component of reusable content intended for learning materials.

Reuse   The practice of using existing components of content to develop new content. See also *reusable content*.

Reuse map   Identifies which elements are reusable, where they are reusable, and how they should be reused, for example, identically, or derivatively.

Reuse strategy   Defines the way content will be reused (manual versus automated), the types of reuse (identical, section, component, conditional, fragment, or variable), the level of granularity, and the reuse governance strategy.

Reviewers   Reviewers check content for such things as accuracy, completeness, and appropriateness. Reviewers are usually limited to making comments about the content without changing it.

Rich text format   A method of formatting text designed by Microsoft and intended as a universal standard for exchanging documents between different programs. Special symbols indicate such characteristics as bold, italic, the formatting of paragraphs, and so on. Microsoft Word files can be saved in rich text format.

RLO   See *reusable learning object.*

Roles   Part of workflow; the people who do the tasks, identified by their roles. See also *workflow* and *task.*

RTF   See *rich text format.*

Schema   A defined structure for a document or type of document. Sometimes used synonymously with document type definition (DTD).

SCORM   See *shareable content object reference model.*

Section-based reuse   The process by which an entire section or grouping of components can be reused at once. See also *reuse* and *reusable content.*

Segmentation   See *bursting.*

Semantic information   A part of an information model; uniquely identifies the content of that element, making it easy for authors to identify exactly what content they should include. Semantic information also enables the identification and reuse of specific content.

SGML   See *standard generalized markup language.*

Shareable content object reference model   SCORM is a model for sharing learning objects; developed by the Advanced Distributed Learning (ADL) network to provide a standard for reusing learning objects.

Standard   A rule, principle, or measure established as a model or example by authority, custom, or general consent. In the computer industry, standards are rules that encourage open systems and provide the basis for portability, interoperability, and manageability.

Standard generalized markup language   Commonly referred to as SGML. "A language for document representation that formalizes markup and frees it of system and processing dependencies" (ISO 8879 4.305). SGML is the parent language of XML.

Static content   Information created in a specific way for a specific purpose; this information remains the same until the author deliberately changes it.

Structural reuse   The process of reusing common content structures across a variety of information products. Structural reuse is defined in content models. Structural reuse facilitates content reuse. See also *reuse* and *reusable content.*

Structure   The hierarchical order in which content occurs in an information product (for example, web page, brochure, or article) or component.

Structured content   Content in which the organizational hierarchy of information has been identified in a systematic, consistent manner.

Structured writing   The practice of writing content following structured writing guidelines, so information can be effectively reused and still fit the "style" of each document. Authors write to meet the structure of the content models, using element definitions to guide them in creating elements consistently.

Stylesheet Structured, controlled content needs to be formatted before it can be read; this formatting is usually accomplished with the use of stylesheets. Stylesheets consist of formatting rules for how particular semantic tags affect the display of a document on a computer screen or a printed page. See also *XSL stylesheet* and *modular stylesheet*.

Swimlane diagrams Show processes in "lanes" (like the lanes you swim laps in) to depict tasks that occur concurrently, illustrating who does what, and when. Used to design workflow. See also *workflow*.

Tablet A tablet is a multifunctional device. Tablets run applications and allow the reading of eBooks. They can handle everything from Basic eBooks to enhanced eBooks to eBook apps. A tablet can also be used to browse the Web, run nonbook applications, and play video and audio.

Task A unit of work within a workflow. Workflows comprise multiple tasks which can be executed serially, in parallel, or on a conditional basis. See also *workflow*.

Taxonomy A hierarchical representation of metadata. The top level is the category, and each subsequent level provides a refinement (detail) of the top-level term.

TCMS See *transactional content management system*.

TEI See *text encoding initiative*.

Text encoding initiative A rich and complex tag set managed by the Text Encoding Initiative Consortium that develops and maintains a standard for the representation of texts in digital form.

TMS See *translation memory system*.

Top-level analysis Part of a content audit; involves scanning representative information products to find common information. See also *content audit* and *in-depth analysis*.

Transactional content management system A CMS that has been designed to manage eCommerce transactions. Usually provides full web content management system (WCMS) capability. See also *content management system* and *web content management system*.

Translation memory system A system that uses pattern matching to match content that's already been translated.

Unified content strategy A repeatable method of identifying all content requirements up front, creating consistently structured content for reuse, managing that content in a definitive source, and assembling content on demand to meet customers' needs. A unified content strategy makes it possible to design modular reusable content that can be efficiently "manufactured" into a variety of information products for multiple devices.

Valid In the context of XML, valid refers to information elements in a document that are allowable, based on the structure defined by the DTD.

Variable Values that can be assigned names and used by referencing the name. Variables are an excellent mechanism for reusing small elements of content (like product names) that are used in large numbers of places and that are subject to frequent or last-minute change.

Variable-based reuse The process by which reusable components can be used where a variable is set up to have a different value in different situations. See also *reuse* and *reusable content*.

Version control   Ensures that each time content is checked in, another version (copy) is created and is assigned a new version number. The version number is incremented to indicate its difference from the previous copy.

W3C   See *World Wide Web Consortium*.

WCMS   See *web content management system*.

Web content management system Assists an organization in automating various aspects of web content creation, content management, and delivery. Delivery to the Web is its primary format, but many WCMS systems also deliver to mobile. See *content management system*.

Workflow   Defines how people and tasks interact to create, update, manage, and deliver content. Workflow helps organizations perform tasks in an efficient and repeatable manner.

World Wide Web Consortium   An international community comprising member organizations, full-time staff, and the public, whose mission is to lead the Web to its full potential. It develops open standards to ensure the long-term growth of the Web.

XML   See *extensible markup language*.

XML early   See *XML first*.

XML first   The point at which content is converted into XML in the workflow to allow production of content for multiple platforms and easy reuse. Sometimes known as XML early.

XMP   See *extensible metadata platform*.

XSL   See *extensible style language*.

XSL stylesheet   A stylesheet written using XSL. See *extensible stylesheet language*.

XSLT   See *extensible stylesheet language transformation*.

Bibliography

"A Manager's Introduction to Adobe eXtensible Metadata Platform, The Adobe XML Metadata Framework." Retrieved from http://www.adobe.com/products/xmp/pdfs/whitepaper.pdf on May 31, 2002.

Baca, Murtha, ed. "Introduction to Metadata: Pathways to Digital Information." Retrieved from http://www.getty.edu/research/institute/standards/intrometadata/index.html on February 13, 2002.

Boiko, Bob. *Content Management Bible.* New York: Hungry Minds, 2004.

Brown, Dan M. *Communicating Design: Developing Web Site Documentation for Design and Planning,* 2nd ed. Berkeley, CA: New Riders, 2011.

Burk, Lisa and Jean Richardson with Lisa Latin. "Conflict Management in Software Development Environments," Proc. PNSQC 2000 (online): 298–357, 2000.

Castledine, Earle, Myles Eftos, and Max Wheeler. *Build Mobile Websites and Apps for Smart Devices.* Collingwood, VIC, Australia: SitePoint, 2011.

Clark, Ruth Colvin. "Four Architectures of Instruction." *Performance Improvement* 39, no. 10 (November/December 2000).

Cleveland, Donald B. and Ana D. Cleveland. *Introduction to Indexing and Abstracting.* Englewood, CO: Libraries Unlimited, Inc., 2001.

Collins, Heidi. *Corporate Portals.* New York: American Management Association, 2001.

Davenport, Thomas H. and John C. Beck. *The Attention Economy: Understanding the New Currency of Business.* Boston: Harvard Business School Press, 2001.

DoD Software Reuse Initiative. "Software Reuse Executive Primer," April 15, 1996. Retrieved from http://dii-sw.ncr.disa.mil/reusic/pol-hist/primer/ on January 1, 2002.

Duck, Jeanie Daniel. *The Change Monster.* New York: Crown Business, 2002.

Fayad, Mohamed and Mauri Laitinen. *Transition to Object-Oriented Software Development.* Hoboken, NJ: John Wiley and Sons, 1998.

Fling, Brian. *Mobile Design and Development.* Sebastopol, CA: O'Reilly Media, Inc., 2009.

Gentle, Anne. *Conversation and Community: The Social Web for Documentation.* Fort Collins, CO: XML Press, 2009.

Goldfarb, Charles F. and Paul Prescod. *The XML Handbook,* 3rd ed. Upper Saddle River, NJ: Prentice Hall, Inc. 2001.

Goodwin, Kim. "Perfecting Your Personas." Newsletter Cooper Interaction Design, July/August 2001. Retrieved from http://www.cooper.com/newsletters/2001_07/perfecting_your_personas.htm on May 1, 2002.

Goodwin, Kim. *Designing for the Digital Age: How to Create Human-Centered Products and Services.* Hoboken, NJ: Wiley Publishing, Inc., 2009.

Gupta, Kavita, Catherine M. Sleezer, and Darlene F. Russ-Eft. *A Practical Guide to Needs Assessment.* Hoboken, NJ: John Wiley and Sons, Inc., 2007.

Hackos, JoAnn T. and Janice C. Redish. *User and Task Analysis for Interface Design.* Hoboken, NJ: John Wiley and Sons, Inc., 1998.

Halvorson, Kristina. *Content Strategy for the Web.* Berkeley, CA: New Riders, 2012.

Handley, Ann and C. C. Chapman. *Content Rules: How to Create Killer Blogs, Podcasts, Videos, Ebooks, Webinars (and More) That Engage Customers and Ignite Your Business.* Hoboken, NJ: John Wiley & Sons, Inc., 2011.

Harvard Business Review. *HBR's 10 Must Reads on Change.* Boston: Harvard Business Review Press, 2011.

Heath, Chip and Dan Heath. *Switch: How to Change Things When Change Is Hard.* New York: Crown Business, 2010.

Hedden, Heather. *The Accidental Taxonomist.* Medford, NJ: Information Today, 2010.

Hoober, Steven and Eric Berkman. *Designing Mobile Interfaces.* Sebastopol, CA: O'Reilly Media, 2011.

Information mapping, structured writing information. Available from www.infomap.com

Instone, Keith. "Information Architecture and Personalization," 2000. Retrieved from http://argus-acia.com/white_papers/personalization.pdf on January 22, 2002.

Kissane, Erin. *The Elements of Content Strategy.* New York: A Book Apart, 2011.

Lyman, Peter and Hal R. Varian. "How Much Information," 2000. Retrieved from http://www.sims.berkeley.edu/how-much-info on April 24, 2002.

Maivald, James J. and Cathy Palmer. *A Designer's Guide to Adobe InDesign and XML: Harness the Power of XML to Automate Your Print and Web Workflows.* Berkeley, CA: Adobe Press, 2007.

Maler, Eve and Jeanne El Andaloussi. *Developing SGML DTDs: From Text to Markup.* Upper Saddle River, NJ: Prentice Hall, Inc., 1996.

Marco, David. *Building and Managing the Meta Data Repository: A Full Lifecycle Guide.* Hoboken, NJ: Wiley Computer Publishing, 2000.

Marcotte, Ethan. *Responsive Web Design.* New York: A Book Apart, 2011.

Marsh, C. Hugh and Eric C. Morris. "Corporate Memory and Technical Communicators: A Relationship with a New Urgency." In *International Professional Communication Conference 2001 Proceedings.*

Martin, Chuck. *The Third Screen: Marketing to Your Customers in a World Gone Mobile.* London: Nicholas Brealey Publishing, 2011.

Morville, Peter and Jeffery Callender. *Search Patterns: Design for Discovery.* Sebastopol, CA: O'Reilly Media, 2010.

Mulder, Steve and Ziv Yaar. *The User Is Always Right: A Practical Guide to Creating and Using Personas for the Web.* Berkeley, CA: New Riders, 2006.

Nakano, Russell. *Web Content Management: A Collaborative Approach.* Upper Saddle River, NJ: Addison-Wesley, 2002.

Nielsen, Jakob. *Designing Web Usability.* Berkeley, CA: New Riders, 2000.

Nielsen, Jakob and Kara Pernice. *Eyetracking Web Usability.* Berkeley, CA: New Riders, 2009.

Redish, Janice (Ginny). *Letting Go of the Words: Writing Web Content that Works.* Boston: Morgan Kaufmann Publishers, 2007.

Rockley, Ann and Charles Cooper. "DITA 101: Fundamentals of DITA for Authors and Managers." Lulu.com, 2010.

Russell, John. "Discovering the Information Model." In *International Professional Communication Conference 2001 Proceedings.*

Self, Tony. *The DITA Style Guide: Best Practices for Authors.* Research Triangle Park, NC: Scriptorium Press, 2011.

Sharp, Alec and Patrick McDermott. *Workflow Modeling: Tools for Process Improvement and Application Development.* Boston: Artech House, 2001.

Sheffield, Richard. *The Web Content Strategist's Bible.* Atlanta: CreateSpace, 2010.

Stewart, Darin L. *Building Enterprise Taxonomies*. Mokita Press, 2011.

Tannenbaum, Adrienne. *Metadata Solutions*. Upper Saddle River, NJ: Addison-Wesley, 2002

Taylor, Arlene G. *The Organization of Information*. Englewood, CO: Libraries Unlimited, Inc., 1999.

Tidwell, Doug. *XSLT*. Sebastopol, CA: O'Reilly Media, 2008.

Vazquez, Julio. "Practical DITA." Lulu.com, 2009.

Walmsley, Priscilla. *XQuery*. Sebastopol, CA: O'Reilly Media, 2007.

Wroblewski, Luke. *Mobile First*. New York: A Book Apart, 2011.

Appendix

Checklist for implementing a unified content strategy

This appendix provides a checklist for implementing a unified content strategy supported by content management:

1. Analysis

2. Developing a unified content strategy

3. Selecting tools and technologies

4. Development

5. Testing and system modifications

6. Pilot

7. Implementation

8. Post implementation

Phase 1—Analysis

Starting with a thorough analysis is key to a successful unified content strategy. Thorough analysis ensures that your strategy addresses your organization's specific needs and goals.

Table A.1 describes the stages of analysis.

Table A.1   Analysis

Stages: What's involved	Tasks: What to do	Deliverables
Identify customer requirements	Interview sales, marketing, and customer support	Analysis report
	Analyze existing customer information	
	Gather new information through web surveys, focus groups, usability testing, and social media	
	Create a persona for each of your major customer categories	
Identify the "pain" in your organization	Ask the following questions:	Analysis report
	What are the top three dangers your organization is facing—or will face—if you don't meet your goals?	
	What are the top three opportunities you hope to take advantage of?	
	What are your organization's greatest strengths?	
	What are your organization's goals for the next year?	
	What are the challenges your organization must overcome to meet those goals?	
Analyze the content creation lifecycle	Identify your current content lifecycle	Analysis report
	Identify who does what within that lifecycle; learn what their issues are	

Table A.1   Analysis continued

Stages: What's involved	Tasks: What to do	Deliverables
Conduct a content audit	Examine the content in your organization to determine how it's used and how it could be reused: Establish the scope of the audit Select representative samples of content Conduct a top-level analysis of samples, looking for structural similarities that indicate where to analyze further Look at selected samples closely, making observations about how content is used and how it could be reused	Analysis report
Formulate your vision for a new, unified content lifecycle	The new content lifecycle is based on the issues you identified in the first three stages—identify pain, analyze content lifecycle, and conduct content audit—and forms the basis for implementing the unified content strategy Identify how to address issues Document a new lifecycle, addressing each phase, such as create, review, manage, and deliver	Recommendations report

Phase 2—Developing a unified content strategy

Design is one of the most critical phases of implementing a unified content strategy. During the design phase, you figure out how you will address the issues you discovered during your analyses, and how you will realize your vision for a new content lifecycle. You design information models that specify how information will be used and reused; you define metadata to ensure that every component of content can be tracked, retrieved, and reused; you design personalized content to suit users' unique needs; you design workflow to ensure that content moves through the content lifecycle; and you plan the change management processes (including security) you'll need to help the changes take place.

Table A.2 describes the stages of developing a unified content strategy.

Table A.2   Developing a unified content strategy

Stages: What's involved	Tasks: What to do	Deliverables
Create adaptive content models	Build adaptive models for each information product and each information component within the product	Content strategy Adaptive content models
	Identify all possible uses for the information	
	Identify the level of reuse required	
	Determine the granularity of the information	
Define metadata	Identify and evaluate industry metadata standards	Content strategy Metadata specification
	Define your taxonomy and controlled vocabulary	
	Define your descriptive metadata	
	Define your component metadata	

Table A.2   Developing a unified content strategy continued

Design workflow	Select start and end points for all the tasks within your content lifecycle	Content strategy
	Determine everything that has to happen in between, assigning tasks to roles	Swimlane diagrams illustrating your desired workflow
	Identify all the interactions and dependencies, notifications and approvals	
	Figure in the what-ifs	
	Document your workflow in swimlane diagrams, showing players' roles in the appropriate swimlanes	
	Examine your documented workflow to simplify where possible	
Stages: **What's involved**	**Tasks:** **What to do**	**Deliverables**
Develop organizational change management plan	Though not part of design, you should begin to address change management during the design phase: • Identify areas where you should focus your change management efforts • Analyze barriers to effective change • Identify change success factors • Identify the roles of stakeholders • Select a change management strategy • Identify change management team members • Identify a communications strategy • Create a change management plan	Content strategy Organizational change management plan

Phase 3—Selecting tools and technologies

Evaluating and selecting tools is a large part of implementing a unified content strategy. There are so many types of tools available and you need to select ones that meet your organizations' needs, your authors' abilities, and what you've decided to do with your information (established during the design phase). Using everything you learned in the analysis and design phases—and referring to your new content lifecycle—evaluate tools and technologies.

Table A.3 describes the stages of selecting tools and technologies.

Table A.3   Selecting tools and technologies

Stage: What's involved	Tasks: What to do	Deliverables
Evaluate tools and technologies	Identify your criteria for selection	Tool selection criteria
	Develop a weighting system for your criteria	RFI/RFP (if applicable)
	Develop a list of vendors to investigate	Tools to support your various authoring, content management, workflow, and delivery needs
	Request a custom demonstration from vendors that interest you	
	Send out an RFI/RFP to selected vendors that includes your detailed criteria and ask them to respond to your questions	
	Evaluate the responses or compare the custom demonstration against your criteria	
	Pick three vendors that most effectively meet your criteria (best ranking)	
	Ask vendors to use a sample of your content to create a content-specific demonstration for you	
	Narrow your selection down to one or two vendors	
	Conduct a proof-of-concept to test the required functionality and determine if the product meets your needs	
	Purchase the product if it performs well in the proof-of-concept	

Phase 4—Development

Moving forward with your unified content strategy means changing the way you work. As you develop your proof-of-concept and pilot, you need to help your authors collaborate and provide them with guidelines and training on how to write and structure content in the same way, and you need to roll out your strategy throughout your organization. You also need to put together your change management plan, implement your models, and install and configure your software and hardware.

Table A.4 describes the stages of development.

Table A.4   Development

Stages: What's involved	Tasks: What to do	Deliverables
Implement collaborative authoring	Identify everyone involved in creating content and what their roles are; hold kickoff meetings at the beginning of projects	Project plans and kick off meetings
	Design collaboration into workflow	Budgets based on content requirements
	Develop resource-focused budgets based on content requirements across the organization instead of department-specific budgets	Information models
	Introduce models to everyone in the organization who creates content; revisit models iteratively	"Buy-ins" from authors
	Make changes to models, authoring processes, and standards by consensus and not by democratic vote; train authors in conflict management techniques	Training in content analysis, modeling, design, and structured writing
	Encourage authors to relinquish ownership of their content; content with a discernible style is not necessarily reusable	Authoring and collaboration tools
	Train writers in information analysis, modeling, design, and structured writing so they all have the same understanding of how to create content and how to write to information models	
	Provide usable tools that support collaborative processes, not impede them	

Table A.4   Development continued

Implement structured writing	Define writing standards that focus on meaning rather than on format	Structured writing standards
	Create standards for each component, so wherever the component appears, it is consistent, and so it is also consistent with the other components contained in the information product	Information models
		Format stylesheets for each output
		Authoring tools
	Train authors in structured writing and support them with tools and comprehensive models to follow	Structured writing documentation and training
	Create stylesheets that are applied when the content is published to its various formats	
Stages: **What's involved**	**Tasks:** **What to do**	**Deliverables**
Address organizational change	Communicate on an ongoing basis: • Why change needs to happen • The plan for implementing the change; the ongoing status of the change • The successes you have achieved in early implementations • The problems you have encountered and how you fixed them or plan to avoid them in the future • Involve "change agents" to help you implement the change • Get a champion on board to help ensure that everyone understands the reason for change and buys into the process	Organizational change plan

Table A.4   Development continued

Implement your design	Create templates	Templates
	Create web forms (if using)	Forms
	Create schemas, DTDs	Stylesheets
	Develop stylesheets	
Install and configure hardware/software	Write configuration specification	System specification
	Configure tools	Installed and configured system
	Write scripts	
Create workflows in CMS	Create workflows using CMS functionality	Workflows created in the CMS
Develop a prototype	Select a short sample (existing content) for prototype testing	A working prototype
	Convert/restructure content according to your new models	Prototype gap analysis report
	Publish (deliver content) using the system	
	Analyze gaps (prototype against requirements)	
	Create a prototype report	

Phase 5—Testing and system modifications

During this phase of the project, you use your prototype to extensively test the functionality of the system, information models, business processes, and workflows. While many of these tasks are required for most project implementations, they are not specific to a unified content strategy and are not covered in this book.

Table A.5 describes the stages of testing and system modifications.

Table A.5   Testing and system modifications

Stages: What's involved	Tasks: What to do	Deliverables
Conduct usability test	Define the objectives of the test (what you want to learn)	Usability test plan
	Define success criteria	Usability test questionnaires
	Define the test questions	List of usability test participants
	Develop any necessary information/training to support the test participants in understanding their tasks	Usability test
	Identify the usability test participants	Usability test report
	Develop the pre- and post-usability test questionnaires and coordinate times with participants	Possibly, a modified system
	Conduct the usability test	
	Summarize the usability test findings	
	Create a usability test report covering results and recommendations	
	Revise the user interface and processes where necessary	
Conduct verification test	Create a verification test plan	Verification test plan
	Test functionality	Problem reports
	Identify problem areas	Engineering change notices
	Document problems (bugs)	
	Determine appropriate changes and create engineering change notices for system changes	

Table A.5   Testing and system modifications continued

Stages: What's involved	Tasks: What to do	Deliverables
Revise specification	Update specification Review	Revised specification
Implement system modifications	Revise information frameworks Revise stylesheets Revise all batches and scripts	Revised stylesheets Revised batches Revised scripts
Implement process modifications	Identify modifications to processes Update process descriptions Update process maps Communicate changes to authors	Revised process descriptions Revised process maps
Implement workflow modifications	Update workflow diagrams Update workflows in the system Communicate changes to authors	Revised workflow diagrams Revised workflows in the system

Phase 6—Pilot

A pilot is required to selectively roll out and test the new tools and processes in a controlled environment that will not impact key deliverables. To conduct a pilot, you select a group, department, or area you will use to roll out a scaled-down version of the unified content strategy so you can thoroughly test the processes and infrastructure. Once the pilot is complete, the rest of the process can be prioritized for implementation.

Table A.2 describes the stages of conducting a pilot.

Table A.6   Pilot

Stages: What's involved	Tasks: What to do	Deliverables
Create pilot plan	Create a pilot plan	Pilot plan
	Create a pilot monitoring plan	Pilot monitoring plan
	Create a pilot schedule	Pilot schedule
	Create a pilot participant agreement	Pilot participant agreement

Stages: What's involved	Tasks: What to do	Deliverables
Select and brief participants	Create pilot selection criteria	Pilot selection criteria
	Evaluate plans against criteria	Selected documents
	Select one or more documents for inclusion in the pilot process	Signed pilot participant agreement
	Meet with the teams to communicate the vision and pilot plan	
	Get signatures of all parties on the pilot participant agreement	
Install pilot on pilot server and participants' machines	Configure pilot server	Configured pilot server
	Install tools	Configured author interface
	Configure tools	
Develop preliminary training plan and materials	Perform task analysis	Training plan
	Identify roles to be trained	Preliminary training materials
	Identify learning styles	
	Identify learning objectives	
	Determine the delivery mechanism	
	Write training plan	
	Write training materials	

Table A.6   Pilot continued

Conduct pilot training	Train staff	Trained staff
	Collect feedback	Feedback report
	Create feedback report	
Develop pilot user documentation	Define user documentation requirements and deliverables	User documentation deliverables report
	Create information product models for each deliverable	User documentation information product models
	Develop preliminary user documentation based on the models	First draft user documentation
Monitor pilot	Conduct pilot kickoff meeting	Pilot kickoff meeting
	Monitor pilot	Pilot summary report
	Summarize pilot	
	Create pilot summary report	
Revise specification	Update models	Updated specifications (models, maps, descriptions, workflow diagrams)
	Update process maps and descriptions	
	Update workflow diagrams	Informed stakeholders
	Communicate changes to stakeholders	
Implement changes	Update work processes	Updated system, processes, and workflows
	Update system workflows, templates, interface, system configuration	Informed stakeholders
	Communicate changes to stakeholders	

Phase 7—Implementation

Proper planning and training are essential to the successful implementation of your unified content strategy.

Table A.7 describes the stages of implementation.

Table A.7   Implementation

Stages: What's involved	Tasks: What to do	Deliverables
Develop rollout plan	Identify all users involved	Rollout plan
	Identify hardware/software requirements	
	Identify training needs	
	Develop rollout schedule	
	Create rollout plan	
Develop final training plan and materials	Perform task analysis	Training plan
	Identify roles to be trained	Training materials
	Identify learning styles	
	Identify learning objectives	
	Determine delivery mechanism	
	Write training plan	
	Write training materials	
Conduct training	Train staff	Trained staff
	Collect feedback	Feedback report
	Create feedback report	
Develop technical support plan	Identify required technical resources	Technical support plan
	Identify tools resource	
	Identify process resources	
	Write technical support plan	
Finalize user documentation	Review user documentation and edit	Final user documentation
	Finalize user documentation	
Roll out solution	As defined in your rollout plan	The rolled out system

Phase 8—Post-implementation

Once your strategy has been successfully implemented, you need to ensure that it continues to run smoothly, and that you keep up-to-date on the latest technological advances. It is also important to analyze your recently completed unified content strategy to determine how you can leverage the experience for future projects.

Table A.8 describes the stages of post-implementation.

Table A.8   Post-implementation

Stages: What's involved	Tasks: What to do	Deliverables
Develop migration/ upgrade plan	Determine migration/upgrade criteria Contact vendors about upcoming product release functionality and schedule Develop migration/upgrade plan	Migration/upgrade plan
Conduct post-project audit	Identify review topics, such as: • Did the final product match the one designed in the project plan and outline? • Did the scope of the project remain the same? • Did the project dependencies remain the same as originally predicted? • What went right? • What went wrong? • How can you build on actions that lead to success? • How can you change actions that caused problems or failures? • Conduct a post-project audit meeting • Create a post-project audit report	Post-project audit meeting Post-project audit report

INDEX